RAILS
TO
ASHBOURNE

HOWARD SPRENGER

Kestrel Railway Books
PO Box 269
SOUTHAMPTON
SO30 4XR

www.kestrelrailwaybooks.co.uk

Printed by The Amadeus Press

ISBN 978-1-905505-29-6

Front cover: The crew of LNWR G2A 0-8-0 49262, a Buxton engine, exchange pleasantries at Parsley Hay on 14th June 1962 while taking a freight turn to Uttoxeter. The locomotive would be withdrawn at the end of the year. (Colour Rail)

*Back cover, top: On 11th May 1963, the "North Midlands Rail Tour" called at Ashbourne on its way from Buxton to Burton-upon-Trent. This leg of the tour was hauled by an unusual visitor to the line, LNER B1 4-6-0 No 61004 Oryx.
(Martin Wilkins/Kestrel Collection)*

Back cover, bottom: Hartington station looking north in 1967, around the time that the last traffic ceased and this section of line closed. The signalbox closed on 25th October that year, and still survives. (Richard Bird)

Three tickets are shown. On the front cover is an LMS day excursion ticket from Hurdlow to Ashbourne. On the back cover is an NSR single from Rocester to Ashbourne dated 27th July 1911 (top) and an LNWR bicycle ticket valid between Hurdlow and Uttoxeter dated 9th May 1913 (bottom). (All, Glynn Waite Collection)

Title Page: Ashbourne in the early 1950s, not long before the withdrawal of passenger services. The buildings (around 50 years old by now) are looking well-kept with all the paraphernalia of a passenger station – seats, trolleys, posters, etc. The up bay is being used to store a three-coach set and cattle wagons are in the down bay. (Eric Brown/Author's Collection)

Contents

Acknowledgements

The opposite ends of the railway were connected not just by a line of rails, but also by the enthusiasm of two medical men and their determination to document and preserve for posterity the scenes that they witnessed. Dr JR (Jack) Hollick was an Ashbourne GP and noted chronicler of the North Staffordshire Railway, being one of the five writers who made up the "Manifold" writing team along with GN Nowell-Gossling, CA Moreton, FM Page and WT Stubbs. Buxton dentist ER (Ray) Morten traversed the country with his camera to become one of the leading railway photographers of the 20th century.   The majority of his subjects were naturally close to home, and his coverage of this line is second to none. Both have left a lasting legacy, and I owe a huge debt of gratitude to them both. Pictures from the Hollick Archive are included with the permission of the Archive's owners, the Foxfield Light Railway Society (www.foxfieldrailway.co.uk) and its associated group, the Knotty Coach Trust (www.knottycoachtrust.org.uk).

I have also been very fortunate to receive a great deal of freely-given help from a large number of individuals who share my passion for the railways of Derbyshire and Staffordshire, and for this line in particular. It would be invidious to call out any one above the others, so I list them all here in alphabetical order. There are some, however, who have gone above and beyond anything that I might reasonably have expected, and I hope that they recognise who they are through my private correspondence with them. My sincere apologies if some names have escaped this list over the considerable number of years that I have been working on this project – my gratitude to them is no less than my gratitude to those mentioned here, many of whom are fellow members of the North Staffordshire Railway Study Group (www.nsrsg.org.uk): Jean Allen, Allan C Baker, Jean Bailey, Mike Bentley, John Blood, Paul Brooks, Roy Christian, Donald Clowes, Steve Crewe, Neil Ferguson-Lee, Dave Harris, John Hillmer, Dr David Jolley, David Moore, Vince Morris, Richard Morton, Roger Newman, Rex North, Mike Price, Dave Scragg, John Sherratt, Mark Smith, Peter Trewhitt, Glynn Waite, Nick Wheat, Stewart Williams, Dr David Woolliscroft.

Railtour information has been verified against that held on the Six Bells Junction website, and I extend my grateful thanks to Gary Thornton for his work on this excellent resource (www.sixbellsjunction.co.uk).

I have made great efforts to trace the copyright holders of the photographs used in this book – never an easy task, and one made almost impossible these days with the advent of technology that allows the indiscriminate copying and dissemination of images which very easily lose any connection with the names of those who took them or who claim to have copyright over them. If anyone believes I have infringed their copyright, please accept my apologies and contact me via the publisher.

Above: The southern end of the line – Uttoxeter, taken around 1908 when the photograph was included in the book "Picturesque Staffordshire". The bearded Station Master with a porter on his left is Thomas Mellor, who served there for over thirty years from 1877. His wife, Emma, is standing behind the barrier, and behind her is platform 3 for arrivals from Ashbourne. Departures were from platform 4 out of picture to the left. (Author's Collection)

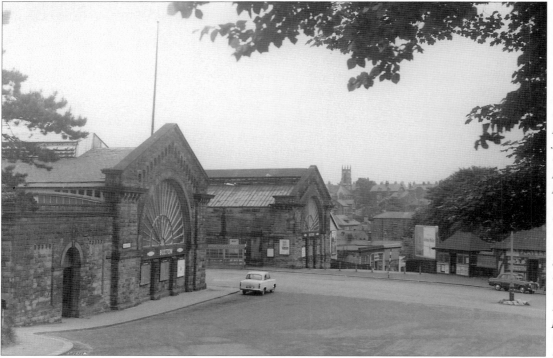

Left: The northern end of the line – Buxton, seen on 5th July 1962 when the town was still graced by the beautiful symmetry of the LNWR station on the left and the Midland station behind. What a pity that no way was found to preserve this scene. The new road that passes through doubtless provides much relief for the town, but visually, the area can hardly be said to have improved. Since losing its twin, the LNWR station has suffered its own indignities, not least the loss of its roof. Ford Populars were clearly popular at the time. (Brunel University/ Mowat Collection)

Introduction

Passing through the beautiful scenery on the border of Derbyshire and Staffordshire from the White Peak landscape of the limestone area surrounding Ashbourne to the grimmer, less-hospitable, Dark Peak of Buxton, the London & North Western Railway's picturesque line from Ashbourne to Buxton has long been a favourite of railway historians and photographers. Along its route, it served remote communities, often isolated by winter snowfalls, and industry in the form of limestone quarries that seem to be eating away north-west Derbyshire to leave a permanent blizzard-white panorama. If the attraction of the scenery were not enough to generate interest in the line, it also had the distinction of being partly aligned on the northern half of the famous Cromford and High Peak Railway.

It has always seemed wrong to me, though, to consider it in isolation, simply because at its southern end, it made an end-on junction with a line built by a different railway company, the North Staffordshire Railway. As part of a through route, it makes more sense to consider the whole line from Uttoxeter to Buxton, and this is the approach taken in this book. The Uttoxeter to Ashbourne section has tended to be overlooked in other published works, so this book will try to redress the balance by viewing the line as a whole between the largely self-contained NSR system and the wider railway network represented by the LNWR.

The two lines were quite different in character. The earlier line, from Uttoxeter to Ashbourne, was very much rooted in the railway mania of the mid-19th century. The later one, from Buxton to Ashbourne, was a comparatively recent addition, built after the railway network of Great Britain had been largely completed. This was a period of consolidation when the sometimes highly-speculative schemes of fifty years earlier had given way to strategic routes that filled in some of the last-remaining gaps on the railway map.

Where the earlier line was built by navvies using only the most basic tools and equipment, the later line had the benefit of half a century of railway-building expertise. Perhaps the most revealing sign of the different eras in which the lines were built is the fact that the construction of the line between Ashbourne and Buxton was recorded by photographers. In historical terms, the line from Uttoxeter to Ashbourne is more contemporary with the original Cromford and High Peak Railway than the extension to Buxton, which largely superseded it.

Howard Sprenger
Southampton, April 2013

Above: NSR class B 2-4-0T No 48 with its train of 6-wheel carriages stands in the platform at Ashbourne after arrival from Uttoxeter in September 1922. (JR Hollick Archive Courtesy of the FLRS)

Below: An unidentified LNWR G2A 0-8-0 stands outside Buxton No 1 box with a freight train to Ashbourne, probably in the mid-1950s judging by the BR 16-ton mineral wagon, but note the Saxa Salt van at the head of the train. (Author's Collection)

Chapter 1

The North Staffordshire Railway – Southern Approaches to Ashbourne

Following the success of early railways such as the Stockton and Darlington and the Liverpool and Manchester, hundreds of ambitious plans were floated by enthusiastic engineers, keen to join the major centres of population with a network of lines criss-crossing Great Britain. One, promoted by John Rastrick (an engineer on the Grand Junction Railway) was for a direct connection between Manchester and London, which was to have run via Stockport, Buxton, Macclesfield, Hartington, Ashbourne and Leicester, with a London terminus at Farington Street. Another scheme was for a line from Manchester to Rugby via Leek, Ashbourne, Tutbury and Burton-upon-Trent, and a third was for a similar line from Manchester to Rugby, but this time via Macclesfield, Leek, Ashbourne and Derby. There was also a proposal for a Liverpool to Derby link (via Warrington, Knutsford, Congleton, Leek and Ashbourne) which would have joined the first Manchester-Rugby proposal between Leek and Ashbourne. Further south, connections were proposed at Rugby with a line to Oxford, and on to Southampton and Portsmouth.

In addition to these north-west/south-east proposals, further schemes suggested lines from Stafford via Uttoxeter and Ashbourne to the North Midland Railway at Ambergate, and the West Midland Railway, which would have run from Crewe through Hanley, Cheadle and Ashbourne, to a junction with the North Midland at Belper. In 1845, the Derby, Uttoxeter and Stafford Railway was proposed, which was part of a grander scheme to link East Anglia with Holyhead. At the same time plans were deposited at Stafford for the Grand Junction and Midland Union Railway to run from the Trent Valley Railway at Colton Mill near Rugeley to the Birmingham and Derby Railway at Burton-upon-Trent, but this would not have passed through Uttoxeter.

In common with so many of these early ideas, the vision of their proponents was not realised (if at all) until several smaller, locally-promoted lines had been built and linked together. Such was the development of the line between Uttoxeter and Buxton. Having featured in many of these "grand schemes", the line was ultimately built in piecemeal fashion, and became a through route in only a limited way.

Our story really starts with the incorporation of the North Staffordshire Railway on 26th June 1846 when the Acts for its three proposed lines received Royal assent. This small but complex system began life with a line between Stoke and Norton Bridge on the Grand Junction Railway (part of the LNWR). By 1849, the NSR had 112 route miles, and made connections with both the LNWR and the Midland Railway. Independent until the Grouping of 1923, it survived proposed mergers with the LNWR, and enjoyed excellent relations with its larger neighbour with extensive (and reciprocal) running powers over the lines of that company.

The first line to pass through the borderlands of Staffordshire and Derbyshire was opened by the NSR from Uttoxeter to Burton-upon-Trent on 11th September 1848, Uttoxeter having been reached from Stoke on 7th August of that year. The building of this line sounded the death-knell for the Derby, Uttoxeter and Stafford Railway, which was wound up at a shareholder's meeting on 19th July 1848. Held at the improbably named George and Vulture in London (a hostelry frequented by Charles Dickens, no less) the meeting largely concerned itself with dividing up the remaining capital, and after presenting the Directors each with 100 guineas plus 2d a share "as a token of respect, and acknowledgement of their services for a period of three years", the shareholders were left with 7s 4d per share.

On 22nd July 1848, the NSR held its half-yearly meeting at Stoke station, and received highly satisfactory reports on the progress of the various lines under construction, including

An early picture of the station at Uttoxeter, clearly taken before the footbridge was enclosed, so probably dating from the late 19th century. (JR Hollick Archive Courtesy of the FLRS)

that from the Potteries to Burton through Uttoxeter. The original line from Stoke to Norton Bridge had opened in April, and in two months, net profits had been £1,668, which was "beyond their anticipations". The meeting ended after a speech by the Reverend Mr Robinson against cheap trains on a Sunday. You can see where he was coming from, but Sunday was the only day of the week that most people could get out of Stoke and into the surrounding countryside. One assumes that the hard-headed businessmen who were the Directors of the North Staffordshire Railway listened politely, and then made up their own minds on the matter.

The Uttoxeter-Burton line was soon followed by a connecting branch from Marston Junction via Egginton Junction to Willington, which opened on 13th July 1849. At Willington, this line joined the MR, over which the NSR (together with the LNWR) had running powers in order to gain access to Derby, where both had a goods depot.

Also on 13th July 1849, the Churnet Valley line was opened along the Derbyshire/Staffordshire border from Uttoxeter (with an additional station called Dove Bank), through Rocester and on to Leek. The Churnet Valley Railway Bill had originally been presented to Parliament in 1845, and in March of that year, the Board of Trade viewed the proposed line as part of a trunk route "from the Metropolis to Ireland, Scotland, Liverpool, Manchester, and the Northern and North Western portions of the Kingdom". It also noted that the line would, "complete a Line of Railway between London and Manchester 19 miles shorter than the present one, and which it is believed to be practically as short a line as any which can be made between the two points."

Civil engineering on the line between Uttoxeter and North Rode would be heavy, but some savings were made south of Froghall by building over parts of the Uttoxeter Canal, a branch of the Trent and Mersey. The abandonment of this 13-mile line of canal was possible because the NSR had acquired it in order to avoid the competition that would

have existed between them. This was a good deal for the canal company, as the threat posed by the new railway was turned into a financially-attractive merger that guaranteed its proprietors a dividend until the NSR opened, followed by an exchange of their shares for NSR Preference Stock afterwards.

Even before the railway reached Rocester, demand was growing for some kind of link from Ashbourne, and to satisfy it, a twice-daily coach service was operated to Rocester by Mr Wallis of the Green Man Hotel in Ashbourne from the opening of the Churnet Valley line. Despite this initiative, the town was slowly but surely suffering a decline in trade due to railway developments elsewhere. Before the growth of railways, Ashbourne had been on a main road route from London northwards, and had always been a busy place. Now though, much business had been drawn away, and property values were falling.

A number of the inhabitants united to press for a railway to the town in order to reverse the decline, and several plans were mooted, none of which was to be realised. Whether it was because of the representations being made by the people of Ashbourne, or whether it was out of a desire to tap a potentially prosperous area with its limestone quarries and agriculture, the NSR started to give thought to building of a line to Ashbourne. The Directors paid a visit to the locality, and satisfied themselves that a branch could be built in connection with their Churnet Valley line.

Things were not going to be that straightforward though, and at a meeting of the board on 20th September 1847, the Chairman, John Lewis Ricardo (also MP for Stoke) "called the attention of the board to the...expediency of avoiding any expenditure as far as possible, and recommended the postponement of the contemplated branch to Ashbourne and extension to Sawley". It was therefore resolved that "the branch to Ashbourne and the extension to Sawley be postponed to a future session". The extension to Sawley, between Derby and Nottingham, was never built, and at the same Board meeting, a letter from the MR was read telling the NSR that any such extension would meet with the "most determined opposition". However, in the same letter, they said that they were happy to oblige over the junction with the MR at Buxton, the inference being that the

Rocester station, looking from Station Road probably around the turn of the 20th century. (JR Hollick Archive Courtesy of the FLRS)

NSR was considering building its own line to Buxton.

The Board's postponement of the line to Ashbourne did not last long, though, for at a meeting on 18th January 1848, Ricardo "laid before the Board a protest against the proposed Ashbourne Branch from certain landowners on the line". Notwithstanding these protests, he was also able to report that "the inhabitants of Ashbourne have expressed a strong desire for this extension and the directors feel confident that a fair return may be expected for the moderate outlay required, and for which the present capital of the NSR will suffice."

As a result, the Board resolved "that as the line is of easy construction, and has been undertaken at the earnest solicitations of the inhabitants of the town of Ashbourne, it is expedient that its merits should be submitted to the judgement of a Parliamentary Committee".

Not all the NSR shareholders agreed, however, being far more interested in generating a healthy amount of through traffic by making links with their larger neighbours. They could not be expected to see 50 years into the future, of course, when the line to Ashbourne would eventually be joined to, and take traffic from, the LNWR – perhaps if they had, the scheme would have been sanctioned with a lot less fuss. As it was, without the benefit of such foresight, there was dissension at the Board meeting held on 29th February 1848. "Mr RH Haywood and Mr Oxley attended and laid before the Board a Memorandum signed by certain Shareholders requesting the Directors to postpone the prosecution of the Bill for the Ashbourne Branch until a future opportunity." The Chairman informed them that further action would depend on the approval of the shareholders at a Special Meeting to be held later that day. At this meeting, held at the London Tavern, Bishopsgate, the renegade shareholders proposed that the building of the branch be deferred until "times of well-secured prosperity". The motion was defeated, but if this was not the first delay to the opening of the

line, neither would it be the last.

At a Board meeting held on 7th April 1848, Ricardo reported that "the two Bills promoted by this company in Parliament had been read a second time, and that he was in negotiation with the principal opposing Landowners on the Ashbourne Branch, and hoped they would be induced to withdraw their opposition".

The 6 mile 66 chain branch from Rocester to Ashbourne was duly authorised by Parliament on 22nd July 1848 (Cap 55). According to the Act, the cost was estimated to be £100,000, but because earlier Acts had authorised the NSR to raise more capital than was required, it was not necessary to provide for additional capital to build the line to Ashbourne. The company was authorised to compulsorily purchase up to 10 acres of land in connection with the construction of the line for which three years were allowed, with a further four years being allowed for the line's construction.

Thomas Houldsworth, Esq received protection for the supply of water to the Rocester Mills, and was also to have a road built for him, but the most stringent conditions were in respect of the line's proximity to St Oswald's, the parish church of Ashbourne. In order to protect its magnificent 212ft spire, the company was prevented from taking any land within 80 yards of the churchyard without the consent in writing of the Bishop, the Vicar and the Ecclesiastical Commissioners for England. The line could come within 60 yards, provided that the station was built further away from the churchyard. More to the letter of the law than in the spirit of it, the NSR came as close as it possibly could!

In the Directors' Report of 20th July, shareholders were told (slightly prematurely) that although the Bill had been carried without opposition in Parliament. "It is not present proposed to incur any expense upon the Ashbourne Branch until the completion of the main line in July 1849." (The "main line" being the Churnet Valley.)

The NSR Board discussed matters relating to the Ashbourne branch again on 6th November 1849, when their Engineer, George Bidder, reported that "a Contractor was desirous of submitting a proposition for making, as a single line, and leasing the Ashbourne Branch which he thought might be found desirable for the Company". The contractor was none other than one of the greatest railway contractors of the time, the eminent Thomas Brassey, so the Deputy Chairman, Robert Chapman Sharp, and another Board member, by the name of Critchley, were instructed to "receive and report upon the proposal". At the same time, it was resolved that "the Parliamentary Committee be authorised to apply for an Extension of time for making, and for powers to lease the Ashbourne Branch".

In the Directors' Report of 30th July 1851,

An early photograph of Norbury station, taken around 1880 and looking towards Ashbourne. Note the smaller building (compared with the view on page 14), the open lever frame to the rear and the normal-height platform. (JR Hollick Archive Courtesy of the FLRS)

shareholders were told of the terms of the contract entered into with Mr Brassey regarding the construction and leasing of the line:

The works on the branch to be constructed for the sum of £48,500, to which is to be added the cost of the land, and upon the entire cost Mr Brassey guarantees to the Company a sum equal to £4 per cent per annum, for a period of five years. Mr Brassey to take the receipts of the branch, and one third of the increase due to the branch on the main line. The land and works to be paid for in bonds bearing interest at £4 per cent per annum. The necessary steps have been taken for placing the Contractor in possession of the land, and the works have been commenced, and it is expected that the line will be opened in July of next year.

In the same report, reference was made to other lines then being constructed, including the Newcastle and Apedale branches. Confidence was high that large quantities of limestone would be carried away from the Ashbourne area to Apedale and Silverdale ironworks, and "the town of Ashbourne must be supplied with coal from the Newcastle mines".

It was in accordance with NSR practice that Brassey should work the line – such arrangements being quite common at this time. Brassey was also responsible for running the London, Tilbury and Southend Railway and the line between Shrewsbury and Hereford, and his agreement to do so with the branch to Ashbourne relieved the NSR of any uncertainty it had about the project. The result of this agreement was that work on the line finally began three years after the Act had been passed.

According to the *Derby Mercury* of 9th July 1851, the original intention was to cut the first sod at Rocester, but in fact the ceremony took place at Sides Mill, Clifton on a sunny afternoon on 2nd July. Soon after 4.00pm, a procession left the

Green Man Hotel in Ashbourne, preceded by "a band of music and banners, and a line of 'navvies' with their wheelbarrows". Among the members of the procession were Mr Jones of the firm Brassey & Co, and Mr Witham, Chairman of the Ashbourne Committee in a carriage and pair. Also present was Mr Forsyth, Engineer to the NSR, other gentlemen connected with the company, and inhabitants of the town. In a fascinating article, which I make no apology for quoting at length here, the *Derby Mercury* continued to describe the events as the procession proceeded to...

...the scene of the action, a plot of ground situate near to Sides Mill, in the village of Clifton, about two miles from the town. Along the line of the road, hundreds of men, women, and children were assembled, and the day being beautifully fine, the scene was of a very animating description. As the procession passed the parish church, and throughout the evening, the bells rang forth joyous peals.

On arriving at the appointed spot, the ceremony of cutting the first sod was at once proceeded with. The honour was conferred upon Mr Witham, who afterwards spoke to the following effect:

He commenced by expressing a hope that the ladies and gentlemen present would excuse him from taking off his hat; his anxiety to bring a railway to Ashbourne had been so intense that it had induced in him a boldness that was foreign to his nature, and he was rather fearful of taking cold. (Laughter.) That day was one of the happiest of his life. It marked the commencement of a great work. When their railway was finished, they would then enjoy the same privileges and advantages as the neighbouring towns. Sure he was that his fellow-townsmen possessed as much talent, industry, and intelligence, as fell to the lot of men in general, but for want of railway accommodation they had not scope for their powers.

There was an important class whose interests were closely allied to the interests of his fellow townsmen. He meant the farmers in the neighbourhood, to whom he firmly believed the railway would be of equal benefit as to themselves, by stimulating them to improve their breed of cattle and the making of cheese. It had long been said, there was a good time coming, and he could not conclude better than by expressing his fervent wish that as far as related to this town and neighbourhood they would all enjoy, by means of railway communications, what they had all been so long and so anxiously looking for – a renewal of prosperity. (Loud and long continued cheers.)

With this, the proceedings were brought to a close, and the assembled company began to disperse. In the evening, a number of gentlemen

Clifton station taken in 1879, 27 years after the opening, and looking towards Ashbourne. (JR Hollick Archive Courtesy of the FLRS)

invited Mr Jones to a public dinner at the Green Man Hotel. The party consisted of members of the Local Committee, officials of the NSR, and several gentlemen of the town. "The dinner, though got up on such short notice, was of the most sumptuous kind, and the wines excellent".

At a meeting of the NSR General Purpose Committee on 16th September 1851, the Engineer reported that the Ashbourne branch was proceeding satisfactorily, and in a report to the Directors on 29th January 1852, the works were said to be in an advanced state, and the line was predicted to be open "at Midsummer next". Things all went very well to plan, and at a board meeting on 3rd May that year, the engineer reported that "the Ashbourne Branch would be very shortly ready for opening". It was therefore ordered that the Secretary give "the Month's Notice to the Board of Trade for opening the Ashbourne Branch as prescribed by the Act 5 Victoria. Cap: 55".

Following a satisfactory inspection by the Board of Trade, the Chairman was able to report to the NSR Board at its 3rd July meeting that the Ashbourne branch had been opened to the public (for passenger and goods services) on Monday 31st May. The *Derby Mercury*, in an article on 2nd June recorded the opening of the line with a long article. It began:

This line of railway – which will open up a communication to some of the most picturesque scenery in the kingdom, and to localities teeming with interest – is now completed, and thrown open to the public. The branch is twelve chains short of seven miles in length, and it consists, at present, of a single line of rails – the company having secured land to lay down a second rail, when the traffic shall have been sufficiently developed to warrant the expenditure.

There then followed some details about the construction of the line, in which the point was made that "so comparatively trifling have been the 'engineering difficulties' that it is said that the line will cost little more than £10,000 per mile, though there are several bridges over the River Dove". A house at Ashbourne, owned by the late Mr Corden had been secured as temporary offices, the projectors "with prudent forethought" having postponed the construction of a passenger station until requirements were better known. A goods station was built, however, being a substantial structure in local limestone measuring 150ft by 36ft. It was thought to be ample to accommodate the mineral traffic, and featured a slate roof, cast iron windows and two canopied loading bays with fretted valences for road traffic. In course of construction was a stone engine shed a little further from the town than the goods warehouse. Following a description of the line (which we shall come back to later) the opening ceremony was recorded.

The ceremony, and the running of the very first train, actually took place on the previous Saturday (29th May 1852) when a preliminary trip was made from Stoke by a party of Directors and their friends, who had been invited by the "spirited contractor" Mr Brassey to participate in an opening banquet. "From an early hour on Saturday morning, the railway station...was a scene of general attraction to the inhabitants of Ashbourn". The extreme end of the station was decorated by a design "consisting of interlacing poles, beautifully bedizened with laurels and flowers, and surmounted by flags". The roof of the goods warehouse was "ornamented by a profusion of gaily coloured flags, and at the eastern end of the building, an avenue, leading from the platform to the entrance, was formed of triumphal arches, elegantly dressed up with flowers, laurels and other evergreens, and surmounted by flags".

The building itself was to be the banqueting hall for the festivities, and three rows of tables were laid from one end to the other with cross tables at each end to cater for the 350 guests. In the centre of the south side, an alcove was erected for the Chairman of the proceedings (Thomas Brodrick a director of the NSR), and at each end of the centre table were placed "recessed canopies" for the Vice-Chairmen. Amid all the floral decorations was a banner proclaiming "Success to the Ashbourn Branch" in gold. The Mayor of Derby, John Dunnicliffe lent a banner bearing the Derby Borough Arms, and the walls were decorated in various places with the Staffordshire Knot. The whole celebration was organised by Brassey's agent, Mr Walker, with the floral arrangements largely the work of Mr John Harding; the dinner itself was provided by Mr R Wallis of the Green Man.

About 100 yards north of the goods warehouse, an extensive marquee was erected to house up to 420 workmen who were "plentifully supplied with roast beef, an ox having been roasted entire for the occasion; and this was plentifully moistened with libations of good ale, in which their worthy entertainer's health was willingly quaffed in joyous numbers". Throughout the day, the church bells rang, and by about 2.00pm, the local inhabitants crowded into every possible vantage point in anticipation of the first train. At about 2.30pm, its approach was signalled, and shortly afterwards, it "glided majestically into the station", completely made up of first-class stock, and headed by two engines. After inspecting the works, the party of worthies made their way to the goods warehouse, and the banquet began.

There were, needless to say, several speeches and toasts to the Queen, Prince Albert, The Army, the Navy, and the Bishop of Lichfield. On his behalf, the Rector of Longton, the Rev Dr Vale, replied with a few lines of his own doggerel:

May railways abound,
And steam engines be found,
And Brassey enterprise all the world round.

They certainly don't write 'em like that any more! Following this toast, there were others to the Lord Lieutenant and MPs for Derbyshire, "Prosperity to the Town and Trade of Ashbourn", and to the contractor, Brassey, who was described by the Chairman as "equal to anything, however great or small, in the construction of railways. He is competent to make the Great Northern, or to lease the Ashbourn Branch. (Loud applause.)" He added that he had known and worked with Brassey for six years, during which time they had been involved with works costing nearly £2m,

"imbued with the importance and efficiency of the contract system, when lately speaking on the subject of the national defence, he said, 'Oh, no fear, let them give that to Mr Brassey, and he will work it' (A laugh)." The early seeds of late 20th century privatisation were clearly being sown in the middle of the 19th century in a goods shed at Ashbourne! Following all the speeches, toasts, and glees from the choir, some time was to elapse before the train returned, and the evening being fine, "a numerous party of ladies and gentlemen joined in the merry dance; and in the inspiriting measures of the polka, waltz, and quadrille, whiled off a few delightful moments." At about 7.00pm, the train started back with the visitors, "and this concluded the business of a most interesting day's proceedings".

yet he had never seen him without a smile on his face, or "without the feeling of benevolence in his heart".

Brassey's reply was modest, and he begged to "apologise for the very imperfect manner in which he was able to express himself; he having been more accustomed to make railways than to make speeches (a laugh)". He then proposed a toast to the NSR, "and begged it might be drank with three times three". Brodrick responded that it was with regret that the Chairman of the North Staffs, Ricardo, had been prevented from attending due to having suffered a "severe accident". (Ricardo evidently made a full recovery, as he continued to be the Chairman of the company for another ten years until his death, when Brodrick himself took over.) Brodrick continued, saying that it would "be affectation of the worst sort...to pretend that in making the Ashbourn Branch, they were actuated by purely disinterested motives; on the contrary, he must admit that they expected to benefit from it; but they also expected that the town and district would be benefited likewise".

Next came a toast to the engineers of the NSR, followed by a drink to the health of Brassey's resident engineer, Mr Jones, whom the Chairman described as being so

An immediate result of the opening of the line was the cessation of the twice-daily coach service to Rocester. The branch then operated for nearly fifty years before the LNWR arrived on the scene to connect end-on with the NSR at a new station in Ashbourne.

Top: Ashbourne station c1880 with class F 0-6-0 No 100 of 1860 on the left and goods shed on the right.

Right: A view of original station at Ashbourne taken around 1890. Note the coaches in the station, the station bus, the NSR delivery drays and a poster advertising excursions to Alton Gardens. The guard's uniform is particularly ornate.
(Both, JR Hollick Archive Courtesy of the FLRS)

Chapter 2

Splendid Isolation

An interesting description of the Ashbourne branch at the opening of the line appeared in the *Derby Mercury* on 2nd June 1852. It is quite long, but is worth including in full here:

We must now give some description of the country through which the line passes. Its junction with the Churnet Valley Branch of the North Staffordshire Railway is at Rocester, a neat village, where the cotton-spinning mills of Messrs Houldsworth are situated, giving employment to a considerable portion of the inhabitants. Rocester was the site of an ancient abbey, founded in 1146, of which there is now no vestige. Crossing the little river Churnet, the line enters the beautiful valley of the Dove, passing over the Ashbourn and Uttoxeter Turnpike Road on the level. The Dove flows peacefully along a little to the right, through a country of exceeding beauty and great fertility. On the left is Barrow Hill, with some well-wooded scenery, the picturesque residence of Mrs White; and on the same side, but about a mile in advance, is 'Dove Leys', the rustic seat of TP Heywood, Esq, son of Sir Benjamin Heywood, of Manchester. At this point we have a considerable expanse of valley, which cannot fail to attract attention from its quietude and sylvan loveliness. In the distance are the Weaver Hills, the boldest heights in Staffordshire; and on the left, but not within range of vision, is the celebrated seat of the Earl of Shrewsbury – Alton Towers. The pretty village of Ellaston is seen in the distance, some three miles from Rocester, with its church and parsonage-house prominent in the landscape; and beyond it, and nearer to the Weaver Hills, we see Wootton Hall, which has obtained some celebrity, as once upon a time having been the retreat of Jean Jacques Rousseau. Adjacent to it is Wootton Lodge, with its nobly timbered grounds. We now reach Norbury, a village on the Derbyshire side, at which it is intended to erect a station. On the brow of the hill, is the fine old church of this village, celebrated among antiquaries, and relative to which we gave some particulars on the occasion of the visit, last year, of the British Archaeological Association. Near to the church stands the old hall of the Fitzherberts, now a farm-house. Crossing a pile-bridge of ingenious construction, over a portion of the river which is considerably expanded, we approach, within an inconsiderable distance, Calwich Abbey, the seat of the Hon and Rev Augustus Duncombe. This is a modern mansion, presenting a rather imposing appearance; the ornamental grounds of which lend charm to the landscape. It is on the Staffordshire side, and was until within a few years, the demesne of the Granvilles, of whose hospitality Handel is said to have been a frequent partaker. Norbury Rectory is on the right, and on the same side we approach Snelston Hall, the noble mansion of John Harrison, Esq. This structure is of modern date, and planned by the eminent architect, Mr Cottingham. Its pleasure grounds and woods are fine features in a landscape of rare beauty. Shortly afterwards,

we approach Clifton Station, which will afford accommodation not only to that village, but also to Hanging Bridge and Mayfield. The latter village, with its pretty church, is visible on the left; and it is in this neighbourhood, at Mayfield Cottage, where the poet Moore penned his Lalla Rookh. Within a pleasant walk of Hanging Bridge, is Okeover Hall, the seat of Houghton Charles Okeover, Esq, and for some time of Robert Plumer Ward, Esq, the celebrated author of Tremaine, De Vere, &c. The new mansion of JG Johnson, Esq - Callow Hall - also comes into view, as does Birdsgrove, the residence of the Rev TAL Greaves. In the distance, we have a glimpse of the hills in Dovedale, and we now gain sight of the spire of Ashbourn Church. Arrived at Ashbourn, the visitor will find many objects of interest upon which to expend his research, and there is scarcely any town which offers more advantages to the tourist in search of the picturesque. Dovedale, Ilam Hall and Church, and other famed localities, are at hand; and this is a neighbourhood which furnishes prominent inducements to the disciples of rare old Izaak Walton.

From the opening, there were five trains each way a day, with two on Sundays, some requiring a change at Rocester in order to reach Uttoxeter. The single third class fare to Derby was around 2 shillings, with first class available at 4s 6d. The respective return fares were 3s and 5s. To get to Derby, passengers travelled via Uttoxeter, and for Buxton it was necessary to go via Leek, Macclesfield and Middlewood on the Macclesfield, Bollington and Marple Railway. This line was jointly owned by the NSR and the Manchester, Sheffield and Lincolnshire Railway (MS&LR – later to become the Great Central Railway).

White's Directory of Derbyshire for 1857 contains the following entry: "Railway Conveyance – The Ashbourn Branch of North Staffordshire Railway, Station Clifton. There are 5 passenger trains to and from Rochester daily." The reference to Clifton station seems a little surprising here, and the spelling of Rocester provides an interesting echo of the early Roman occupation of the area, and the possible derivation of the name of the village.

In addition to the passenger service, the railway served local industries and agriculture in the region, and the NSR profited by considerable milk and limestone traffic from Ashbourne. The 1857 *White's Directory* also contained a description of the branch:

This branch commences from a junction with the Churnet Valley line...at Rocester, 3½ miles from Uttoxeter, and proceeding in a northeasterly direction for a distance of 6¾ miles, chiefly up the valley of the Dove, terminating at the market-town of Ashbourne, in this County. This branch was constructed in a great measure for the accommodation of visitors to the celebrated scenery of Dovedale, about 4 miles from Ashbourne.

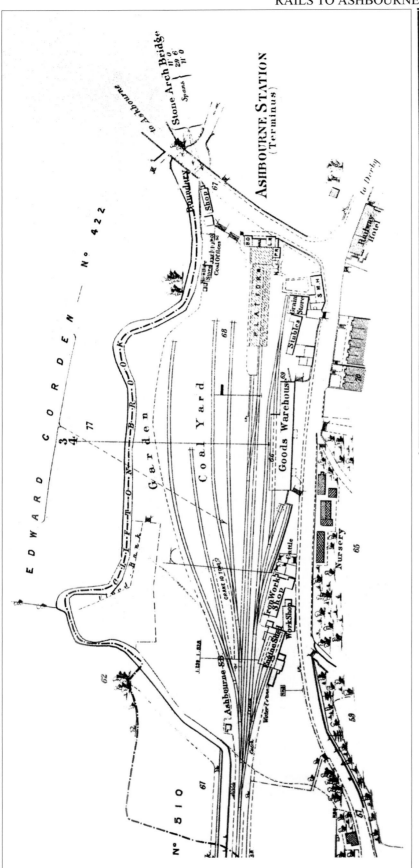

Above: An estate map of the original Ashbourne station. The exact date is unknown, but it probably dates from the opening of the line, although such maps were "living documents" and often received alterations and additions over time.

The timetables date from February 1863, just over ten years after the line was opened (below) and November 1879 (right).

Three photographs of the original station at Ashbourne taken at around the same time.

At the top, photographed around 1885, we see the station in front of St Oswald's church with the original road that served the terminus (known as Church Lane or School Lane). By the tree on the right, the road crosses School House bridge over the Henmore Brook. Behind the station building is a shop, covered in hoardings, to the left of which are the coal offices. In the left foreground is the Station Master's house.

The next picture gives us a close-up view of the hoarding-bedecked shop outside the station, probably taken a few years after the previous photograph.

Finally, taken around 1895, we see a view taken in the opposite direction. Compared with the view on page 6, the lamp on the station building has been repositioned, and there has been a slight proliferation of bills advertising excursions to Derby and Buxton amongst other places. The excursion to Buxton will be taking a circuitous route, as the LNWR extension is still some years away. This will cut across the road, which will become known as Old Station Road, and a footbridge will be built to allow pedestrians to cross the new line. (All, JR Hollick Archive Courtesy of the FLRS, Ticket: Glynn Waite Collection)

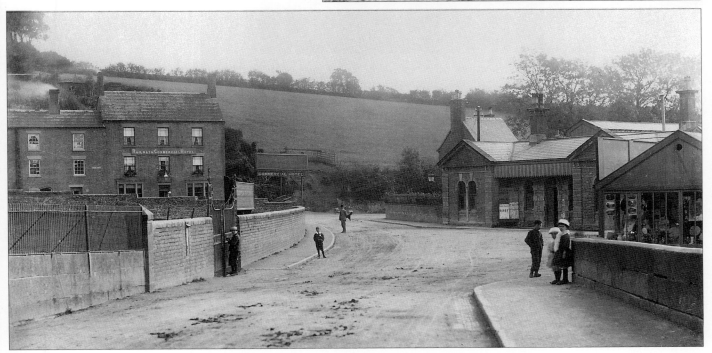

Left: Something of a mystery surrounds these photographs of 2-2-2 No 21 which is said to have been derailed between Rocester and Norbury in 1882 (during the summer months judging by the amount of foliage on the trees). No mention of the incident has been found in NSR records, nor is there any record of a Board of Trade enquiry into the accident. No 21 was built as a 2-4-0 in 1850 and rebuilt as a 2-2-2 a year later. It was renumbered from 53 in 1870, and withdrawn in 1882, which would accord with the date of the photographs. As mentioned in the text, a derailment is believed to have befallen an excursion in May 1894, but again, no "official" evidence of this incident has been found. Despite all this, the two photographs are of sufficient interest to include here, and it would be nice to think that further information about what happened might yet be forthcoming.
(Both, JR Hollick Archive Courtesy of the FLRS)

Opposite page: Taken just after the turn of the century, this view of Rocester shows the Redhill Brick and Tile Co with its siding from the Churnet Valley line (dating from the Spring of 1901). Also to be seen on the left is the Ashbourne branch and the crossing-keeper's house where it crossed Alton Road.
(JR Hollick Archive Courtesy of the FLRS)

The *Bemrose Guide to Derbyshire*, published in 1878, was not as enthusiastic, describing the line as an "inconvenient branch from Uttoxeter", and *Baddeley's Guide to the Peak District*, published in 1894 said:

Visitors to the south will do well to make Ashbourne...their starting point, remembering that the routes to Ashbourne or Dovedale, from Rocester or Alton, are worth a much more close exploration than can be made from the windows of a railway carriage.

In the Directors' Report of 29th July 1853, under general revenue, a sum of £1,280 had been received from Brassey in rent, but a year later, at the Board Meeting on 20th July 1854, it was reported that Brassey was willing to give up the lease despite it having been favourable for the previous year. The NSR Board seemed quite happy to agree to this, noting that a good deal of paperwork would be saved by running the line themselves. It was resolved, therefore, to "cancel the contract and that the Secretary communicate with Mr Brassey

and the London and North Western Company that such a step is in contemplation". Although relishing its independence, the NSR seemed anxious to remain on equitable terms with its larger neighbour, and to inform it of its intentions.

The railway mania that surrounded the building of the line was to continue for a few more years, and yet more plans were made for additional railways in the area. One such was the North and South Staffordshire Junction Railway in 1862, which would have left the Trent Valley line at a triangular junction near Rugeley to connect with the NSR at Uttoxeter. Jointly operated by the LNWR and the NSR, the line would have carried traffic from the Cannock Mineral Railway to the Potteries. Additional to the scheme was a branch to Abbots Bromley. The support given by the LNWR and NSR to this route proved the downfall of a very similar line that had been proposed earlier in the year to link Rugeley and Uttoxeter. It too proposed a branch to Abbots Bromley, but only by seeing it as a way of persuading the Parliamentary Committee to turn down the North and South Staffordshire Junction

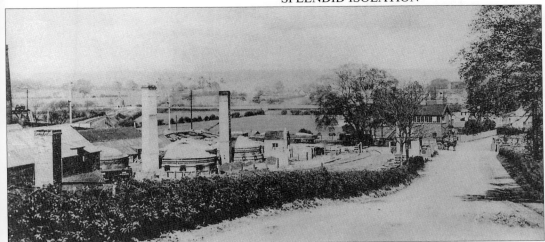

Keane Ltd of Derby portraying scenes around Ilam – the Memorial Cross, Ilam Hall from the north-east and the River Manifold.

It might be thought that the NSR and the LNWR had things pretty-well sewn up in this part of the world, and in truth they did, which explains why both companies saw advantages in staying close to each other. At the end of 1867, however, a new line opened which was to be a thorn in the side of both companies. The Stafford and Uttoxeter Railway was steadfastly opposed by both the NSR and the LNWR, but it not only succeeded in gaining Parliamentary authorisation, it also obtained running powers over the LNWR into Stafford, and over the NSR into Uttoxeter. Neither company liked the idea, and routinely failed to keep connections with Stafford and Uttoxeter trains at their stations. In addition, the NSR simply refused to accept through consignments, even if they were prepaid.

After less than nine years, things became impossible for the Stafford and Uttoxeter, and a receiver was appointed. The line eventually became part of the Great Northern Railway, but isolated from it, so to gain access to its far-flung western outpost, the GNR agreed reciprocal running powers over the NSR's lines – a mutually-beneficial deal that enabled a reliable service to be provided between Stafford and Derby. The Stafford and Uttoxeter remained isolated when the LNER took over, and continued to be so after Nationalisation under British Railways (Eastern Region) until London Midland Region took over in 1950.

If relations had initially been frosty between the NSR and its new neighbour, those with the people of Ashbourne were deteriorating as well. This was demonstrated in 1876, when the NSR felt the need to increase fares on the line, a move that resulted in the citizens of Ashbourne retaliating by starting their own competing bus service. However, it was not successful, and closed down just a week later. The early months of 1881 saw severe flooding, and parts of the branch were raised that year by as much as two feet to eradicate the problem. However, the following year there was further flooding resulting in the line being raised at Norbury.

Throughout this period, Ashbourne station had been the subject of much criticism, not least from a Colonel Jelf, who in August 1898 described it as a disgrace. There was no waiting room, and only a small booking hall, in which small children were said to gather to warm themselves. The Chairman of the NSR, now Sir Thomas Salt, admitted that the company had been concerned about the station for some years, but that improvements had consistently been postponed in anticipation of a new station when the LNWR arrived in the town.

scheme.

The February 1863 *Bradshaw* shows six trains each way along the branch on weekdays, with two each way on Sundays. The railway also started to run excursions from Ashbourne, and trips were available to various seaside towns and London. The line even inspired a song, sung by children in the area:

Clifton, Norbury, Rocester and Uttoxeter,
Change here for Potteries, and off we go again.
Take your leave and in you pop,
Mind you don't your luggage drop,
If you do you're sure to stop,
The excursion train.

The people of Ashbourne, although no doubt pleased with their arrival on Britain's railway map, must have had some regret that the line went to Uttoxeter in the east, where most looked towards Derby and the west for commerce. Not surprisingly, therefore, the 14th August 1869 edition of the *Staffordshire Sentinel and Commercial & General Advertiser* reported that a meeting had been held at Ashbourne Town Hall to discuss a proposed line from Ashbourne to Idridgehay with stations at Atlow and Hognaston. Joining the MR's Wirksworth branch would give a 16½-mile journey to Derby rather than the existing 33-miles, and it was to the Midland that the plans would be proposed, as it was felt that the NSR would not be interested. An extension to Ambergate or Belper to provide a better links with the Derbyshire coalfields and Yorkshire's manufacturing districts was also proposed, but sadly, nothing was to become of this enterprising scheme.

In the 1870s, a local vicar, Rev Wilfred Stanton, travelled regularly from Rugeley to Clifton, returning the same day. This involved a LNWR train from Rugeley to Stafford, followed by a Stafford and Uttoxeter train to Uttoxeter Bridge Street. From here he was able to take the NSR train to Clifton, sometimes changing at Rocester – quite a convoluted journey to cover a distance of some 20 miles, but there was little alternative.

The NSR was keen to attract tourists and day trippers into the area, and many of its carriages were adorned with photographs of beauty spots served by its trains. One such was a series of three "Permanent Photographs" by Richard

A rare survivor from the original NSR line in Ashbourne is the goods shed, seen here on 21ˢᵗ November 2006. Since this picture was taken, the redevelopment of the area and the subsequent use of the building, has made it virtually impossible to take a corresponding photograph due to the amount of "clutter" around the building. This view makes an interesting comparison to the one at the top of page 6. (Ted Millward)

Both the MR and the LNWR were interested in London traffic from the Ashbourne district, and in the 1880s there was a daily through carriage from Ashbourne to St Pancras, the average journey time being five hours. There was also a train service from Manchester to Ashbourne, run by the MS&LR. During the month of October 1882, the 1.30pm (SO) from Manchester to Macclesfield was extended to Alton, and in July 1883, the service was retimed to depart from Manchester at 2.00pm and further extended to Ashbourne, where it arrived at 4.15pm. The return journey left Ashbourne at 8.15pm. Similar services were run from July to September in 1890, again in July 1891, and periodically after that until the arrival of the LNWR at Ashbourne. In GCR and LNER days, a vestige of this service survived in a regular working from Manchester to Uttoxeter on race days.

There were also excursions from Manchester, one of which was timed to arrive in Ashbourne at 7.40am on 3ʳᵈ June 1882. Another two excursions were run that year, with five more taking place in 1883, and a derailment on 29ᵗʰ May 1894 is thought to have afflicted a similar excursion.

Between 7ᵗʰ and 9ᵗʰ November 1882, special trains were laid on to take the Earl of Shrewsbury and his guests from Alton to Ingestre on the Stafford and Uttoxeter line. The return working each day required a NSR locomotive to travel light engine from the Ashbourne branch to Ingestre accompanied by a GNR pilot engine to pick up the party's family saloon and brake.

On 1ˢᵗ July 1890, the LNWR started competing with the MR in earnest with four through trains a day each way from Ashbourne to Nuneaton (via Burton-upon-Trent) where they connected with the Euston trains. Just like the MR's daily through carriage service between Ashbourne and St Pancras in the 1880s, the service resulted in a journey time of five hours. From 1ˢᵗ November 1890, there was a through carriage between Ashbourne and Euston on one of these trains each way.

The 6.40am train was worked to Nuneaton by a NSR locomotive which returned on the 10.05am from Nuneaton; the 10.20am was worked by a LNWR engine to Nuneaton, returning on the 7.20pm from Nuneaton and stopping overnight at Ashbourne. The 2.05am and 4.20pm departures from Ashbourne were worked by NSR engines to Burton and thence by the LNWR, a similar arrangement taking place on the return workings. All trains were made up of LNWR coaching stock. On the branch service itself, it was not unusual to see trains made up of a mixture of NSR and LNWR stock.

New proposals continued to surface, and in 1895, a deputation from Lichfield, Uttoxeter and Abbots Bromley unsuccessfully petitioned the LNWR to build a railway from Lichfield to Uttoxeter. It was suggested that such a line would open up the milk trade with London from the area around Abbots Bromley, Newborough, Hoar Cross, Yoxall, King's Bromley and Hamstall Ridware. It was also seen as an alternative route between Birmingham and Manchester via Lichfield, Ashbourne and Buxton.

Another interesting proposal also first saw the light of day in 1895, when on 16th August, a meeting was held at St James's Hall, Derby to discuss the proposed Derby and Ashbourne Electric Light Railway. Amongst the attendees were Lord Scarsdale of Kedleston Hall, Mr John Shaw and Mr GF Meynell of Meynell Langley Hall. Mr Shaw was evidently one of the more enthusiastic proponents, and he read a lengthy report about the economic viability of an electric tramway over a conventional railway between the two towns: "…various schemes for a railway had been proposed, but they had all been abandoned on the ground of initial expense and the improbability of their paying any interest as a commercial undertaking".

He quoted figures of between £60,000 and £80,000 per mile for a conventional railway, whereas he believed that a tramway could be laid for only £2,000 per mile (excluding the overhead lines and generating equipment). Furthermore, there would be no need for very much infrastructure as passengers could be picked up and set down anywhere along the route. The travelling time by existing railway between Derby and Ashbourne was said to be 1¾ hours ("if punctual, which they seldom were") but he predicted a journey time around 30 minutes less for the direct light railway.

It was proposed to build a generating station near the Brailsford Brook, about 7½ miles from Derby, which was thought to be the best site due to the heavier gradients being at the Ashbourne end of the line, and "if sufficient hydraulic power could be obtained from the brook, a large saving might be made in generating the current". Maintenance costs were thought to be very small, and the number of vehicles proposed were six motor cars, six "travelling cars" (presumably passenger trailer cars) and six goods cars. The rolling stock would cost £6,100, and all cars would be electrically lit. The most optimistic forecast for the use of the line was 100,000 passengers a year, which was based on estimates that had been made about 15 years previously when a conventional railway had been planned.

Shaw maintained that no Parliamentary approval was necessary for such a line, but that it could be built under existing County Council powers. If necessary, the success of the line could be further exploited by building branches to settlements that lay off the main route.

Mr R Finney was present as the representative of the Derbyshire Dairy Farmer's Association, and stated that his organisation believed that the proposed railway would be of the greatest benefit to the locality. However, Mr WR Holland was rather more sceptical, and with a remarkably perspicacious view of the future, said that he thought the day was not far off when he would be able to drive from Derby to Ashbourne "in his car without horses, and in which the motive power would be mineral oil or electricity", further noting that "the balance of opinion appeared to be in favour of mineral oil". Mr TO Farmer doubted whether the tourist traffic to Ashbourne would be very great, but it was pointed out by Mr Shaw that it was intended that the railway would eventually be extended to Dovedale.

The result of the meeting was that a committee was formed to look further into the proposal, and in 1896 (despite the previous assertion that Parliament need not be involved) a Light Railway Order was obtained for the line to be built to a gauge of 4ft 0in. After a public inquiry in October 1897, the plans were revised to build the line to standard gauge, and although the scheme eventually failed through lack of capital, plans were also made to extend the line to Leek via Waterhouses. Quite how the overhead wiring was expected to withstand the winter weather on the moors around Ashbourne can only be imagined, but the line would have been an interesting addition to the area, and bears comparison with the Burton & Ashby Light Railway and the Nottinghamshire & Derbyshire Tramway, both of which were similar rural tramways built not far away.

More successful were plans to build a narrow gauge (2ft 6in) line from Waterhouses to "Hulme End for Sheen and Hartington". Opened on 27th June 1904, the Leek and Manifold Valley Light Railway was built partly because of the failure of the Derby to Ashbourne scheme, and also because traders in Leek feared that the LNWR line from Buxton to Ashbourne would take trade from the Moorlands and Upper Manifold Valley to markets in those towns. There were plans to extend the line to Buxton via Longnor, Hollinsclough, Earl Sterndale and Harpur Hill, but due to financial pressures and the engineering difficulties that would have been encountered, the NSR dropped its plans in 1907, although there was a connecting bus service in the summer of 1909. Perhaps significantly, the LNWR had refused to assist with the scheme, but had it gone ahead, there would have been another magnificent viaduct in Buxton.

In preparation for the connection with the LNWR, the NSR had obtained authorisation to extend to a new joint station on 4th August 1890 (the same day that the LNWR Buxton and Ashbourne Railway was authorised). It had also decided, under the original Act of 1848, to double the line, initially between Clifton and Ashbourne, in anticipation of the line's new importance, but Board of Trade approval was only granted on condition that the work did not interfere with any plans made by Staffordshire County Council (whatever they might have been). No such problems arose, and plans went ahead, even though there was still a long time to wait until the LNWR arrived. Finally, on 7th November 1898, the Secretary of the NSR was able to write to the Board of Trade: "I beg to give you notice of this Company's intention to open the additional line, or widening of that portion of their Ashbourne Branch Railway, that lies between Ashbourne and Clifton Station, and I will in the course of a week or two send the necessary tracings with the second notice."

An acknowledgement was received from the BoT the next day, and on 10th December 1898, the Secretary wrote again: "In further reference to my letter of the 7th ulto and your reply of the 8th R12901, I have now the pleasure to enclose tracings of the proposed widening between Ashbourne and Clifton."

In the view of the NSR, the double line would be completed by 12th December, and on the 13th the Board of Trade replied that Lt Col HA Yorke had been appointed to inspect the works, which he did on 27th December. In his report, Yorke mentions the intention of the NSR to double the branch throughout, and notes that the new line between Clifton and Ashbourne will form the up line of the branch (the existing track becoming the down line). As noted in the *Derby Mercury* article on the opening of the branch, Yorke comments that no extra land was purchased for the doubling of the line. Both Ashbourne and Clifton stations remained "single sided", with only one platform each, and Yorke remarks that in the case of Ashbourne (a terminus) this arrangement "is not in accordance with the requirements of the Board of Trade, and could not be approved as a permanency". However, because a new station was to be

built, the requirements of the BoT would not be enforced.

Yorke then discusses the signalling arrangements at the two stations, and it is here that he makes his only recommendations. The alterations were to be completed within a fortnight, and on 7th January 1899 (although the minute is dated 1898 – how often do any of us overlook the turning of the year when writing a date in January!), the Secretary of the NSR duly wrote to the BoT confirming that "the necessary alterations required by the Inspecting Officer have now been complied with".

The new station, in contrast to the original stone station, was made almost entirely of wood to a similar design to the stations the LNWR had built on the line from Buxton (although to a larger scale). It was opened for passengers and goods at the same time as the LNWR line on 4th August 1899, 33 chains of line through the new station and along to the old station being jointly owned by the two companies. With the opening of the new station, the road from School Lane to the Clifton road was cut by the railway and blocked, a footbridge being provided to maintain the right of way. The original station closed, but the stables and the goods shed were retained as a goods depot for the town, as was the small engine shed, which was a sub-shed of Stoke, and housed one engine. The old station building was converted into offices and a milk platform.

Norbury and Ellaston station, taken after 1901 when the name was changed from Norbury, but before 1904 when the lever frame on the open stage was replaced by a "proper" signalbox. Compared with the picture on page 3, the single storey building has gained an additional gable, and the low section of platform (not in the earlier photograph) looks very odd after the extension of the platform at normal height in 1900. (JR Hollick Archive Courtesy of the FLRS)

Chapter 3

The London and North Western Railway –
The Advance from the North

The nearest the LNWR had come to Ashbourne in the years after the opening of the NSR branch was when it obtained a perpetual lease of the Cromford and High Peak Railway in March 1861. Somewhat bizarrely, a passenger service ran on the line until 1877 when it was withdrawn following a fatal accident. *White's Directory of Derbyshire* for 1857, in its entry for Buxton, advised:

Railway Station – High Peak Railway, Ladman's Low, 1½ mile SW from Buxton. There is one Passenger train to Cromford, daily at 2.30pm, and to Whaley, at 11.30pm. Fras. Barton, manager, and Peter Jepson, clerk.

It might be assumed that "11.30pm" is a misprint, but since there was only one "fly" carriage for use by passengers, it is quite likely that the timing reflects a round-trip to Cromford and back, and thence to Whaley Bridge.

Bearing in mind the length of time needed to make the journey (over 8 hours for 27 miles) it is not surprising that the service was poorly patronised. In 1862, for example, monthly passenger receipts were sometimes as little as 14s 9d. Prior to the LNWR taking the lease, a proposal had been made to convert the whole line to main-line standards as a link between Manchester and the Midlands, but although the LNWR was keen to develop a line of this nature, good sense prevailed, and it began a series of more modest improvements. However, it is interesting to look at some of the other schemes that were being proposed around this time.

In 1864, the Chesterfield, Sheffield and Stafford Railway was proposed. This line would have run to Baslow, Bakewell or Rowsley, Ashbourne and Stafford, and from Sheffield there would have been a branch to Chesterfield. Although it opposed the main line, the branch actually got the backing of the MR. The main line was supported by Sheffield Corporation, but opposed by the MS&LR and the NSR. Eventually, the Bill was withdrawn due to the promoters having insufficient funds.

The LNWR made a proposal in 1866 for the Sheffield, Buxton and Liverpool Railway which would have left its Buxton branch at Chapel-en-le-Frith and reached Sheffield via Castleton and Padley. This line would have linked with another proposed line, the Macclesfield, Buxton and Sheffield Junction Railway, which was proposed at the same time, and had the backing of the NSR. Nothing came of these, as the LNWR gained running powers into Sheffield over the MS&LR.

Five years later, and in a similar vein, came a proposal for the Sheffield and Buxton Narrow Gauge Railway. With a gauge of 3ft, this 24-mile long line starting at Chapel-en-le-Frith would have reached Sheffield by way of Castleton, Bamford and the Rivelin Valley. The unbroken climb at 1 in 50 from Sheffield to the summit of 1,180 feet at Hollow Meadows was the downfall of the scheme, but what a fascinating tourist railway that would have been today if it had been built (and if it had survived)!

Back in the real world, and at the suggestion of William Smith, Secretary and Engineer of the C&HPR (and still Secretary after the LNWR took the lease) the LNWR first sought to upgrade the northern part of the C&HPR. Smith's

*Taken on 26th June 1902, this wonderful photograph shows a dray drawn by six horses and carrying a 2 ton 18 cwt block of Shipley coal, which was delivered to Ashbourne to take part in the procession celebrating the coronation of King Edward VII. Behind the dray is a wagon with its side dropped down, from which the block of coal has presumably just been unloaded. Next to it is private owner wagon No 651 from EM Mundy Shipley Collieries, and next to that we get an excellent view of wagon No 6 owned by Ashbourne's own JO Jones & Sons.
(JR Hollick Archive Courtesy of the FLRS)*

An early view (undated) of the viaduct over Duke's Drive at Buxton (Author's Collection)

DUKES DRIVE, BUXTON.

"The Hindlow Tunnel, 500 yards in length, has been pierced by the contractors, Naylor Bros, and the work of lining has now commenced. Considerable progress is being made with the works all along the new route from Buxton."

In the same year, the *Buxton Advertiser* reported: "We understand that an effort will be made to open the new railway from Buxton to Hindlow at the commencement of April next. Goods and minerals will thenceforth be dispatched by this

recommendation was made in 1864, and proposed a deviation between Hurdlow and Dowlow to avoid Hurdlow incline. His estimate of a total cost of £7,300 for a single track line was approved on 15th September of that year, and the works were authorised by Parliament in the LNWR Act of 5th July 1865 (Cap 333). The contract was given to G Farnworth of Matlock for £4,211 on 20th December 1866, and the new 2-mile long line was opened on 4th January 1869.

Further improvements were required, and on 30th June 1874, an Act of Parliament (Cap 159) was passed that gave the LNWR powers to build a connecting line to the C&HPR from Buxton. The Buxton and High Peak Junction Railway was to be 5m 15ch long, and would run from the LNWR station at Buxton to the C&HPR south of Hindlow, with another 76-chain connection two miles south of Buxton to the C&HPR at Harpur Hill. Work did not begin immediately, however, and the LNWR obtained extensions of time in Acts passed in 1877 and 1880. Finally, in an Act of Parliament passed on 19th July 1887 (Cap 131), which also resulted in the LNWR completely absorbing the C&HPR, powers for the new line were revived.

On 18th July 1888, Naylor Bros of Denby Dale were hired as contractors to make the junction lines for a fee of £73,346. The main line was built as double-track, and the spur to Harpur Hill was to be single-track. The work involved some major engineering projects including a new triangular junction, the 353-yard long Hogshaw Lane Viaduct at Buxton, the 176-yard long viaduct at Duke's Drive, a 514-yard tunnel at Hindlow (which went under the existing C&HPR line) and various other bridges numbering about twenty. All this on a line which in its first 4½ miles out of Buxton ran on a ruling gradient of 1 in 60 to the summit near Hindlow. As a final sting in the tail, immediately before the summit was a short stretch of line at 1 in 41. By early 1889, work was well in hand on the viaducts and tunnel and the other excavations were also in progress.

On 22nd January 1890, the *Derby Mercury* reported that:

new route. At a later date, the line will be opened to passenger traffic, and progress will be made with the continuation of the line to Ashbourne. The platform of the station at Hindlow will be considerably longer than at Buxton, and provision is being made for dealing with the large volume of traffic that is expected at this country station."

The LNWR was now looking for a fast route to London, and the "LNWR (New Works) Act" of 1867 had given it powers to run over all existing and future parts of the NSR. It saw that by joining that company at Ashbourne, it could bring Buxton within 5 hours of London, and could possibly tap the traffic then using the MR, whose route was 37½ miles less than the shortest LNWR route to the capital. This traffic was of great importance at this time, as well-healed Victorians found it desirable to retire periodically to inland spas such as Buxton, Cheltenham and Harrogate where they would "take the waters".

In addition to attracting some of this lucrative traffic away from the Midland, the LNWR also envisaged opening up the countryside to general tourism, and increasing revenue by transporting limestone and agricultural goods, particularly milk to London. However, more important than this was its belief that a route through Stockport, Buxton, and Ashbourne to Lichfield would provide a shorter main line between London and Manchester than the existing routes through Crewe or Stoke-on-Trent. A new link from Ashbourne to Lichfield would have allowed trains to completely avoid having to use NSR metals on the existing route between Macclesfield and Colwich Junction, and it is interesting to consider that if this line had been built, Virgin Pendolinos would now be running over an electrified line through Parsley Hay on their way from London to Manchester and beyond.

In 1890, while the Buxton to Hindlow work was still in progress, the LNWR sought further powers to extend from Parsley Hay to Ashbourne. The Act for the Buxton and

Ashbourne Railway was duly obtained on 4th August 1890 (Cap 154), and when built would result in the completion of the 33½-mile route from Uttoxeter to Buxton. The Act also signalled the abandonment of most of the C&HPR north of Ladmanlow. News of the authorisation of the line was reported in *The Times* and reprinted by the *Derby Mercury* on 24th September 1890:

A pretty but remote bit of Derbyshire is about to be opened up by the London and North Western Railway Company. They have obtained powers to construct a line, 18 miles and three furlongs in length, from Ashbourne, by Dovedale and the old-fashioned village of Hartington, to their Cromford and High Peak track; and this undertaking will not only develop the agricultural and industrial capabilities of a district entirely new to railway travelling, but place Buxton practically nearer town.

Following this is a lengthy and prosaic piece about the district, including references to the possibility of Izaak Walton "quaffing Derbyshire ale, may be, at the inn at Hartington with the quaint sign of 'The Silent Woman' (a headless female)" and Jean Jacques Rousseau thinking out some of his "confessions" on the Derbyshire-Staffordshire border. Interestingly, though, there is also reference to the abandonment of part of the scheme, namely the upgrading of the lower part of the C&HPR to provide a passenger service to Cromford, Wirksworth and Matlock.

By 1892, the new line from Buxton to Hindlow was complete, and goods trains began running to Parsley Hay on 27th June of that year, rendering the Dowlow to Harpur Hill section of the C&HPR redundant. Naylor Bros then began doubling the section from Hindlow to Parsley Hay, and in May 1893, a goods station was opened at Higher Buxton where progress was also being made on a passenger station. Further stations were to be provided at Hindlow, Hurdlow and Parsley Hay. A single line was reported as complete by 18th October 1893, and following an inspection on 29th May 1894, the line from Buxton to Parsley Hay opened for passenger traffic three days later on 1st June. Initially, the new line was served by just two trains each way daily with a bus service connecting Parsley Hay with Hartington and Ashbourne, and an article in the *Buxton Advertiser* of 2nd June 1894 described Parsley Hay as "an admirable centre for excursions by road to Hartington, Beresford Dale, the Manifold Valley, Arbor Low, Lathkill Dale, Youlgreave, etc."

These first trains used a small terminal platform by the main road at Parsley Hay, and an awkward curved extension of No 2 platform at Buxton. The buffer stop of this bay was right up against the gentlemen's lavatory - a situation that led to the death of an unfortunate man availing himself of the facility when, in the early days of the branch, a mineral train from Hindlow ran out of control and completely demolished the building.

An interesting consequence of the new line was that the C&HPR, which had hitherto been measured from zero at Cromford Wharf, was remeasured with zero at Buxton. All the old stone mileposts of the C&HPR were replaced by concrete ones by the LNWR, who also installed concrete gradient posts along the line.

While this activity was taking place north of Parsley Hay, plans for the southward extension to Ashbourne were being drawn up by Francis Stevenson, and were presented to the LNWR board in June 1893. However, it wasn't until 10th December 1895 that the chosen contractors (Naylor Bros once more) were awarded the contract to build the line.

Work commenced in January 1896, and it was to be an arduous task with up to 500 navvies at a time working on the line over the next 3½ years. Construction was done in two sections, the northern one being five miles long and the southern, eight, with work being started simultaneously at each end. Due to the particularly heavy nature of the work, the northern section, although a good deal shorter than the southern one, swallowed up almost half of the total cost.

In contrast to some of the construction work that had taken place half a century previously, by the end of the 1800s, it was actually quite difficult to find enough navvies willing to work so far away from large centres of population, and labour costs were correspondingly high in an effort to attract sufficient numbers. The only notable big towns were Ashbourne and Buxton, and both were at times swamped by the influx of workers. At Ashbourne, many were simply unable to find accommodation, so they slept wherever they could, including in the half-finished station buildings – literally "on the job". Special trains conveyed the labourers to and from the extremes of the line every day.

Some were evidently housed near Hartington, as in December 1896, the Vicar of Hartington, Rev William Fyldes, wrote to a Mr Challinor mentioning the Navvy Mission Fund, of which he was the local secretary. He seems to have been particularly concerned about the drinking habits of the navvies, writing, "Some day before long I want your advice about tackling the drink that is sold in the Navvies' Huts. I know very heavy fines are imposed if found out. Should the Excise people be informed?"

All blasting was done using gelignite, which had been invented some 20 years before, and which significantly aided the excavation of the line compared to earlier manual methods. Details of the locomotives used by Naylor's are given in Appendix A.

Among the many bridges on the line was Hand Dale Viaduct, just north of Hartington. While digging the foundations for this viaduct, the navvies uncovered some old mine workings at the western end of End Low vein containing the skeletons of miners who had been trapped after a roof fall. In addition to the difficulties encountered in building the line across the difficult limestone terrain, winter snowstorms often halted progress altogether, and at least one resulted in a week's lost work as the labourers were completely occupied clearing the snow away sufficiently to make any progress at all.

By March 1898, Naylor's had been awarded the contract to build the stations at Hartington, Alsop-en-le-Dale, Fenny Bentley, Thorpe Cloud and the new station at Ashbourne. The proposed site for the new station was not entirely to the satisfaction of the locals, as it took up part of the Paddock, a

Two views of the construction of Hand Dale viaduct, Hartington, with the temporary wooden trestles used in its construction prominent. The view above, taken after the piers had been completed, is looking south, and shows the trestle carrying the contractor's line and some timber framing for the arch centres in the background ready to be moved into place. The station will be built beyond the viaduct. On the opposite page, the arch centres have been installed on the piers, and the wooden trestle appears to have been dismantled and replaced by a lighter construction resting on the arch centres themselves. (Both, National Railway Museum/Science & Society Picture Library)

venue for many sporting events in the town. Construction was to the simple LNWR design for wayside stations, being of timber with slate roofs on wooden platforms. The goods sheds were more robust, being brick with tiled roofs.

In the meantime, the *Derby Mercury* on 13th June 1894 was reporting on the possibility of upgrading or replacing the C&HPR south-east of Parsley Hay in terms that suggested that much of the traffic that might be expected to be using that line was in fact going by road: "Hope is now entertained of an extension of the new Parsley Hay and Buxton branch of the London and North Western Company to Wirksworth in conjunction with the old High Peak Railway. A mineral and agricultural traffic would thus be facilitated, which is now only carried on by road."

By 1896, the 386-yard Ashbourne tunnel was partly complete and some of the other excavations had been started. In September 1898, the *Railway Magazine* published a report

by Francis Stevenson, Chief Constructive Engineer of the LNWR: "Ninety per cent of the earthwork is finished, and 36 of the 41 bridges and viaducts are constructed or in hand. The works have been commenced for the intermediate stations at Thorpe Cloud, Fenny Bentley, Tissington, Alsop-en-le-Dale and Hartington."

Apart from Ashbourne tunnel, several rock cuttings were needed, the major one being Coldeaton Cutting approximately half-way between Hartington and Alsop-en-le-Dale stations, which was ¾ mile long and up to 60 feet deep. Over 200 navvies and eight steam cranes were used in the building of this part of the line alone. Further south, the seven-arch viaduct between Ashbourne and Thorpe involved the removal of more than 200,000 cubic yards of boulder clay.

The line was designed to be double-track, but although the Buxton to Parsley Hay section had been doubled (and the

NSR was considering doubling the Ashbourne branch) single track only was laid down to Ashbourne, with passing loops at all stations except Thorpe Cloud. Double track was, however, laid through Ashbourne tunnel and into the station. No doubt this was intended to be a temporary measure, but in fact the line remained like this until the end. All stations between Parsley Hay and Ashbourne had two platforms, except for Thorpe Cloud, and there were separate booking offices on each platform as was LNWR practice at the time.

Just as the line rose from Buxton to Hindlow on a ruling gradient of 1 in 60, the ruling gradient from Ashbourne in the south to the summit at 1,268ft was a more sustained, and slightly steeper, 1 in 59. This, together with a sharpest curve of 20 chains radius, severely limited speeds of northbound trains, and was probably the reason why the route never lived up to the high expectations of the LNWR.

According to a *Railway Magazine* article of October 1899, prior to the opening of the line, the railway company conveyed all the inhabitants of Hartington to Ashbourne and back in a special train, free of charge, "an outing that was much appreciated, seeing that the majority of the villagers had certainly never travelled by train before in their lives".

On 1st August 1899, the Chairman and Chief Officers of the LNWR toured the Ashbourne extension, and the next day the line was inspected by the Board of Trade, who "expressed themselves well satisfied with it", according to the *Derbyshire Advertiser*. Presumably also on the same occasion as the LNWR officials' visit, or possibly the free trip for the Hartington residents, Edward Bradbury (who wrote under the pen name, "Strephon") traversed the line and wrote an article for the *Daily News*, also printed in the *Derby Mercury* of 2nd August 1899. He reported that the opening of the railway would be an "event of more than local importance, and one affecting a district far wider than that covered between the towns that are the objective points".

Commenting on the engineering works, he noted that there was only one tunnel (at Ashbourne) and gave special mention to the extreme engineering works that had to be undertaken at Coldeaton cutting. Overall, the new line required 43 bridges "of one kind or another: under, over, public or accommodation". He also mentioned the two resident engineers, Mr Hull, who had been responsible for the northern half, and Mr Hirst, who had been in charge of the remainder. "The solid character of the work superintended by these gentlemen gives emphasis to the first portion of the compound word: permanent-way, and is a credit to the

Ashbourne tunnel in the course of construction. The view above shows the stone-faced southern portal with Church Street bridge taking shape in front of the camera. On the opposite page is the northern portal with its engineering brick contrasting starkly with the way the other end has been treated. Mapleton Road runs across the top of the tunnel, and the bowler-hatted gentleman appears in both photographs, suggesting that he is possibly Mr Hirst, the engineer responsible for the southern half of the new line. (Both, National Railway Museum/Science & Society Picture Library)

persevering contractors, Messrs Naylor and Sons."

Each new station is mentioned including Fenny Bentley, which "will be served by a goods station". At Alsop-en-le-Dale, Lord Hindlip, head of the Burton brewing firm, Samuel Allsop & Sons Ltd, had "provided a commodious hotel that might be a private mansion playing at being a public house, or a public house playing at being a private mansion". This is believed to be the New Inns Hotel (now Newton House), although some references show that building to date from the 18th century.

Between here and Tissington, the cuttings were "of peculiar interest to the geologist" as they consisted of "various clays that are of a brilliant colour when first exposed; limestone, iron, and lead, and shale and green sand also enter into the composition of the strata".

Anticipating the problems that would beset the railway during winter, Bradbury waxed lyrical on the subject of Coldeaton cutting: "'Cold' is an appropriate prefix for this bleak, hungry fissure, and the spot is likely to give the snow

plough some work in the winter, when the heavy, whirling snows peculiar to the district make a white world, and paths and sheep are alike lost in the beleaguering drifts that obliterate the stone wall fences, bulge the hills and choke the valleys. Winter arrives early and tarries late in those Derbyshire uplands."

His description of the line ended with an account of the official luncheon provided by the Chairman and Directors of the LNWR at Hartington, to celebrate the opening on the 1st August. On 4th August 1899, the *Derbyshire Advertiser* carried a large article on the opening of the line, beginning: "The new railway from Ashbourn to Buxton which has been constructed...at a cost of over a million and a half of money, was formally opened on Tuesday, in weather of a tropical character. As many of our readers are aware the new line runs in the immediate vicinity of Dovedale, and this fact alone should cause the railway to be extensively used."

As is customary, the opening celebrations were described, and the following selected extracts give some idea

of the proceedings:

It was decided the actual opening ceremony should take place at the luncheon to be held at Hartington... A special train was to leave Ashbourne at a quarter past twelve to convey those gentlemen who had been invited to the luncheon. Shortly before this, a special train arrived bringing amongst others, Sir Thos. Salt (Chairman of the North Staffordshire Ry Co).

The special train comprised several saloon carriages and the engine (No 930) was in charge of driver C Smith. There was quite a crowd of ladies to see the train start and as it moved out of the station, it immediately ran into a country rich in beautiful scenery of hill and dale, moorland and mountain. As the train passed Sandybrook Hall, several ladies waved their handkerchiefs, and here and there along the banks small knots of country folk had gathered to see the first passenger train proceed along the new line.

At Tissington...amongst the spectators was an old lady named Sharratt who was present at the opening of one of the first railways in the country, namely the old High Peak line. It should be mentioned that the stations on the new line are

not yet completed but will be in a few days. The painters are hard at work but by the time the railway was to be opened for public traffic (Friday August 4th) the buildings will have assumed a more finished appearance.

The train arrived at Hartington at about 1.00pm, but as the *Derbyshire Advertiser* said, "The scene of the actual opening ceremony, if ceremony it can be called, being situated at a point midway along the line, it was necessary that a special train should also be run from Buxton". This was a corridor train of ten saloons, which left Manchester at 11.30 am, under the charge of driver Bethall, and carried yet more LNWR and NSR dignitaries to Hartington.

Here everyone alighted and inspected the station, the only one along the whole line which is completely finished. An air of newness pervaded the atmosphere, and struck one more forcibly than anything else. Porters in spick and span uniforms hustled about the spotless platforms, whilst the newly painted signal box and waiting rooms glistened in the summer sun.

Luncheon was served at 1.00pm in a marquee erected in a

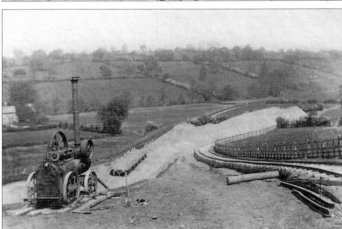

Because the Ashbourne-Buxton line was not built until very late in the 19th century a remarkable photographic record exists of its construction – particularly the Ashbourne to Parsley Hay section. Some were taken by the railway's official photographer, and others by a local amateur. On this page (top) we see one of the contractor's locomotives, Manning Wardle 0-4-0ST "Tissington", being hauled by two traction engines up Dove House Green to commence work at the north end of Ashbourne tunnel, a third traction engine followed behind to act as a "banker" if necessary. A "steam navvy" is seen (middle-left) digging out a cutting and loading the spoil onto a wagon for use elsewhere on the line where embankments were needed; the foreman can be seen in his bowler hat. Next (middle-right) we see a shot that would not be out of place in an Ealing comedy as "Tissington" jauntily propels materials towards the site of Seven Arches viaduct. With a stretch of temporary track on the right and Tan Yard Farm on the left, a stationary engine is standing by Mapleton Road above the north end of Ashbourne tunnel, with the embankment that will lead onto Seven Arches viaduct taking shape below (bottom-left). Finally (bottom-right) we see preparations underway on Church Street for the digging of the tunnel. (All, JR Hollick Archive Courtesy of the FLRS)

Top: A wooden trestle bridge carries the temporary line over Spend Lane on the approach to Thorpe Cloud station (left), while navvies' accommodation at Parsley Hay is pictured right. (Both, JR Hollick Archive Courtesy of the FLRS)

Above: The cutting being excavated at Fenny Bentley with another "steam navvy" at work, and a rake of wagons similar to the one seen on the opposite page. (National Railway Museum/Science & Society Picture Library)

Officials of the LNWR together with invited guests as described in the "Derbyshire Advertiser" article; FW Webb is the bearded gentleman standing to the right of the group. The poster nailed to the tree announces the "Opening of the New Line Between Ashbourne and Parsley Hay" (Author's Collection)

field adjoining Hartington Station. As was usual on these occasions, there were several toasts and speeches, the first, by Mr HA Hubbersty, JP, Chairman of Buxton Lime Co, who noted that dynamite had made light work of the excavation of the cuttings. Lord Stalbridge (LNWR Chairman) then replied, and made reference to the old C&HPR: "If a passenger arrived at the station too late for the train he only had to walk on to the next station and catch it up again (laughter) but he did not think they would be able to say that about the new Buxton and Ashbourne line. (Hear, hear.)"

After the luncheon, "the guests grouped themselves under a tree and were photographed by Mr Webb of Crewe, the official photographer of the L and NW Company". The great LNWR Chief Mechanical Engineer, FW Webb, was certainly in attendance at the luncheon, but the LNWR's official photographer at the time was John Astles, so it looks as though the *Derbyshire Advertiser* reporter was a little confused.

Shortly afterwards, the special trains left Hartington, that from Buxton running to Ashbourne before returning over the whole length of the line in order that its passengers could

view the southern section. Exactly nine years after its Act had been passed, the first passenger trains began to run on the line on 4th August 1899 with goods services being operated from the same date. After driving a line 22½ miles from Buxton to Ashbourne, the LNWR was now able to run through services between Euston and Buxton (the same distance to St Pancras via the MR) and the fortunes of both the LNWR and NSR lines were to be forever intertwined. Although NSR trains occasionally used the line, this was to be the exception rather than the rule.

As mentioned previously, the opening of the new line was featured in a ten-page article in the October 1899 issue of the *Railway Magazine*. This pre-eminent monthly periodical, which is still published today, had itself been established just two years previously, and new lines of the size of this one were becoming something of a novelty. It is not surprising, therefore, that it was given prominence in this way. Regrettably, the article contains a number of very obvious errors, but it is an interesting contemporary account of the building and opening of the line.

It begins: "The iron horse is for ever seeking out new

FW Webb is seen again standing next to his personal departmental saloon in this picture taken at Hartington. There is no evidence here of the other special trains that ran that day, so Webb must have arrived separately (possibly with the LNWR photographer) before the arrival of the rest of the guests. (Author's Collection)

country, penetrating fresh districts, and giving access to hitherto inaccessible spots. Each fresh advance excites corresponding opposition on the part of conservative landowners and all those selfish people who would fain exclude the many from a participation in the pleasures of the few. But notwithstanding the efforts of the anti-progressivists, that which makes for the ultimate good of the greatest number invariably triumphs, and hence it comes about that each year witnesses the opening up of some new beauty-spot in the British Isles, the gift of some new lung to England's gasping cities of toil."

Apart from the observation that much could be said over a century later in respect of HS2, the proposed high-speed rail link between London, the West Midlands and the North, it is interesting to note that the line was immediately being viewed as a way for the masses to escape industrial conurbations such as Manchester to seek respite in the unspoilt beauties of the Peak District.

Completely overlooking the incursion of the GNR through Derby (and indeed, the LNWR's existing presence by dint of its line to Buxton and the Cromford & High Peak Railway) the article went on to assert that, "Derbyshire has hitherto been the special preserve of the Midland, the North Staffordshire alone among the railway companies venturing to dispute its sway, though dispute is perhaps hardly the word, seeing that the North Staffordshire line makes no attempt to compete with any of the Midland Company's iron roads."

Though it made much of the line's ability to attract tourist traffic to the area, the *Railway Magazine* article also emphasised the value of the line for through traffic between London and Manchester, observing that what at first sight might seem to be a somewhat unimportant matter was in reality an event that might was destined to produce far-reaching results. It was anticipated that this could become the LNWR's primary route between the two cities, supplanting the company's existing routes.

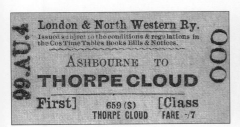

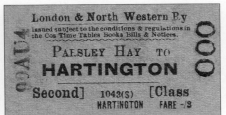

Tickets from the first day of operation of the Buxton line, and indeed the first ones to be issued from Ashbourne to Thorpe Cloud and Parsley Hay to Hartington (number 000 in each case). (Glynn Waite Collection)

Above: The LNWR/NSR Joint station seen shortly after the opening of the extension to Buxton. The original station is out of the picture on the left, and the road serving it has been blocked by the railway, so a footbridge has been added to provide access. The signals are by the LNWR, and the contractor's locomotive (possibly "Tissington") can be seen in the short siding beneath the bridge. In the station is an NSR train from Uttoxeter and an LNWR train from Buxton. The footbridge was later moved to Tutbury where it is still in use today.

Below: Photographed at the same time, the down bay has not yet been built, nor has the Station Hotel. Horse boxes from both companies are in the horse dock to the right, and in the up bay four LNWR carriages are sandwiched by a North Staffordshire Railway milk van and carriage. (Both, JR Hollick Archive Courtesy of the FLRS)

Chapter 4

Two Lines United

The years immediately following the opening of the line were marked by a series of connections being added to serve the various quarries and works along the route that began to thrive as a result of the railway's arrival. Each resulted in an inspection by the Board of Trade, and details can be found in later chapters where features along the line are described.

The first effect of the arrival of the LNWR in Ashbourne was the abandonment of the old NSR station in the town. In recent years, we have become used to reading of the closure of lines and stations, but in 1899, this was a very rare event. On 4th August 1899 the *Derbyshire Advertiser* supplemented its coverage of the opening of the new line with a report of the last train to use the NSR station. By all accounts, the scenes were more appropriate for the complete closure of a branch than the closure of a station that was being replaced:

The last train run into the old station on Sunday night (31st July) was witnessed by a large crowd of spectators. On the platform, and also on the new footbridge, people crowded on each other to see the final act in the drama. In some the sentiment was carried even further, as the train was simply crowded with people, the greater part of whom had apparently no other object in travelling than to ride upon the last train that came into the station. The carriages had no sooner been shunted out of the station than a large gang of workmen commenced connecting the new main lines to the new station, and breaking up the old platform. In a very short time the connection was made, and the platform broken up beyond recognition. This work is still being continued, the platform being converted into a milk wharf. The old booking office and waiting rooms are to be used as goods offices.

At the opening of the new line, there were four stopping trains a day between Buxton and Ashbourne, with the addition of an extra service on Saturdays. A feature of the first timetable of 4th August 1899 was a 10.25am departure from Buxton to Uttoxeter, which remained a constant feature almost throughout the whole time that the passenger services operated over the line.

Amongst the first services over the new line, introduced on 1st October 1899, was a through coach from Buxton to London, which ran via Ashbourne, Uttoxeter, Burton and the Ashby & Nuneaton Joint Railway, to Nuneaton where it was picked up by the 8.30am train from Manchester. In the opposite direction, a through coach from London to Buxton left with the 11.00am departure from Euston and was slipped at Nuneaton, from where was taken back over the same route as the up service to reach its destination at 3.22pm. From the same date, an early afternoon train left Buxton at 1.20pm and carried a coach that was attached at Rugby to the 4.35pm departure to Euston, arriving there at 6.25pm. This had a corresponding return service as well.

The October 1899 *Railway Magazine* noted that it was not proposed to improve very much on existing times until the track had thoroughly consolidated and settled (usually achieved by opening new lines to goods before passenger services) but that "no doubt the through expresses will be accelerated later on". The article also noted that cheap weekend and excursion tickets were available from Manchester to stations on the new line.

Interestingly, the through coach service to London was not shown in the NSR timetable as it was a competitor to that company's own (somewhat roundabout) service from

A few years after the line opened throughout, an LNWR "Watford" 0-6-2T moves its train towards the yard to run round for the return trip to Buxton. Note the LNWR 6-wheeled close-coupled coaches and the additional wall that has been added by the footbridge forming a small compound next to the Station Master's house (compare with the photograph on page 23). The Station Hotel (opened in November 1901) is also now evident.
(JR Hollick Archive Courtesy of the FLRS)

Webb's 5ft 6in 2-4-2T locomotives were introduced in 1890, and saw use on the line to Parsley Hay and later Ashbourne. Newly-built 427 has just been allocated to Buxton, and is seen on the turntable at the site of the old shed in around 1894, after the new shed had been opened on the Stockport line. The earlier shed has been demolished, and a temporary water tank provided. The new fence and signal rodding in the foreground is in the area that will become the Ashbourne bay. Although difficult to make out in the photograph, behind the loco is a line of wagons belonging to the contractors, Naylor Bros, who were busy building the line south of Buxton at the time. (RS Carpenter Photo Collection)

NSR class D 0-6-0 No 124 is seen leaving Ashbourne with the goods shed visible behind. Beyond the goods shed is quite possibly the corn mill built for JO Jones & Sons. The reason for the locomotive being decorated is not know with certainty, but the locomotive number does not have the suffix "A", which was added in 1904, so it is quite possibly celebrating the coronation of Edward VII in 1902. (Author's Collection)

Buxton, which ran via the LNWR to Disley, then over the Manchester, Sheffield and Lincolnshire and North Staffordshire Railways' joint line through Bollington to its own metals at Macclesfield before rejoining the LNWR again at Colwich. Because of this LNWR connection, that company effectively controlled the through service, and similarly, the MS&LR was the major partner on the joint line north of Macclesfield. As a result, it was difficult for the NSR to make a success of these services. A first class ticket on the LNWR route between Buxton and London cost £2 3s 4d for the 168½-mile journey.

At this time, milk was carried to London via the GNR line from Egginton Junction, drawing comment from the *Railway Magazine* who, in March 1906, wrote:

A good many readers...will be surprised to learn that London and North-Western rolling stock works regularly over the Great Northern Railway to King's Cross. Every day, a van is loaded with milk at stations between Buxton and Ashbourne, on the London and North-Western Railway, and travelling over the North Staffordshire Railway is handed over to the Great Northern Railway at Eggington (sic) Junction, the milk being consigned to Finsbury Park, etc. It says a good deal for the power that the customers of our railways wield that consignors of milk can insist on their traffic travelling thus by such a route. In the ordinary way one would expect the

A lovely period piece taken at Ashbourne, probably soon after the new joint station was opened. The footbridge is in its original state with its overall roof, and a sign has been fixed to the down side staircase giving directions to the Station Hotel and refreshment rooms. On the right of the picture is the WH Smith bookstall. (Glynn Waite Collection)
The advert is from the "Derbyshire Advertiser" for 4th August 1899, the day the line opened.

Above: Ex-LNWR non-corridor brake third carriage (LMS No 22478) is pictured in the up bay platform at Ashbourne in 1927.
(HMRS Jim Richards Collection Ref No AAH205)

Left: Although not directly associated with the branch to Ashbourne and Uttoxeter, these photographs of the aftermath of a boiler explosion at Buxton were too compelling to leave out. On 11th November 1921, Webb 4-cylinder compound 0-8-0 No 134 had just backed onto a goods train bound ultimately for Oldham when the catastrophic explosion occurred. The Board of Trade's inspecting officer, Major Hall, put the blame on a number of factors each of which, individually, would not necessarily have been regarded as dangerous. Even large pieces were found up to 670 feet away, and Driver W Holmes and Fireman W Fletcher were killed instantly. (Author's Collection)

Opposite page top: Ashbourne is seen here in 1924, with a train arriving from Buxton made up of NSR coaching stock hauled by an LNWR 0-6-2T. The station is still in almost pristine condition, but the take-over by the LMS is demonstrated by the removal of the LNWR/NSR notice board – ironically advertising LMS holidays. (JR Hollick Archive Courtesy of the FLRS)

Opposite page bottom: LMS 3P 0-4-4T No 1436 at Uttoxeter on 25th May 1933.
(Ronald G Jarvis/ Midland Railway Trust)

London and North-Western Railway would insist on the whole of the journey being performed over its own system, and require the consignee to take delivery at a London and North-Western Railway station in London.

This might have been true, but in practice, traffic would have had to travel by a very circuitous route to avoid using the Great Northern or Midland Railways to reach (say) the Trent Valley Line – even if travel over the NSR was regarded as being "over its own system". A cheese factory at Hartington was also served, and this dairy traffic, together with limestone and cattle, formed the mainstay of the freight traffic on the line for most of its life.

The gradients on the line made it unsuitable for express passenger work, and except as a diversionary route, the line was unnecessary for through traffic between London and the North, so even at its height, the usual daily service was six local passenger trains each way, with up to two through carriages from Euston. Apart from the very early days, when close-coupled sets of four-wheeled (and later six-wheeled) coaches were the norm, the standard coaching stock comprised three-coach trains of bogie stock, of which the middle coach was all third class, and the two end coaches were brake composites with first, second and third class seating. In these coaches, the two first and second class compartments had lavatories between them, and the third class compartment was at the end of the coach. When second class was abolished in 1913, those compartments became third class. These were originally main line coaches that had been downgraded, and they were peculiar to the Buxton to Ashbourne line. The train sets were lettered "Buxton Ashbourne and Manchester Set No 1" (or 2 or 3) on the ends, but it is not certain that they never actually made trips to Manchester. After the grouping in 1923, their runs were extended to Uttoxeter, and it is difficult to see how they could have found time to leave the line to travel north of Buxton. Six-wheeled stock (except water tanks for the Locomotive Department) was prohibited between Hindlow and Ladmanlow according to the April 1916 LNWR *Appendix to the Working Timetable*.

Before the grouping, the passenger engines were Webb 5ft 6in 2-4-2Ts from Buxton shed, later supplemented by 5ft 2½in "Watford" 0-6-2Ts, which quickly established themselves as the locomotive of choice on the branch until the mid-1930s. This was a type found only in a few districts – London, Birmingham, Leeds and Manchester – with this little enclave at Buxton. London trains consisted of two corridor coaches hauled by "Jumbo" 2-4-0s, and excursions from Manchester were worked by 4-6-2Ts. A regular visitor to the line was the Manchester inspection saloon hauled by a 2-4-0 named *Engineer Manchester*. Stone trains were worked down to Ashbourne by High Peak 2-4-0Ts, and a particularly interesting working was of a Webb 0-6-2T that ran light from Buxton to Parsley Hay to pick up a train of stone wagons each evening. This was said at the time to be the longest regular light engine working in the British Isles.

South of Ashbourne at this time, the usual engines were 2-4-0Ts, class D 0-6-0Ts and 2-4-2Ts. However, 2-4-0 tender engines, with inside and outside cylinders, were used occasionally. Class DX 0-6-2T No 76 was shedded at Ashbourne for years, and worked freight traffic, while class E 0-6-0s sometimes appeared on goods and excursion trains, and 4-4-0s were occasionally used on excursion trains to North Wales; some NSR trains worked through to Buxton.

The July to September 1914 NSR working timetable shows the following goods services to and from the branch, listed here as they appeared at Uttoxeter (not all Churnet Valley services are shown, just those that served stations described in this book). These services were conditional, and only ran when required.

- Weekdays NSR ordinary goods from Ashbourne to Burton, arrives Uttoxeter at 2.42am. (Does not run between Rocester and Burton on Saturdays.)
- Weekdays NSR passenger and goods (mixed) from Ashbourne to Uttoxeter, arrives Uttoxeter at 6.56am.
- Weekdays NSR ordinary goods from Uttoxeter to Rocester, departs Uttoxeter at 11.15am.
- Weekdays NSR ordinary goods from Rocester to Uttoxeter, arrives Uttoxeter at 1.05pm. (Calls at Uttoxeter Gas Works, 12.50 to 1.00pm.)
- Weekdays NSR ordinary goods and milk vans from Burton to Ashbourne, passes Uttoxeter at 1.50pm.
- Weekdays (except Saturdays) NSR ordinary goods from Ashbourne to Burton, arrives Uttoxeter at 2.42pm, departs at 3.10pm. (Attach at Scropton when required.)
- Weekdays (except Saturdays) NSR ordinary goods from Uttoxeter to Burton, departs Uttoxeter at 6.20pm.
- Weekdays NSR ordinary goods from Ashbourne to Burton, arrives Uttoxeter at 6.27pm, departs at 8.26pm. (Works engine and brake van, Uttoxeter to Cresswell, returning with milk vans. Also on Tuesdays, when Meir Auction, works to Blythe Bridge for cattle, attaching milk vans at Cresswell on return.)
- Weekdays (except Saturdays) NSR ordinary goods from Burton to Ashbourne, arrives Uttoxeter at 7.25pm, departs at 7.40pm. (Conveys tranship road vans lettered Macclesfield, Uttoxeter and Ashbourne.)
- Weekdays LNWR ordinary goods from Parsley Hay to Burton, arrives Uttoxeter East Junction at 9.55pm. (Works 2 hours earlier over NSR lines on Saturdays only, and runs into Horninglow Yard.)
- Weekdays NSR express goods from Burton to Manchester, departs Uttoxeter at 11.45pm. (Calls at Rocester on Saturdays only, and on that day runs 30 minutes earlier.)
- Sundays NSR engine and van from Uttoxeter to Tutbury, departs Uttoxeter at 11.00am. (Return at 11.30am with milk vans.)

During the First World War, trains of guns were run through Ashbourne to be tested on the moors, and German prisoners of war from Ashbourne Hall Hotel were sent to work in the quarries in a Great Eastern Railway six-wheeled coach at the front of the train. A poem was published in

BUXTON, HARTINGTON, and ASHBOURNE.—London and North Western.

Up.	Week Days.							Suns.		
				S	E					
	mrn	mrn	mrn	aft	aft	aft	aft	mrn	aft	aft
Buxton .. ....dep.	7 25	9 15	1035	1 25	1 45	230	5 53	10 0	130	4 35
Higher Buxton ...	....	9 17	1037	1 27	1 47	232	5 55	....	...	....
Hindlow	7 34	9 26	1046	1 36	1 56	241	6 4	10 9	139	4 43
Hurdlow §	7 45	9 36	1053	1 44	2 4	249	6 12	....	...	4 59
Parsley Hay.......	7 51	9 43	1059	1 50	2 10	255	6 18	1021	151	5 7
Hartington	7 57	9 50	11 5	1 55	2 15	3 1	6 22	1027	157	5 14
Alsop-en-le-Dale †..	8 10	10 2	1114	2 6	2 32	312	6 33	1038	2 8	5 26
Tissington	8 19	10 8	1121	2 15	2 39	318	6 44	1043	213	5 38
Thorpe Cloud †....	8 25	1013	1127	2 21	2 45	323	6 54	1048	218	5 51
Ashbourne 603arr.	8 37	1021	1136	2 30	2 54	332	7 2	11 0	230	6 0

Down.	Week Days.							Suns.		
			S	E						
	mrn	mrn	mrn	mrn	aft	aft	aft	mrn	aft	aft
Ashbourne ....dep.	7 45	9 15	11 5	1150	1 45	4 10	7 45	1140	3 0	6 30
Thorpe Cloud †	7 52	9 22	1112	1157	1 52	4 17	7 52	1147	3 7	6 38
Tissington	7 58	9 28	1118	12 3	1 58	4 23	7 58	1153	313	6 45
Alsop-en-le-Dale †..	8 7	9 37	1127	1211	2 6	4 31	8 8	12 2	322	6 54
Hartington	8 19	9 48	1138	1222	2 18	4 42	8 19	1212	332	7 6
Parsley Hay	8 25	9 56	1144	1227	2 25	4 49	8 26	1218	338	7 14
Hurdlow §	8 31	10 2	1151	1233	2 34	4 55	8 33	....	...	7 22
Hindlow	8 40	1010	12 0	1241	2 42	5 6	8 42	1231	352	7 31
Higher Buxton 639	8 47	1017	1216	1254	2 49	5 14	....	....	...	....
Buxton 634, arr.	8 53	1025	1223	1 0	2 55	5 19	9 0	1245	4 5	7 45

E Except Saturdays. **S** Saturdays only. † Station for Dovedale. § Station for Longnor (3 miles) and Monyash (1½ miles).

ASHBOURNE and UTTOXETER.—North Staffordshire.

Miles.	Up.	Week Days.																Sundays.			
		mrn	mrn		mrn	mrn		aft	aft	aft (Saturdays only.)	aft	aft					mrn		aft	
	483 Buxton ....dep.	....	7 25	....	9 15	1035	....	....	2 30	....	5 53	....	....	....	....	....	....	....	4 35	....
—	**Ashbourne**..............dep.	7 35	9 10	....	1057	1145	....	1 35	4 15	5 22	7 5	9 0	....	....	....	....	9 30	....	6 10	....
1¼	Clifton (Mayfield)...........	7 39	9 15	....	11 1	1149	....	1 40	4 19	5 26	7 10	9 5	....	....	....	....	9 35	....	6 15	....
4¼	Norbury and Ellastone......	7 46	9 22	....	11 7	1155	....	1 47	4 27	5 32	7 17	9 12	....	....	....	....	9 42	....	6 22	.. .
6¾	**Rocester 601**.......... arr.	7 51	9 28	....	1112	12 1	....	1 52	4 32	5 37	7 22	9 17	....	....	....	....	9 47	....	6 27	....
	dep.	8 4	9 29	....	1122	12 2	....	1 54	4 34	....	7 23	9 19	....	....	....	....	9 50	....	6 30	....
11¼	**Uttoxeter 597, 602** .. arr.	8 12	9 37	....	1130	1210	....	2 2	4 42	....	7 31	9 27	....	....	....	....	9 58	....	6 38	....
24¼	596 Burton (Station St.) arr.	9 50	1032	....	1 5	1 5	....	3h20	6 1	....	8 30	11s10	....	....	....	....	1115	....	8 0	....

Miles.	Down.	Week Days.														Sundays.			
		mrn	mrn	mrn		mrn	aft	aft (Saturdays only.)	aft (Saturdays only.)	aft (Except Saturdays.)		aft	aft			mrn		aft	
	597 Burton (Station St.) dep.	....	9 12	....	....	1053	1 30	2 35	4 25	4 25	....	5 25	7 10	....	....	9 30	....	6 20	....
—	**Uttoxeter**...............dep.	7 50	1015	....	....	1240	3 9	4 50	5 30	5 45	....	6 15	8 25	....	....	1050	....	7 30	....
4½	**Rocester**............ arr.	8 5	1023	....	....	1248	3 17	4 58	5 33	5 53	....	6 23	8 33	....	....	1053	....	7 38	....
	dep.	8 10	1025	1130	....	1250	3 19	5 0	5 35	5 55	....	6 25	8 35	....	....	11 1	....	7 40	....
7	**Norbury and Ellastone**......	8 16	1032	1136	....	1257	3 26	5 6	6 2	6 2	....	6 32	8 42	....	....	1111	....	7 48	....
10	Clifton (Mayfield)...........	8 23	1040	1143	....	1 5	3 33	5 13	6 10	6 10	....	6 40	8 50	....	....	1119	....	7 54	....
11¼	**Ashbourne 483** ....arr.	8 27	1044	1147	....	1 9	3 37	5 17	6 14	6 14	....	6 44	8 54	....	....	1123	..	7 58	....
33¾	483 Buxton ....arr.	1025	1 A 0	1 e 0	....	2 55	5 19	....	....	....	....	9 0	....	....	....	1245	....	....	....

A Arrives at 12 23 aft. on Saturdays. *e* Except Saturdays. *h* Wednesdays and Saturdays. *s* Saturdays only.

The July 1922 timetables for Buxton-Ashbourne and Ashbourne-Uttoxeter.

Punch describing an escape from the worries of war by choosing a peaceful branch line from the pages of *Bradshaw*. The writer chose this branch, and referred to the "peaceful sound" of Hindlow, Hurdlow, Parsley Hay and Hartington.

The May 1920 NSR *Appendix to the Working Timetable*, noted that the LNWR allowed a maximum of only ten coaches on NSR trains between Ashbourne and Buxton, and if this number was exceeded, the train had to be divided. The same *Appendix* showed that although mixed trains were run elsewhere on the NSR, there was only one such train per day on the Ashbourne branch, this being the 7.50am Uttoxeter to Ashbourne service. Cattle trucks could be attached to passenger trains on the Ashbourne line on Wednesdays (3.09pm Uttoxeter-Ashbourne) and Thursdays (1.35pm Ashbourne-Uttoxeter), and the 10.15am Uttoxeter departure was allowed to carry a "Tranship Van" and an MR van from St Pancras.

Further reading of this *Appendix* reveals more information about the line between Uttoxeter and Ashbourne, for instance, Rocester ("Up Churnet") was included in a list of principal stations, whereas neither Uttoxeter nor Ashbourne was. We also learn that there were no catch points anywhere between Uttoxeter and Ashbourne, and the number of places where tow-roping of vehicles was permitted "if absolutely necessary" included Clifton Yard and Norbury milk dock.

More interesting, perhaps, are the signalling details included in the book. For instance, there were no track circuits on the line between Ashbourne and Rocester, but there were on the Churnet Valley line. The single lines between Rocester and Norbury, and between Norbury and Clifton were worked by electric staff or tablets, and the block posts were listed as the signal cabins at Ashbourne No 2 (LNWR), Ashbourne No 1 (NSR), Clifton Yard, Norbury, Rocester Junction, Spath Crossing and Uttoxeter North Junction; telegraph instruments were situated at all stations.

Water columns (or tanks) were located at Uttoxeter and Ashbourne, but not at the intermediate stations, while an interesting note relates to the joint NSR and LNWR ownership of Ashbourne station. Here, it was specified that if the line through the station became blocked by a failed engine or derailed train, the North Staffordshire breakdown gang would attend and clear the line, whether the culprit was one of its own or an LNWR train.

In 1922, just before the grouping, the line from Rocester to Ashbourne was recorded as being 1m 36ch of double track

BUXTON and ASHBOURNE

Miles	Up — HOUR	mrn 7	8	S 9	10		E 1	S 1	S 3	S 6	E 5	S 6	aft S 7	Sundays mrn 10	aft 1	aft 4	aft 7
—	**Buxton** ....dep.	7	.	15	35	.	45	55	15	.	55	0	50	1020	1 35	4 48	7 54
½	Higher Buxton............	10	.	17	37	.	47	57	17	.	57	2	.	..	..	..	..
3¾	Hindlow	18	.	26	46	.	56	**6**	26	.	**6**	11	59	1029	1 44	4 57	8 3
4½	Dowlow Halt...............	22	.	30	50	.	**0**	10	30	.	10	15	**3**	1033	1 48	5 1	..
6¾	Hurdlow **D**...............	27	.	35	55	.	5	15	35	.	15	20	8	1038	1 53	5 7	8 9
9	Parsley Hay..............	33	0	41	**4**	.	11	21	41	.	21	26	14	1044	1 59	5 13	8 15
10¾	Hartington...............	.	5	46	9	.	16	26	46	.	26	30	22	1049	2 4	5 18	8 20
15½	Alsop-en-le-Dale **F**........	.	15	55	18	.	25	35	54	10	34	38	31	1058	2 13	5F33	8 29
18¼	Tissington................	.	22	**1**	24	.	31	41	**1**	16	N43	D50	37	11 4	2 19	5H45	8 35
19½	Thorpe Cloud **F**..........	.	27	6	29	.	36	46	6	21	48	55	42	11 9	2 24	5 50	8 40
22¼	**Ashbourne 572**........arr.	.	32	11	34	.	41	51	11	26	53	**0**	47	1114	2 29	5 55	8 45

Miles	Down — HOUR	mrn 7	10		S 11		1		4	S 5	S 7	7	S 9	aft	Sundays non 12	aft 3	aft 7	aft 9
—	**Ashbourne**...........dep.	50	28	.	8	.	35	.	18	40	10	50	15	.	12 0	3 20	7 5	9 42
2¾	Thorpe Cloud **F**..........	57	35	.	16	.	43	.	26	48	18	57	23	.	12 8	3 28	7 13	9 50
4	Tissington................	**4**	41	.	26	.	49	.	32	54	24	**4**	29	.	1214	3 34	7 19	9 56
6¾	Alsop-en-le-Dale **F**.......	14	49	.	36	.	57	.	40	**1**	32	12	37	.	1222	3 42	7 27	10 4
11½	Hartington................	24	58	.	48	.	**6**	.	49	.	41	21	46	.	1231	3 51	7 36	1013
13¼	Parsley Hay...............	28	**2**	.	52	.	10	.	53	.	46	25	50	.	1235	3 55	7 40	1017
15⅝	Hurdlow **D**..............	33	7	.	59	.	15	.	58	.	.	30	55	.	1240	4 0	7 45	1022
17¾	Dowlow Halt...............	39	13	.	**5**	.	21	.	**4**	.	54	36	**1**	.	1246	..	7 51	..
18¾	Hindlow...................	42	16	.	8	.	24	.	9	.	59	40	5	.	1251	4 7	7 56	1029
21¾	Higher Buxton............	50	24	.	16	.	32	.	17	.	.	.	.	.	..	..	..	..
22¼	**Buxton**................arr.	58	28	.	19	.	35	.	20	.	**6**	47	12	.	1258	4 15	8 3	1037

C Station for Golf Links. Alighting Platform only. **D** For Longnor (3 miles) and Monyash (1½ miles). D Arr. 6 44 aft. **E** Except Sats.
F For Dovedale. F Arr. 5 26 aft. H Arr. 5 38 aft. **H** Change at Stockport. K South Junc. Platform. **L** Sats. only. One cl. only N Arr. 6 39 aft.
P Mayfield. **S** or S Sats. only. T Dep. Mayfield on Sats. U Dep 2 18 aft on Sats. Y Arr. Mayfield on Sats.
Y On 9th inst only. **Z** On 16th, 23rd, and 30th inst.

UTTOXETER and ASHBOURNE

Miles	Down — HOUR	mn 8	A 9		A 12	3	S 5	E 5	7	aft S 8	Sun. aft 3 A	3	6	9 A
—	**Uttoxeter** ....dep.	23	56	.	50	12	10	43	0	36	.	0	35	.
4½	Rocester..................	30	**3**	.	57	19	17	50	8	43	0	8	43	22
7	Norbury and Ellaston....	37	10	.	**4**	26	24	57	16	50	6	15	50	28
10	Clifton, for Mayfield......	44	17	.	11	33	31	**4**	23	57	13	27	57	35
11½	**Ashbourne 523** .....arr.	49	23	.	16	38	36	9	28	**2**	18	34	**2**	40

Miles	Up — HOUR	mn 7	9	11		1	4		7	aft S 9		Sun aft 2 A	6	8 A
—	**Ashbourne** ....dep.	25	2	36	.	40	25	.	20	15	.	30	0	50
1¼	Clifton, for Mayfield.....	28	5	39	.	43	28	.	24	18	.	34	3	53
4¼	Norbury and Ellaston...	35	12	46	.	50	35	.	31	25	.	41	10	**0**
6¾	Rocester **519**............	41	18	52	.	56	41	.	37	31	.	47	16	6
11¼	**Uttoxeter 526, 528**.arr.	50	28	**1**	.	**5**	50	.	45	40	.	.	25	.

A Through Trains to and from Buxton, page 523. **E** Except Sats. **S** Sats only
OTHER TRAINS between Uttoxeter & Rocester, p 519

Above: The July 1938 timetables for Buxton-Ashbourne and Ashbourne-Uttoxeter.

Below: Ex-LNWR 0-6-2T 6899 is seen at Higher Buxton with the 1.45pm Buxton to Ashbourne train in June 1930. (ER Morten)

Two photographs taken at Ashbourne showing the platform of the old station in use as a loading dock for milk and other items. At the top of the page, we see ex-MR Johnson 2-4-0 237 on a train of horse boxes on 25th September 1929 – notice the NSR signal attached to the goods shed on the right. Below is ex-LNWR 4-6-0 5672 on 29th June 1930 with an assortment of what appear to be empty churns on the platform. (JR Hollick Archive Courtesy of the FLRS)

Above: Fowler 2-6-4T 2319 arrives at Buxton with a train from Ashbourne and pulls into platform 2, having just passed Buxton No 2 signalbox in 1935. (ER Morten)

Below: In connection with Territorial Army exercises around Hindlow in the 1930s, many military specials were run by the LMS, usually using ex-LNWR 0-8-0s such as this one, seen here having just passed Beswick's Sidings signalbox in June 1936. (ER Morten)

Driver Joe Norton and Fireman Jack Baker are seen next to their locomotive, Fowler 2-6-4T 2370, at Uttoxeter in 1931 shortly before taking the train to Buxton. Not long after Jack Hollick took the photograph, Fireman Baker tragically lost his life when he was struck by a passenger train at Disley. (JR Hollick Archive Courtesy of the FLRS)

(between Clifton and Ashbourne) and 5m 30ch of single, in addition to the 33 chains of joint line at Ashbourne. On the Churnet Valley line at Rocester, four passenger trains connected with Uttoxeter to Ashbourne services each weekday, with one connecting on Sundays. The MR provided a through coach between London and Ashbourne, which ran as the 11.55am Ashbourne to St Pancras (arriving at 4.30pm), and the 2.00pm St Pancras to Ashbourne (arriving at 6.42pm).

Almost immediately after the grouping in 1923, the LMS cut back services on the line, so that only a local link was preserved between Uttoxeter and Buxton. Staff numbers at the stations were cut back, and many augmented their earnings by having allotments and smallholdings, which they tended between trains. Nevertheless, the take-over meant that the line was generally worked more as a unified whole, with a few extra trains working into and out of Ashbourne to the north and to the south. Rowsley Control, which had previously covered the Midland line from Whatstandwell to Buxton and Peak Forest Junction, now took over responsibility for the C&HPR and the line from Buxton to Ashbourne (excluding Ashbourne).

Webb 0-6-2Ts and the Buxton coaches worked most of the trains with later occasional appearances from MR class 2 4-4-0s, and for a short time, a Midland 0-4-4T worked from Buxton to Ashbourne on Saturdays. The NSR locomotives were replaced by new class L 0-6-2Ts, but Ashbourne class DX (numbered 2238 by the LMS) lasted into the late 1920s. A Midland 2-4-0 was used to work a through evening passenger train from Derby to Ashbourne, and then returned with the milk train. This train was later altered to become a through train from the NSR "loop line" north of Stoke-on-Trent, and finally became the 5.3pm from Crewe, which changed engines at Uttoxeter. NSR railmotors worked to Ashbourne during the General Strike of 1926. Later, LMS Fowler 2-6-4Ts came into general use, and the daily goods

trains between Uttoxeter and Buxton, and Walsall (later Burton) and Buxton, were worked by ex-LNWR 0-8-0s or LMS 0-6-0s.

Until its final years in the 1930s, the Sunday milk train was worked by the Willesden engine off the Willesden to Uttoxeter milk train. Engines noted on this service at this time included ex-LNWR 4-4-0s and "Prince of Wales" class 4-6-0s (some with outside Joy valve gear), LMS compounds and 2-6-0s, and occasionally 2-6-4Ts – a long working for a tank engine. On a couple of occasions, the Willesden engine was even seen working the weekday afternoon Uttoxeter to Buxton passenger train – once with a compound and once with a 2-6-0.

Excursion traffic continued to be a feature of the line, and an example of this was in 1932, when a special train organised by the firm of Mather and Platt ran from Manchester to Friden (on the C&HPR) via Buxton and Parsley Hay.

The March 1937 *Appendix to the Working Timetable* contained the following restrictions: "All passenger trains working locally between Parsley Hay and Ashbourne must be worked by tank engines and stop at each station. This will not apply to the through passenger trains, but tender engines working passenger trains must run engine first. All goods trains over this line must be worked with 20-ton brake vans."

The Second World War resulted in further curtailments of the service over the line, including the withdrawal of all milk trains in 1941, and Stanier 2-6-2Ts and 2-6-4Ts became the standard motive power. The 2-6-2Ts, however, came to be used less and less as they had a habit of derailing themselves on suspect turnouts and crossings on the North Staffordshire section of which, regrettably, there were a few. Ammunition trains were worked over the line to RAF Harpur Hill, Jack Hollick noting one on 26th May 1940 and several others on subsequent days. They were hauled by class 4Fs, but had to wait at Ashbourne for a class D 0-8-0 to arrive light engine from Buxton to assist. In April 1943, the third class single fare between Ashbourne and Buxton was 3s 7d.

The presence of reversing triangles at both Buxton and Uttoxeter made the line suitable for testing purposes, and one such occurrence was the testing of an experimental refrigerator car adapted from an ex-LNWR coach. More testing would take place on the line in forthcoming years, and this will be described in the next chapter, but the severe winter of 1947 saw one of the most unusual experiments ever witnessed on a British railway. The line was blocked so badly, and for so long, that an experiment was tried whereby two Rolls-Royce Derwent Mark 1 jet engines were attached to a wagon, and taken to the worst blockage at Hurdlow cutting in the hope that they would thaw the solid ice. The experiment was conducted on 1st March with the co-operation of the National Gas Turbine Establishment, Ministry of Supply, and while it was moderately successful, it was not felt to be sufficiently viable to warrant continued development. A shame – it must have provided quite a spectacle!

db.

LONDON MIDLAND AND SCOTTISH RAILWAY COMPANY.
(WESTERN DIVISION)

ERO.46108.

No. 147.G.

S P E C I A L   N O T I C E.

SATURDAY, MARCH 1.

SPECIAL TEST TRAIN, DERBY TO BRIGG'S SIDING. (SNOW PLOUGH GOING TO CLEAR THE LINE).

	arr. a.m.	dep. a.m.		arr. a.m.	dep. a.m.
Derby		8.50	Clifton for Mayfield		10X17
Stenson Jn.	pass	9. 5	Ashbourne	10.23 W	10.28
Marston Jn.	pass	9.22	Tissington		10X40
Tutbury	pass	9.27	Alsop-en-le-Dale		10X48
Uttoxeter E. Jn.	9.47 L	9.48	Hartington		11X 0
Rocester		10X 0	Parsley Hay		11X 5
Norbury & E.		10X 8	Brigg's Sdgs.	11.20	

To return to Derby on completion of work.
To be signalled "Express Passenger".
To be marshalled :-

> Engine,
> Service Coach for Officers,
> Pipe-fitted Brakevan with Verandah trailing,
> Rail Tank (Fuel Supply),
> Container Flat (Apparatus vehicle).

To be worked by Class 4 Engine.
MIDLAND DIVISION P.. ENGINEMEN & G. to Uttoxeter, return as required. UTTOXETER ENGINEMEN & G. forward to Brigg's Sdgs., return as required.
The following special arrangements to apply :-

1. The C.M.E. will provide screw couplings for the apparatus vehicle and the rail tank containing the fuel, which must be properly screwed up before the train runs over the main lines.
2. A Guard will ride in the brakevan in order to keep the rail tank and the apparatus vehicle under observation as these two vehicles are not fitted with the continuous brake.
3. Authority is given for this train to run throughout without brakevan in rear in accordance with the provisions of Rule 153 (a).

BREAKDOWN VAN TRAIN, BUXTON SHED TO BRIGG'S SIDINGS.

	dep. a.m.		arr. a.m.	pass. a.m.
Buxton Shed		10.25	Buxton No. 3	pass	10.32
" No. 1	pass	10.29	Brigg's Sdgs.	10.50	

To be worked by a G.2 Engine.
BUXTON P & G.
On arrival of the Test Train at Brigg's Sdg. the Service Coach and Pipe Fitted Brakevan to be detached and the snow clearance test to be carried out by the G.2 Engine propelling the apparatus and rail tank vehicles over the up line between Brigg's Sdgs. and Parsley Hay.
The Buxton Breakdown van with jacks, six men and a Foreman Fitter to stand at Brigg's Sdg. during the course of the experiment.
After the test, the train will be marshalled at Brigg's Sdg. in the same order as on leaving Derby and will proceed to Buxton to turn on the triangle there, in order that the vehicle containing the apparatus may return in rear of the special test train via Ashbourne and Uttoxeter to Derby.

Above and right: The trials using jet engines to blast away snow drifts were dramatic if not too effective. One can't help wondering what the effect of two Rolls-Royce Derwent jet engines spinning up to maximum revs might have had on the rest of the train and particularly the locomotive that was supposed to be propelling them towards the snowdrifts! Presumably, the speed of the engines had to be carefully governed. As it was, the track ballast was badly disturbed in places, as was some point rodding.
(Both, Author's Collection)

Opposite: The Special Notice that covered the working of the train over the branch, although nowhere is the use of jet engines actually mentioned.
(Glynn Waite Collection)

Chapter 5

Nationalisation and Rationalisation

The Second World War had taken a heavy toll on the nation and its infrastructure. Much of the railway network had been run into the ground, with little or no investment unless a project could be justified as being in the country's strategic interest. The result was that post-war services were a shadow of their former selves, and in many cases they never got back to pre-war levels. This was certainly true of the Uttoxeter-Buxton line, which enjoyed only three passenger trains each way per day in the second half of the 1940s. With no obvious way for the "Big Four" to find the level of investment required to recover from years of conflict and neglect, it came as no surprise for the Government to step in and nationalise the railways at the beginning of 1948, a year after it had taken the coal industry under State control.

Under nationalisation, the line from Buxton to Ashbourne became part of the Manchester Division of the London Midland Region. South of Ashbourne, the line was part of Stoke Division, which also looked after the Churnet Valley line. Given the ancestry of the lines north and south of Ashbourne, these centres of control were entirely appropriate, of course. At around this time, the line gained another mention in Punch, when the writer of an article called *On Getting Out at Chorlton-cum-Hardy* described his joy at being able to retain the third class ticket he had used between Parsley Hay and Ashbourne.

Beginning on 11th November 1948, and continuing into 1949, the line saw fuel consumption tests using ex-Lancashire and Yorkshire 2-4-2T No 10897, which was shedded at Uttoxeter while the trials took place. The locomotive was coupled to LMS coach No 5245 and LMS Mobile Test Unit (MTU) No 1, and was fitted with a self-weighing grate, which had sensors sufficiently sensitive to detect the weight of each additional shovelful of coal. Continuous readings were electrically transmitted to the MTU, as well as being able to measure the weight of the fire before and after the tests. The outward journey from Uttoxeter would usually start at 10.55am, arriving at Buxton at 12.43pm and then returning at 2.40pm to arrive at Uttoxeter at 4.30pm. Additional tests were carried out on WD locos, 2-8-0 90464 and 2-10-0 90772 (not on the Uttoxeter-Buxton line) and on 3rd March 1950, 10897 underwent further tests between Rugby and Peterborough with ex-LMS MTUs 1, 2 and 3, but although the device worked satisfactorily, it was not fitted to any further locomotives.

1949 marked the half-centenary of the Ashbourne to Buxton line, and the event was celebrated in the *Derbyshire Advertiser*:

This section of the line...no doubt was intended as another twenty miles towards the fulfilment of a pipe dream to open up a new part of England and carry the message of progress and speed over hill and dale. However, there was to be reckoned with a new force of road transport which within the next twenty years challenged and was victorious. Today the line goes on, three passenger trains a day, either way, a few goods trains and an occasional Bank Holiday rush, this is about the sum total of the activity on the Ashbourne and Buxton line. The line has none of the glamour of the great

Opposite page, top: Ex-Lancashire &Yorkshire Railway 2-4-2T 10897 is seen here at Ashbourne on 8th July 1949 working the test train towards Uttoxeter with MTU 1 at the rear of the train. The locomotive was nicknamed "Jane" by the Derby test personnel, and was often used with the Mobile Test Plant based at Derby under the direction of Dr Ivor Andrews. (JR Hollick/FW Shuttleworth Collection)

Opposite page, bottom: 10897 languished for several years in a siding by the Picknall Brook at Uttoxeter shed, before finally being cut up in 1956, still with its LMS logo and number. It is seen here on 22nd January 1955. (FW Shuttleworth)

Right: The Special Notice covering the tests carried out on 8th and 10th December 1948. (Glynn Waite Collection)

WEDNESDAY & FRIDAY, DECEMBER 8 & 10

TEST SPECIAL.

		arr. p.m.	dep. a.m.			arr. p.m.	dep. p.m.
Uttoxeter			10.55	Buxton			2.40
Rocester	pass		11.11	Briggs Siding	pass		2.55
Norbury	pass		11.18	Parsley Hay	pass		3.10
Clifton Yard	pass		11.27	Hartington	pass		3.15
Ashbourne	pass		11.32	Alsop-en-le-Dale	pass		3.30
Tissington	pass		11.45	Tissington	pass		3.38
Alsop-en-le-Dale	pass		11.54	Ashbourne	pass		3.50
Hartington	pass		12. 8	Clifton Yard	pass		3.58
Parsley Hay	pass		12.13	Norbury	pass		4. 8
Briggs Siding	pass		12.28	Rocester	pass		4.17
Buxton		12.43		Uttoxeter		4.30	

Conveys Brake Van No. 5245, Mobile Test Unit No. 1. Worked by engine No. 10897
SIGNALLED "PASSENGER"
UTTOXETER P.& .G.

BUXTON and ASHBOURNE

Miles	Week Days only	J a.m T		Z a.m T		a.m T		p.m T	
	Buxton .... dep	7 7	..	7 25	..	1035	..	5 55	..
½	Higher Buxton	7 9	..	7 27	..	1037	..	5 57	..
3½	Hindlow	7 16	..	7 36	..	1044	..	6 4	..
4½	Dowlow Halt	7 20	..	7 41	..	1048	..	6 8	..
6¾	Hurdlow **A**	7 24	..	7 47	..	1052	..	6 12	..
9	Parsley Hay	7H59	..	7H59	..	1059	..	6 18	..
10¾	Hartington	8 4	..	8 4	..	11 4	..	6 23	..
15½	Alsop-en-le Dale **B**	8 14	..	8 14	..	1113	..	6 31	..
18¼	Tissington	8 20	..	8 20	..	1119	..	6 40	..
19½	Thorpe Cloud **B**	8 24	..	8 24	..	1123	..	6 44	..
22¼	**Ashbourne** .... arr	8 30	..	8 30	..	1129	..	6 50	..

Miles	Week Days only	a.m	E a.m	S a.m L	S a.m P		E p.m U	p.m V	
	Ashbourne .... dep	7 50	1045	11 5	11 5	..	4 10	4 18	..
2¾	Thorpe Cloud **B**	7 57	1053	1112	1112	..	4 17	4 25	..
4	Tissington	8 5	1059	1120	1120	..	4 23	4 31	..
6¾	Alsop-en-le-Dale **B**	8 13	1112	1128	1128	..	4 30	4 38	..
11½	Hartington	8 23	1122	1138	1138	..	4 41	4 48	..
13¼	Parsley Hay	8 28	1127	1149	1149	..	4 46	4 53	..
15½	Hurdlow **A**	8 33	1132	1154	12 4	..	4 50	4 58	..
17¾	Dowlow Halt	8 39	1138	12 0	1214	..	4 56	5 4	..
18¾	Hindlow	8 42	1141	12 3	1217	..	4 59	5 7	..
21¾	Higher Buxton	8 49	1148	1210	1224	..	5 6	5 14	..
22¼	**Buxton** .... arr	8 52	1151	1213	1227	..	5 9	5 17	..

A For Longnor (3 miles) and Monyash (1½ miles)
B For Dovedale
E Except Saturdays
H Arr. 7 30 a.m.
J Will not run 1st November, 1948 to 5th March, 1949, inclusive
L Will not run 6th November, 1948, to 5th March, 1949, incl.
P Runs 6th November, 1948, to 5th March, 1949, inclusive.
S Saturdays only.

T Through Carriages between Buxton and Uttoxeter (Table 131). **U** Runs 1st November, 1948, to 4th March, 1949, inclusive.
V Runs daily to 30th October, 1948; Saturdays only 6th November, 1948, to 5th March, 1949, inclusive, and daily afterwards. **U** Arr. 7 53 a.m.
Z Runs 1st November, 1948, to 5th March, 1949, inclusive.

The September 1948 timetables for Buxton-Ashbourne and Ashbourne-Uttoxeter showing a reduced service compared to the years before Nationalisation.

UTTOXETER and ASHBOURNE

Miles	Week Days only	a.m		a.m F		p.m Sats. only		p.m F Except Sats.		p.m F Sats. only		p.m	
	Uttoxeter .... dep	8 28	..	1015	..	1 5	..	3 33	..	3 43	..	6 17	..
4½	Rocester	8 35	..	1022	..	1 12	..	3 42	..	3 52	..	6 24	..
7	Norbury and Ellaston	8 42	..	1029	..	1 19	..	3 49	..	3 59	..	6 31	..
10¼	Clifton, for Mayfield	8 49	..	1036	..	1 26	..	3 56	..	4 6	..	6 38	..
11½	**Ashbourne** .... arr	8 54	..	1041	..	1 31	..	4 1	..	4 11	..	6 43	..

Miles	Week Days only	a.m		a.m F		a.m F		p.m Sats. only		p.m Except Sats.		p.m F			
	Ashbourne .... dep	7 20	..	9 2	..	1134	..	3 35	..	4 10	..	6 55	..	..	..
1¾	Clifton, for Mayfield	7 23	..	9 5	..	1137	..	3 38	..	4 13	..	6 59	..	..	..
4½	Norbury and Ellaston	7 30	..	9 12	..	1144	..	3 45	..	4 20	..	7B12	..	..	..
7	Rocester	7 38	..	9 19	..	1150	..	3 51	..	4 26	..	7 18	..	..	..
11½	Uttoxeter .... arr	7 47	..	9 28	..	1159	..	4 0	..	..	..	7 27	..	..	..

B Arr. 7 6 p.m
F Through Carriages to and from Buxton (Table 127)

For **OTHER TRAINS** between Uttoxeter and Rocester, see Table 129

trains speeding north, but it is an engineering job of which those hundreds who worked on it can be proud. It is finely built, and, although single track throughout, most of the way, the builders showed their optimism by making their bridges and embankments wide enough for the addition of another track. This line, typical of many small lines throughout the country, could only have been built in a period of superb optimism. Some might see in it a waste of resources and time. Rather one should see in it a monument to that England which had resources to waste, but have now gone from us forever.

A particularly interesting special ran over the line on 28th June 1952 in the shape of ex-GWR diesel railcar W14W. Organised by (or for) "Birmingham area miners", the tour ran from Solihull to Burton-on-Trent, Ashbourne and Buxton, returning via Millers Dale and Derby.

There was a notable special working over the northern part of the line on 25th April 1953, when a train hauled by class 3F 0-6-0 43618 was run jointly by the North Western Area of the Stephenson Locomotive Society and the Manchester Locomotive Society over the section from Parsley Hay to Buxton. So successful was the trip, that it was repeated on 27th June of the same year, this time with class 3F 0-6-0 43387 providing haulage on the Parsley Hay to Buxton section. Further similar tours were subsequently organised over the Cromford and High Peak Railway by the SLS (with or without the involvement of the MLS) as will be seen later.

Sunday 17th May 1953 saw two excursions over the line

On 28th June 1952 ex-GWR diesel railcar W14W, having arrived at Buxton from Solihull over the Ashbourne line, now leaves past Buxton No 2 signalbox (hidden behind the unit) to run over Spring Gardens viaduct, after which it will take the Midland main line through Millers Dale to Derby and back to the Birmingham area. (ER Morten)

Stanier 2-6-4T 42440 in the up bay at Ashbourne at the head of a three-coach train bound for Uttoxeter on 9th April 1952.
(ER Morten)

– one from Nottingham to Ashbourne and Buxton was hauled by two 4F 0-6-0s, 44436 and 44030, and the other, from the Western Division, was hauled by class 4 2-6-4T No 42542. The two trains passed at Tissington station. Between 4th July and 6th September that year, BR in the Potteries marketed "Excursions to Local Resorts" with a train leaving Longport each Saturday at 11.45am for Ashbourne, Thorpe Cloud (for Dovedale), Tissington and Alsop-en-le-Dale. It picked up passengers at Etruria, Stoke, Longton, Meir, Blythe Bridge and Uttoxeter.

LMS class 8F 2-8-0s were allowed to work from Buxton to Ashbourne, but no further. In the last years that Alsop Quarry was working, a daily stone train ran from Alsop to Northwich, powered initially by a class 4F 0-6-0. Unfortunately, this was not up to the job, and had great difficulty getting the train moving away from Alsop. Double-heading with 0-6-0s was tried next, and then a class 8F 2-8-0 was put in charge. Even this wasn't enough, and the final solution was to provide two 8Fs, one hauling and the other banking, as the heavy train made its way up the climb from Alsop to Coldeaton cutting. Passenger trains by this time consisted of an ex-LMS class 3 mixed-traffic 2-6-2T with two non-corridor coaches.

On 18th December 1953, the *Derbyshire Advertiser* carried two articles about the imminent closure of the line from Uttoxeter to Buxton. One was a "leader", carrying the announcement that the British Transport Commission was proposing that passenger services be withdrawn, and bemoaning the fact that the line (and several like it) had been built in the first place. "If only internal combustion had been foreseen", it commented, "how many thousands of pounds might have been saved in building these lines, and how much worry to future generations!" A somewhat less romantic view than that portrayed by the same paper only four years previously, and rather an ill-informed opinion, it has to be said, considering that the limitations of road transport in adverse weather conditions were even greater than those of the railway.

The second article in the paper reflected this rather more balanced attitude to the question of closure, and observed that the announcement by the BTC had produced a swift reaction from councils in the area. At a meeting of Bakewell Council on the previous Monday, a letter from the District Commercial Superintendent of the BTC, Mr WB Carter, had been read out. It claimed that a review of services on the line had concluded that the cost of operating the service greatly exceeded the revenue derived from the passengers carried. "The necessity for taking this step is very much regretted, but I feel you will appreciate in the interests of economy, this financial loss cannot continue indefinitely." In the interests

Token exchange at Tissington

In a couple of posed shots taken at Tissington in the early 1950s, we see (top) class 4F 0-6-0 44176 heading a goods train to Buxton with the Webb and Thompson staff being exchanged with the Station Master (probably Bert Morritt).

The shot below is most likely a southbound passenger train standing outside the signal box hauled by Fowler 2-6-4T 42367. The Fireman is not known, but the Driver is Jim Thorpe and Peter Featherstone is the Signalman.

(Both, Eric Brown/Author's Collection)

Passengers and freight at Buxton. Above we see an unidentified 2-6-4T, still carrying its LMS lettering, hauling its train out of Buxton towards Ashbourne in May 1951, and crossing the Midland line as it does so. The MR signalbox and goods shed can be seen through the bridge.

Left is 3F 0-6-0 43268 on 10th June 1952 bringing a freight train from Ashbourne across Spring Gardens viaduct, and passing under the distinctive signal gantry at the Buxton end of the viaduct.
(Both, ER Morten)

of economy, note, not in the interests of the local people, for many of whom the line was a vital link with civilisation.

The news of the proposal was received with much concern by Ashbourne Urban District Council when they met the next day, and they determined to obtain accurate passenger figures as soon as possible so that they could oppose the move. It was noted that there was not an adequate bus service, and that a small local bus company that had

wanted to provide a service from Tissington to Ashbourne had been unable to do so because of the monopoly of a larger company.

A further article in the *Derbyshire Advertiser* for 19th February 1954, (accompanied by a sympathetic leader for the road lobby) reported that Ashbourne Urban District Council had now heard, in full, the case for closing the line. BR asserted that with an average number of only 180 passengers

A shadow hangs over the future of passenger services on the branch as Fairburn 2-6-4T 42233 pulls away from Clifton with a Uttoxeter to Ashbourne train on 4th April 1954. (Pat Webb)

per day in the summer, and 149 in winter, receipts only totalled £2,000 a year (plus another £900 in "cartage" receipts) against annual operating costs of over £19,000. Over £16,000 a year could thus be saved by closing the line. The main concern of the local councils, of course, was how the district would be served by public transport in the event of bad weather blocking the roads. Winters were so notoriously bad in these parts that stories grew up about signal arms being bent around their posts. Whether or not this was true, the locals had a justifiable fear of isolation, and were assured that in the event of a bad snowfall making road travel impossible "everything possible" would be done to run emergency train services.

The staff took an extremely pragmatic view of the harsh conditions experienced through the west Derbyshire winters. A lengthman who had started his working life as a stone-waller on the C&HPR later became responsible for the stretch of line between Tissington and Hartington. For walking this stretch between 7.30am and 5.00pm every day, he earned £5 per week, but supplemented his earnings by catching rabbits, which he traded with the drivers. The winter working was not easy, but it had its compensations in the overtime that could be worked when snow blocked the line. Another nail in the line's coffin, perhaps!

A very strong case for the provision of an emergency service was made by Jack Hollick who had previously campaigned for Ashbourne No 2 signalbox to be closed after he found the duty signalman literally dying from hypothermia (he was immediately admitted to Ashbourne hospital) and now he pointed out to BR that if he was unable to reach a patient by road, they would have to put on a special train for

him. Perhaps BR thought he was bluffing; if so, they were to be proved wrong. An assurance was duly given by the BTC that, "we should be prepared to institute an emergency rail service...in the event of snow causing a total road blockage, provided of course the railway line was clear". This naturally presupposed the continued existence of the line for goods services – something that wasn't even questioned at the time.

A memorandum was prepared by the BTC for the use of the East Midlands Area Transport Users' Consultative Committee (TUCC), in which many facts about the line and its use were recorded. One of these was the mistaken assertion that Fenny Bentley was open for goods and passenger traffic, when in fact passengers had never been handled there. There were said to be five passenger trains each way on weekdays, six down and five up trains on Saturdays, and no Sunday service.

At the same time, it was reported that the Trent Motor Traction Company ran thirteen buses a day at an interval of one hour (half-hourly at peak periods). Five buses were also run between Ashbourne and Uttoxeter. Other Trent services were detailed, including those between Derby and Uttoxeter, and Derby, Ashbourne and Dovedale. Services between Ashbourne and Buxton (North Western), Ashbourne, Ilam and Dovedale (Hulley's), Burton, Clifton and Ashbourne (Stevenson's) and Ashbourne, Load Mill and Ilam (Warrington's) were all given great prominence in the memorandum, which must have left the reader wondering why the passenger train service had lasted as long as it had.

At a meeting of the TUCC shortly after the Ashbourne UDC meeting, BR amended its figure for the loss on the Uttoxeter-Buxton section, so that savings were then reported

Last day scenes along the branch on 30th October 1954

Above: Fowler 2-6-4T 42365 arrives at Buxton with the 11.40am departure from Ashbourne. (ER Morten)

Below: The same locomotive (and possibly the same train) arrives at Alsop-en-le-Dale en-route to Buxton with a train from Ashbourne. (Midland Railway Trust)

Above: Stanier 2-6-4T 42667 is seen here at Ashbourne on the last day of passenger services over the branch. (Pat Webb)

Below: The same loco is seen coming off the branch at Rocester with a train from Buxton. (Pat Webb)

Opposite page, top: Stanier 2-6-4T 42667 arrives at Alsop-en-le-Dale with the 10.25 departure from Buxton. (Midland Railway Trust)

Opposite page, bottom: The last train to Buxton prepares to leave Uttoxeter behind Stanier 2-6-4T 42665. (Bernard Mettam photograph, Industrial Railway Society)

to be (a remarkably exact) £18,612, rather than the £16,000 originally reported. This figure was repeated at a further meeting, held on 17th March 1954, between Ashbourne Urban Council, Ashbourne Rural Council, parish councillors on the route of the line, the Ashbourne Chamber of Trade, and the Ashbourne branch of the NUR. Mr Carter, who was present to answer questions on behalf of BR, was bombarded with questions, but remained resolute to the end. The closure had to be viewed as purely economic, he said. If it wasn't for the parlous state of the line's finances, BR would have no desire to close it.

At a further meeting of the East Midlands TUCC held on 2nd June, Mr FH Thomas, Clerk to both the Ashbourne Urban and Rural Councils, questioned BR's figures. He pointed out that cheap-day returns were not available on the line, bemoaned the adverse effect of the line being controlled by different divisions, and questioned whether other economies (such as running diesel trains) had been considered. Perhaps Mr Thomas's greatest regret, however,

Taken from an unidentified train on the last day of passenger services, the tablets are exchanged at Norbury and Ellaston. (Pat Webb)

was that despite repeated requests for further information, no breakdown had been forthcoming to show how the figures quoted had been arrived at.

As we have seen, a diesel railcar had run over the line in 1952, and the same unit, ex-GWR diesel railcar W14W, returned on 19th June 1954 to operate a railtour organised by the Birmingham Locomotive Club. It ran between Birmingham Snow Hill and Buxton via Derby and Matlock, returning over the Ashbourne line. On 16th July, Ashbourne Secondary Schools ran a day excursion to London Euston, which must have been one of the last before regular passenger services were withdrawn; the price for under-16s was 15s 6d.

Resistance to closure was useless, however, and it was with a large sense of inevitability that the last scheduled passenger service between Uttoxeter and Buxton ran on Saturday 30th October 1954, passenger services having been withdrawn with effect from the following Monday, 1st November. The withdrawal of the service left Ashbourne (with a population of 5,000 people) as the largest town on the former North Staffordshire Railway system to lose it train service, but winter emergency trains and Sunday excursions for ramblers and visitors to the Tissington well-dressings would continue to use the line until 1963.

The end of regular passenger services was marked by no special train, just the timetabled 6.20pm Buxton to Uttoxeter service (which left four minutes late) boosted to four coaches instead of the usual two, and hauled by Stanier 2-6-4T No 42665. Earlier in the day, the last down train had left Uttoxeter at 3:50pm (also four minutes late) arriving in Buxton at 5:34pm. The passing of the service did not go unmarked, and the *Derbyshire Advertiser* of 29th October was the first to report on the demise of passenger services that would occur the following day.

As usual for the *Advertiser* at this time, there was little sentiment in its columns for the loss of the service: "let us face it, the line from Uttoxeter to Buxton...has never been a very profitable concern", it wrote. Interestingly, in the light of the assurances made when the line was first proposed for closure, neither of the largest bus companies, Trent and North Western, planned to add any new services on the route to compensate for the loss of trains. Perhaps, not unreasonably, they figured that the passenger levels on the trains were so low that there was unlikely to be a huge influx of passengers – at any rate, they could wait and see.

On Monday 1st November, the *Derby Evening Telegraph* also reported on the last train under the headline, "The last passenger train carried 'a year's load'". With 500 passengers on the train, perhaps 'a week's load' would have been more accurate, but the point was well made, and it neatly summed up the situation. The driver of the train (and the man responsible for the ironic quote about his load) was Arthur Dowler, a 53-year old Uttoxeter-based man who had worked on the line for 28 years. He remarked to the paper that he had been as busy signing autographs as driving the train, and it was reported that his fireman, John Hirst of Ashbourne, had worked on the line for ten years.

One passenger, Mrs DA James, who had organised a special train from Ashbourne to London for the Coronation the previous year, rued the fact that they could have chartered a dining-car if only they had thought about it in time, and ticket enthusiasts were observed throughout the morning driving to stations along the line buying up tickets for the last journey.

The following Wednesday, the *Ashbourne News Telegraph* marked the end of the line's life with just a few column inches, but on the 25th anniversary of the closure in 1979, the paper recalled the events in rather more detail:

Hundreds of people travelled on the last regular train between Buxton and Uttoxeter, a journey which marked the end of the 50-year old service from Ashbourne to Buxton and the 100-year old service from Uttoxeter to Ashbourne. When the train passed through Clifton, about half the village's inhabitants turned out to help the station master, signalman and porter perform their last duties. Trumpets blew and exploding detonators and fireworks added to the festive air, and there were farewell scenes in other villages. Among the passengers from Ashbourne was 83-year old Mr EW Hurd, of Derby Road, who travelled on the first Ashbourne to Buxton train (the Derby Evening Telegraph report also added that Mr Hurd's father had also been on the first train from Ashbourne to Uttoxeter). In the wake of the withdrawal of

the train service, Ashbourne Urban District Council and Rural District Council appointed a committee to approach the appropriate bus companies for extra services.

Significantly, it was also reported that Mr W Warrington, an Ilam bus owner, had withdrawn his offer to run a workers' bus service from the village to Ashbourne, because he was only attracting 14 regular passengers.

Rex North recalls the last train. On the final day his mother took him from Ashbourne to Uttoxeter, and they returned on the last northbound train from Uttoxeter. He still has the tickets which cost 3s 6d adult and 1s 9½d child return, and was treated to a Dinky toy observation coach to mark the occasion! He also remembers seeing a large group of well-wishers on the Stoke-bound platform at Uttoxeter seeing off a pair of newlyweds – complete with confetti!

So ended a relatively brief passenger service (brief north of Ashbourne, at least) but it was not long before BR had to honour its commitment to Dr Hollick to run an emergency train for him. At 2 o'clock one morning in January 1955, the weather was so bad that he called the Stoke Divisional Manager, George Dow (himself, a celebrated railway historian, and no doubt on familiar terms with Jack Hollick) to request a special train. He was not disappointed.

Freight services continued, and in 1955, there was one through goods train a day each way between Uttoxeter and Buxton, together with one each way between Buxton and

Fowler 2-6-4T 42362 departs from Buxton with the return leg of the Gloucester Railway Society tour on 21st May 1955.
(Glynn Waite Collection)

Ashbourne, and two each way between Uttoxeter and Ashbourne. The engines of the Uttoxeter-Ashbourne workings (2-6-4Ts based at Uttoxeter) also did the morning and afternoon shunting at Ashbourne.

1955 saw a rail tour in the shape of a Gloucester Railway Society visit to Buxton on 21st May. Having reached Wirksworth via the Midland line, passengers walked to the top of Middleton Incline to transfer to open wagons on the C&HPR for the next leg to Buxton, initially behind ex-North London Railway class 2F 0-6-0Ts 58850 and 58856, but from Friden to Buxton (via Harpur Hill) by class 3F 0-6-0 43618. 2-6-4T 42370 hauled the train to Ashbourne, Uttoxeter and Burton, whence the tour returned to Gloucester (arriving nearly 13 hours after it had left in the morning) behind class 2P 4-4-0 40416, which had brought the train as far as Wirksworth.

In January 1956, the afternoon working was changed and was henceforth worked by a Derby-based class 3F or 4F 0-6-0. Rail tours continued to use the line, and on 14th July 1958 a special train was organized for the Cadet Force of King Edward's School, Birmingham. Hauled from New Street to Uttoxeter by class 4F 0-6-0 44099, Fowler 2-6-4T 42362 was added to the train before it ran to Hartington and back. 42362 was removed at Uttoxeter, and the train made its way back to Birmingham with just 44099 in charge.

On 9th May 1959, another rail tour ran over the southern end of the route between Uttoxeter and Rocester on its way from Paddington to Macclesfield via Derby. Organised by *Trains Illustrated* magazine (Ian Allan), the "Potteries Express" was hauled by "Royal Scot" 4-6-0 46154 *Hussar* to Derby and 2-6-0 42922 on the Churnet Valley line. It also included the Devon Belle observation car (by then renamed the Welsh Chieftain Lounge).

The line between Briggs Sidings and Parsley Hay was singled in June 1959, and electric key token working was introduced on the section. Special trains continued to use the line, the Manchester and Liverpool areas of the Ramblers Association advertising a "Ramblers Special" on 21st August 1960 from Liverpool Central to Ashbourne via Warrington Central.

The SLS (Midland Area) ran its "North Staffs, Buxton and Cromford & High Peak Rail Tour" on 15th April 1961. This comprised a Cravens 2-car set and a Derby Lightweight 2-car set, which ran from Burton-upon-Trent to Buxton via Uttoxeter and Ashbourne, returning to Parsley Hay for a trip over the C&HPR (not by DMU!) before returning to Burton via Wirksworth and Derby.

Exactly a week later, the SLS (NW Area) joined forces with the MLS to run the "High Peak Rail Tour" from Chinley to High Peak Junction via Buxton and Parsley Hay. Hauled

The SLS (Midland Area) "North Staffs, Buxton and Cromford & High Peak Rail Tour" is seen here at Ashbourne on 15th April 1961. Despite the withdrawal of passenger services, the station was kept in pretty good order through the 1950s, but was starting to show some signs of neglect by the time this photograph was taken. (David Lawrence/Photos from the Fifties)

Above: Testing returned to the line between 14th November and 17th December 1958 when BTH 800HP Diesel-Electric locomotive D8208 underwent trials with the ex-LMS Mobile Test Plant. It is seen here near Dowlow with LMR Dynamometer Car No 3 and MTUs 1 and 3. (ER Morten)

Left: On 7th April 1959, 350hp 0-6-0 diesel-mechanical shunter 12006 is seen on trial at Parsley Hay with a trip to Friden on the Cromford & High Peak Railway. (ER Morten)

from Chinley by Fowler class 4 2-6-4T 42371, the tour included the added attraction of a detour to the Harpur Hill Mines Research Centre on the way to Parsley Hay.

Later the same year, on 23rd September, the Lancashire branch of the Railway Correspondence and Travel Society (RCTS) ran its "Four Counties Rail Tour" on a circular route from Manchester Victoria to Oxford Road. It traversed the line behind Fowler class 4 2-6-4T 42372 on its way to Leek and Stoke, reversing at Uttoxeter in order to regain the Churnet Valley line for its northward journey.

Just a week later, on 30th September, the SLS and MLS repeated their "High Peak Rail Tour" from Chinley to High Peak Junction (and thence to Matlock by bus) via Buxton and Parsley Hay, hauled between those places by Fowler 2-6-4T 42379. Again, the tour included a visit to the Harpur Hill Mines Research Centre, but perhaps learning from experiences of the first running of the tour, it was assisted on this part of the journey by class 3F 0-6-0 43822.

On 8th September 1962, the SLS/MLS organised the "Leicestershire Rail Tour", which ran from Manchester Piccadilly to Burton via Buxton, Ashbourne and Uttoxeter hauled by Fowler class 4 2-6-4T 42343. After spending the day running over branches in the Leicester area, it returned to Manchester via the Churnet Valley line and Stockport.

11th May 1963 saw the "North Midlands Rail Tour" traverse the line. Jointly organised by the RCTS and the Locomotive Club of Great Britain, this train had worked its way up the Midland main line to Buxton from St Pancras before returning over the Ashbourne line to reach Burton, and ultimately St Pancras. Between Buxton and Burton the train was hauled by ex-LNER B1 4-6-0 No 61004 *Oryx*.

Rex North recalls the special trains that ran over the line during the last 10 years of its life. A favourite Bank Holiday day outing for members of his family was to take the train from Ashbourne to Buxton, paying a penny or two to enter the Pavilion Gardens.

Schools in the Ashbourne area also hired trains for their annual trips, and Rex remembers two in particular. The first went via Buxton to Liverpool Lime Street where it was met by trams for the onward journey to Pier Head, whence the party transferred to the Liverpool Overhead Railway for a complete round trip along the waterfront. Once back at Pier Head, they caught the New Brighton ferry, *Royal Iris*, across the River Mersey while their train ran empty to New Brighton to collect them. The return was via Crewe, and Uttoxeter. The other day out was again to Liverpool, but this time they boarded the Isle of Man packet steamer, *St Tudno*, to Llandudno pier, and took a tram up the Great Orme before catching the return train home.

The last excursion trains on the line ran to Tissington for the Well Dressings on Sunday 26th May 1963 from Hinckley, and Alsager (going on to Buxton) and from Colne and Manchester Piccadilly (going on to Ashbourne). A proposed excursion from Birmingham did not run, and the line was subsequently declared as unavailable for further passenger trains.

The SLS and MLS "High Peak Rail Tour" on its repeat performance on 30th September 1961 is seen here at Parsley Hay, hauled by Fowler 2-6-4T 42379. (DJ Norton)

Views of the last excursions to traverse the line on 26th May 1963 are rare – these photographs are among the very last ones taken of passenger trains on the line.

Top: Taken from the footbridge at Ashbourne, two DMUs are seen stabled away from the main running lines. Easily identified by its white cab roof – a feature unique to DMUs allocated to Buxton depot, the Birmingham RC&W unit (later class 104) is awaiting its return to Manchester Piccadilly. The Cravens unit (later class 105) over by the goods shed has come from Colne. (Matthew Burnby)

Middle: The return excursion to Colne was the penultimate departure from the station. Note that the up platform was being used for both arrivals and departures at this time. (Matthew Burnby)

Bottom: With reporting number 1Z19, the last passenger excursion to run over the line (and almost certainly the last passenger train of any description) prepares to leave Ashbourne to return to Manchester Piccadilly. (JW Sutherland, © Manchester Locomotive Society Collection)

On 30th September 1963, the Line Manager at Crewe wrote to the General Manager at Euston proposing to close the line between Uttoxeter North (exclusive) and Ashbourne (inclusive) completely. Among many reasons to justify his proposal, he mentioned that the Redhill Brick and Tile Co that was served by a siding at Rocester was derelict and that the only other private siding belonged to Nestlé at Ashbourne. There were no passenger services, and not much in the way of parcels and freight traffic. Such traffic that did remain could, in any case be handled by a goods vehicle transferred from Rocester to Uttoxeter, and Ashbourne could be covered by Derby. Although this might result in an additional cost of £450, the loss of £12,422-worth of business would be more than compensated for by the estimated annual savings of £11,853 rising to £14,803. It is interesting to see how the savings were calculated:

Loaded train miles 13,700
Engine miles (including
shunting)   21,800
Staff   2 drivers
                        2 firemen
                        2 guards
Engines   1 class 4MT tank
Rolling Stock   6 covered vans
                        4 open wagons
                        20 16-ton mineral wagons
Terminal staff   2 class 4 clerks
                        2 shunters
                        1 checker
                        2 motor drivers
Signalling staff   3 class 4 signalmen
                        3 class 2 relief signalmen
                        1 porter/signalman
                        1 checker/porter/ signalman
                        6 crossing keepers
                        2 porters (also relief for crossing keepers)
CCE staff   3 men, gang 109, Ashbourne
                        4 men, gang 108, Rocester
                        1 man, gang 106, Marchington
Additional staff   2 motor drivers
                        2 loading goods porters

The request was received by Euston evidently with some consternation, as they immediately contacted the Line Manager, Derby, who replied on 2nd October that they "do not appear to know anything of this submission by Crewe – and in fact are seeking to develop Ashbourne as a concentration depot". Do we detect an element of "Derby v Crewe" here? Indeed, could it be possible that Derby was so annoyed at Crewe's meddling in its business that its response was calculated to "drop Crewe in it"? If so, it had the desired effect, as Euston replied to Crewe somewhat testily:

With reference to your letter of 30th September and subsequent conversations between our representatives; pending your official reply to the suggestion put to you that Ashbourne should not have been included for closure in the submission in view of it being under consideration by the Line Manager, Derby, for development as a concentration depot, I am taking no action on your proposals. Will you please endeavour to get the matter cleared up quickly and also arrange in future to obtain the approval of the Line Manager concerned before submitting proposals to me relating to the closure of a depot or section of line which falls outside your jurisdiction.

Until 7th October 1963, there were two freight trains each way between Uttoxeter and Buxton, worked by ex-LNWR 0-8-0 locomotives, with the crews changing over at Alsop-en-le Dale, but from that date, no further services ran. The fate of the line still lay in the balance, however, and on 14th October, it was reported that Shell-Mex & BP Ltd felt unable to implement proposals for the development of their Ashbourne depot until the future of the line between Uttoxeter and Ashbourne had been decided.

On 4th November, a (presumably chastened) Line Manager at Crewe wrote again to the General Manager at Euston: "Up to the time of the submission, no mention had been made by the Nottingham Divisional Manager to my Stoke Divisional Manager that Ashbourne was being considered as a concentration depot. The Nottingham Divisional Manager has now raised the question of the line being retained on the cheapest possible basis…any recommendation made by him must be on the basis that Ashbourne bears the whole cost of the line from Uttoxeter."

So much for "one railway"! If Derby had made its point about Crewe's proposal, Crewe had firmly put the ball back in Derby's court by effectively saying "You want it? You pay for it!" Derby, it seems, was not prepared to put its money where its mouth was, and a note added to the 4th November letter by the General Manager, Euston, reads: "It was agreed at the Regional Rationalisation Committee meeting held on 12th November 1963 that Ashbourne would be retained as a non-rail connected depot. Proceed therefore with the proposals as originally submitted."

Derby was thwarted and Crewe got its way – but it didn't end there! Having informed the Line Manager, Crewe, of its decision on 22nd November, Euston had to write to the Line Managers at Crewe, Derby and Manchester on 28th November, less than a week later: "Urgently need to resolve where locations are to be for distribution of animal feeding stuffs for R Silcocks & Sons Ltd, currently performed from Rocester and Ashbourne."

This had clearly been overlooked, but was evidently dealt with to the satisfaction of Silcocks, as there is no further mention of it. There was, however, the matter of the assurances given to the local population at the time of the line's closure to passengers, which had also been overlooked. On 5th March 1964, the Line Manager at Derby (still presumably fighting to save the line) wrote to the General Manager, Euston:

Enclosed copy of Transport Users Consultative Committee minute of June 1954 regarding closure to passengers and provision of emergency services in winter. Emergency

Freight services in BR days

Top: Class G2a 0-8-0 49132 passes Norbury and Ellaston with a Uttoxeter-bound goods train on 17th June 1958. Also known as "Super Ds", this was a final development by Charles Bowen-Cooke of an original LNWR design, and was seen all over the former LNWR section of the LMS and BR(LMR). (Hugh Davies/Photos from the Fifties)

Middle: Stanier 2-6-4T 42454 eases an afternoon Uttoxeter to Ashbourne goods service through Clifton on the same day. (Hugh Davies/Photos from the Fifties)

Bottom: Another "Super D", 49439, is seen at Alsop-en-le-Dale in May 1962 with a southbound goods train. This locomotive would be withdrawn from Buxton shed at the end of the year. (G Harrop/J Suter Collection)

services have been operated from time to time and were in fact operated on 6 occasions during Jan/Feb 1963 (1963 was a particularly harsh winter – Hartington had been snowed in, and provisions had to be sent by rail from Ashbourne and Buxton). The line was abandoned between Ashbourne and Hartington on 7th October 1963 – the track is still there, but no maintenance has been done.

The letter also noted that Derby had written to Nestlé regarding the termination of its siding at Ashbourne. It was used only very occasionally, and no reply had been received.

By now, Euston must have been getting rather frustrated over the obstacles being put in the way of its plan to close the line. On 9th March, it replied to the Line Manager at Derby: "Looking at the wording, it would appear that we are not under a definite obligation to provide emergency services. Therefore unless our proposals envisaged the running of such services, I think we may be home and dry on the use of the words, 'without conditions or qualifications'. In other words, we can go ahead and close the section entirely if we wish."

The defence of the local population's case (albeit somewhat half-hearted) came from, perhaps, an unlikely source, for it was the Line Manager at Crewe who replied on 13th March. Perhaps he was simply using the opportunity to get his own back. He wrote: "Whether we are under a definite obligation to provide emergency services or not, the fact remains that we undertook the obligations which were entered into. Circumstances have changed since then, however, and the state of the line and stations is such that I suppose we could get out of our obligations on the grounds that the permanent way, etc, is not in good enough condition to run passenger trains."

So far, the discussion over the future of the line had only been between railway officials at Crewe, Derby and Euston, but Ashbourne Urban District Council had got wind of the proposals and on 19th March, the Clerk to the Council wrote to the Manager at Derby asking for clarification of the position regarding the emergency services. In reply, he was told that the future of the line was still under investigation (a little disingenuous, given that its fate had virtually been sealed) and that BR had only "agreed to run an emergency train service when roads were impassable *so long as the line was available for use*". (My italics – this seems a little like making a promise with your fingers crossed behind your back! BR was in the habit of making such promises at this time, a similar assurance having been given to users of the Wensleydale branch, which resulted in a special train running over that line on 2nd January 1962.)

On 2nd April 1964, the Line Manager at Derby wrote to his opposite number at Crewe to say that he had learned that Nestlé had agreed to the termination of their siding with effect from 6th April, and that "this will no doubt clear your way for the closure of the above line". This was followed by a letter from Crewe to Euston on 13th April stating that "arrangements are being made for the closure of the portion of the line from Rocester Junction to Ashbourne to take place on Monday 1st June 1964."

The General Manager at Euston duly informed the BR Board on 7th May that the line would be closed with Ashbourne remaining as a non-rail connected depot. The closure of the section between Uttoxeter and Rocester, however, was dependent on the withdrawal of the passenger service between Uttoxeter and Leek.

On 3rd June 1964, the *Ashbourne News Telegraph* carried an article entitled "End of Ashbourne Station – Town says an official farewell". Accompanied by two photographs, the piece related the events of the previous Friday 29th May, when the "final locomotive used the lines before they were ripped up". The pictures show Stanier class 4 2-6-4T 42605 standing at the south end of the station with a carriage immediately behind it; the rest of the train is not visible. A witness to the events was John Blood, who worked for H Lee and Son, the undertakers, in Bellevue Road. When the news came through that the last train was at the station, he and his boss, Billy Lee, went down to the station to see it. "A lot of people were there", John remembers, "including all the 'worthies' from the town."

The question is – what was this train? Passenger services had long gone and it does not appear to have been an excursion or enthusiasts' special. The most likely explanation is that it was a demolition train, but why was it thought to be the last? The engine carried a class K headcode lamp, and it is known that 42605 was used on the demolition trains. Photographic evidence shows that for part of the time the train was at the station, someone had put a crude hand-made headboard reading "Dr Beeching's Axe" with a drawing of an axe. However, as we shall see later, demolition trains were still operating on the line in October. Whatever prompted the commemoration of the train on that day, the local "worthies" certainly pulled out all the stops. The newspaper article read:

Some fifty people gathered to say farewell to what had been a flourishing line. Councillor AE Dawson, Chairman of the Ashbourne UDC, was there to say an official farewell and he was supported by other councillors and officials of the council, together with railway workers and representatives of most of the businesses in the town. Coun. Dawson said the last locomotive…was a break with the past which was deeply regretted. He also added that it was a great pity that his first job as Chairman of the Council (he was elected only three days earlier) was to see something closing. Said Coun. Dawson: "I well remember the Station bookstall, the passengers hurrying over the footbridge and the good old steam locos proudly puffing into place. In its day this Station served the town well, and my heart is heavy to see the havoc that time and conditions have wrought."

The Chairman then offered his sincere thanks to all the railway staff, past and present, for their good services, and after shaking hands with the engine driver, Mr H Hodgetts of Uttoxeter, and the fireman, Mr K Sherratt, also of Uttoxeter, the locomotive pulled out of the station. Amongst those at the station was Mr AJ Millard…who remembers the opening of the station and started work there himself in 1900, when Mr David Dean was stationmaster. Stories of the past glories of

The events of 29th May 1964 were fortunately captured by the cameras of some of those who were in attendance that day. The train is seen (top) with some of the dignitaries who gathered to witness what was said to be "the last train" to call at the station, even though the justification for this claim is dubious (both, John Blood). Above is a close-up of the headboard that was attached at some point in the proceedings, although it has to be said that the closure owed nothing to the findings of the Beeching Report (JR Hollick Archive Courtesy of the FLRS).

the Ashbourne line were being repeated by some of the business men at the station. Mr FP Birch, recalling the days when the station was built, and when the stones and rubble dug out of the tunnel were used as a foundation for Station-road; Mr RF Wright telling of the occasion when the firm of Frank Wright Ltd and the local branch of the NFU ran a trip to the Glasgow Exhibition in the 1930s, the only train he believes to run from Ashbourne with a dining car; and the day a truck ran away from Alsop Station and gathered so much speed that it went through Ashbourne Station at about 70 miles an hour, finally crashing at Norbury.

Given his close association with the line, it seems inconceivable that Jack Hollick could not have had something to do with the organisation of the event. He appears to have been present on the day, but I have come across no firm evidence that he played any part in its organisation, so an air of mystery surrounds the whole proceedings some 50 years later.

Hartington officially lost its goods facilities on 6th July 1964, but goods trains continued between Buxton and Hartington until 5th September 1967 for quarry traffic, and to bring fresh water from Buxton to the signal boxes and railway houses at Parsley Hay and Hartington. The last delivery to the coal yard is believed to have taken place on 2nd October 1967, and the signal box remained open until 25th October.

This water traffic had been a feature of the northern part of the line throughout its life before the new line had opened. Wells in this part of the world are notoriously unreliable as the water table is deep down in limestone pockets from which it leaks out through fissures. Rivers can often go underground to surface again miles away (the Manifold, for example) and the only reliable sources of water were at Hindlow and Cromford. Water therefore had to be transported to meet the needs of locomotives (and winding engines on the C&HPR) and also for domestic water supplies. These were required at Parsley Hay and Hartington (as mentioned) but also in earlier days at Hurdlow and Alsop-en-le-Dale.

The water was transported either in ex-LNWR tenders adapted for the purpose, or in specially-built tanks mounted on old tender underframes. Six-wheeled tenders and frames had their centre pairs of wheels removed, but from the early 1960s, ex-MR tenders appeared, and these retained all three axles. A buffer beam was added at the front of each water carrier, together with buffers, drawhook and three-link couplings, and a handrail for shunters. In LNWR days, the tanks were numbered in a series from 1 to 19, but later arrivals simply retained their LNWR or LMS tender number. Because their underframes dated back so far, these water tanks were of considerable interest when they were still running in 1967.

How the local population viewed the line's final closure, especially in light of the assurances given in 1954, can only be imagined. Meanwhile, north of Parsley Hay, the line was still usable for rail tours, and on 27th June 1964, the RCTS ran its "High Peak Rail Tour" from Sheffield Victoria. After reaching Buxton via the Woodhead route, the train ran to Parsley Hay behind class B1 4-6-0 61360 before taking a trip over the C&HPR to High Peak Junction and thence back to Sheffield. The tour was repeated on 29th August.

BR lost no time arranging to have the railway infrastructure south of Hartington removed as soon as possible – presumably before the onset of the next winter. On 14th July, the Chief Civil Engineer at Manchester informed Euston that a tender had been accepted from Messrs Leonard Fairclough Ltd to remove 23 miles of track (later corrected to 18¾ miles – whether this was correcting an error, or whether it was decided to leave some track in place is not known), signalling and telegraph equipment for £19,750. Incidentally, lest *Coronation Street* fans raise an eyebrow at the name Leonard Fairclough, it is quite genuine! The value of materials to be recovered was estimated at £46,197, resulting in a net credit to BR LMR of £26,447; the work was planned to be completed by October 1964.

A memo dated 5th/6th August records the following materials to be recovered:

Fairburn class 4 2-6-4T 42160 brings a track-lifting train through Ashbourne in September 1964. (Midland Railway Trust)

Track
37,735 lineal yards of running lines and sidings
2,771 lineal yards of points and crossings
21 buffer stops
5 sets of level crossing gates

Signalling
6 signalbox structures and contents
3 ground frames and contents
Miscellaneous signal posts, telegraph poles, signal wires and point rodding

All did not go smoothly, however. On 19th October 1964, while track-lifting operations were in progress, three wagons loaded with sawn-up rails and a number of sleepers, ran away. The demolition men were working near Ashbourne station at the time, and the wagons gained speed on the downward gradient, demolishing the crossing gates at Clifton Cross and Clifton station. It was estimated that by this time, the wagons were travelling at 40mph, and they continued careering down the line, rumbling over the bow-string girder bridge across the River Dove, and demolishing the next set of gates at Norbury and Ellaston. By this time,

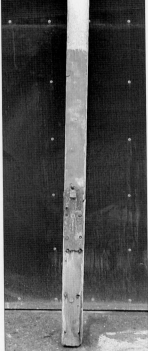

the police had been informed, and the station staff at Rocester were able to stop all traffic, and open the gates ready for the runaway to pass through. However, an adverse gradient slowed the wagons down, and they came to a halt within a few yards of the Ashbourne road crossing, with the remains of three sets of gates hanging off the leading wagon. The current owner of the station building at Norbury still has part of the remains of the level crossing gates (see left).

With the closure of the line confirmed, and demolition trains about to perform the last rites, the Estate Rating Manager received an interesting letter from Mr J Eyre. Sent on behalf of Derbyshire Railway Society on 6th August, his letter read:

We are approaching all Railway Societies in an attempt to get together and make a united effort to preserve a length of line as a working museum. Can you please let me know if the line from Buxton to Uttoxeter is available for renting for such a purpose together with the two engine sheds at each end, and if so, the annual rent. Apparently

there is some traffic between Buxton and Hartington during the week, but as most of the enthusiasts would only have weekends to spare, that need not be a stumbling block. The choice of the Buxton-Uttoxeter line has been made because of its central position. It should be possible to run trains there from all main points.

The reply, sent on 14th August, pointed out that the line was already closed between Rocester and Hartington, and that arrangements had been made for the removal of track, etc. "In any event, the Board would only be prepared to dispose of such a branch line, for private operation by a Preservation Society, by outright sale."

Undaunted, Mr Eyre wrote again on 25th August: "I have been asked to enquire the sale price of this line so that we can put the matter before a meeting of railway enthusiasts at an early date. It is to be hoped that the removal of the track from Hartington to Rocester can be deferred until time has been permitted for our own appeal to be made for its preservation on a National scale."

His appeal fell on deaf ears, however, for on 28th August, the following reply was sent: "I regret that it is not possible for the removal of the redundant track to be deferred as you request."

Was it naïve of the Derbyshire Railway Society to believe that it could take over the running of a line that BR no longer wanted? Perhaps it was in the context of the time. Railway preservation was very much in its infancy, and railway enthusiasts were looked upon with some disdain by professional railwaymen. However, with the benefit of hindsight, and bearing in mind the success of numerous heritage railways throughout the UK, this could be seen as a proposal that was simply ahead of its time. Perhaps the only naïvety was in believing that such a request would be taken seriously by BR management, and that the demolition of the line could be halted.

Such was the atmosphere at the time that it wasn't just BR who did not take the proposal seriously. The following scathing article appeared in the November 1964 edition of *The Mercian*, the newsletter of the Railway Preservation Society, with the headline "We are not responsible":

One may have read in the Railway press that the 'Railway Preservation Society' is to attempt to purchase a 30 mile stretch of line between Uttoxeter and Buxton. This is entirely due to a misuse of the Society's name. The Society which appears to be responsible for this irresponsible scheme is the Derbyshire Railway Society, who used our name, and this month, November, has changed it to the 'National Railway Preservation Society'. We deplore such use of our Society's name, or any name which might be remotely confused with ours. Has this Society yet looked at current branch line prices? A line of this size would cost at least £100,000. How could such a line be purchased, and if by some miracle it was, how could any Society afford to maintain it, yet alone run their own trains over it? Railway enthusiasm in this country does not justify such a hair-raising scheme, as that Society will find out – to their cost!!!

With no support from any quarter, it is not surprising that the proposal went no further, but it was not a bad idea. It was a very good idea that just happened to occur at the wrong time.

On 5th October 1964, the General Manager at Euston wrote to the BR Board, this time regarding the proposal to withdraw the Uttoxeter to Leek passenger service on and from 7th December. It was intended to withdraw freight services from Oakamoor at the same time. The next day, the Line Manager at Derby wrote to Euston proposing to close Ashbourne as a freight depot completely. Euston replied with its approval on 13th October, and the depot closed on and from 1st February 1965.

Churnet Valley line passenger services had actually been withdrawn between Uttoxeter and Macclesfield (Hibel Road) on and from Monday 7th November 1960, the last trains running on Saturday 5th November as there was no Sunday service. However, a workmen's service had been retained from Leek southwards, and this was the service proposed for withdrawal in the October 1964 letter. Freight services had been withdrawn from most of the Churnet Valley line from 1st June 1964, except over the short stretch between Leek and Oakamoor, which continued until 30th August 1988 despite Euston's wishes. Much of this traffic was sand from Oakamoor and limestone from the Caldon Low branch.

Rocester station remained open to passengers until the workmen's service was withdrawn with effect from 4th January 1965. Rail tours were traversing the Churnet Valley line during this period, including the RCTS "North Staffordshire Rail Tour" on 30th May 1964, which used the Uttoxeter-Rocester section on its way from Birmingham Snow Hill to Caldon Quarry hauled by class 5 4-6-0 45020.

On 8th December 1964, Fairclough's tender was extended by £478 to cover the removal of redundant assets, such as cranes, and one wonders whether these had been overlooked in the original tendering process. It wasn't until 21st March 1966 that it was noted that the demolition contract had been completed for a total sum of £20,986 16s 3d, which included an additional £758 16s 3d for "extra rail cutting at the direction of the Supplies Manager".

On 4th March 1967, the SLS/MLS returned to the Buxton line with another "High Peak Rail Tour", which started from Manchester Central, and used the line as far as Parsley Hay to reach the C&HPR, over which its passengers were transported down to the Midland main line at High Peak Junction. Haulage from Manchester to Parsley Hay was by Fairburn class 4 2-6-4T 42079, and this loco was also waiting at High Peak Junction for the return trip, having returned to Manchester in the meantime.

Parsley Hay had been closed to goods traffic on 6th July

The SLS/MLS High Peak Railtour on 4th March 1967 would be the last to traverse the line south of Hindlow, the enthusiasts transferring from coaches to open wagons and brake vans for the journey over the Cromford & High Peak Railway. On the left is Fairburn class 4 2-6-4T 42079 arriving with the train from Manchester, while on the right, C&HPR Guard Arthur Millward (the author's great uncle) looks on as J94 0-6-0 68012 prepares for the onward journey. (Both, Richard Bird)

1964, but the junction remained open to serve Friden brickworks on the C&HPR until 5th September 1967. By November of that year, the curve between Buxton No 2 Junction and platform 3 of the LNWR station had been lifted, and the line south had been cut back as far as the site of Dowlow Halt.

The ICI Hindlow plant is served by Briggs Sidings, which until 18th May 1969, was the limit of the double track section from Buxton. This had been worked under the absolute block system, but from that date, the section was singled, Briggs Sidings and Higher Buxton signal boxes were closed, and electric key token working was introduced as far as Hindlow station; from there to Briggs Sidings and Dowlow, one-train working came into force. In 1972, two new 990-ton limestone trains were introduced between Dowlow and Teesside, and at about this time 40% of the annual tonnage produced by the quarries in this area was being sent away by rail.

From Hindlow station, a 1¾-mile branch led to various quarries in the Harpur Hill area but this, and the block post at Hindlow, were closed on 19th September 1973. From that date, the line between Buxton and Dowlow therefore became worked as a long siding, and one-train working was instituted over the whole length. At Higher Buxton, an intermediate ground frame controlled access to Buxton South goods depot, which closed in September 1987, and on 7th October 1987, signalman key token working was introduced over the whole line from Buxton to Dowlow. This change paved the way for the introduction of twice-daily stone trains from January 1988.

100 years after the line was opened between Buxton and Ashbourne, the northern section still sees regular stone traffic. There is a regular service from Tunstead Quarry which, like the Hindlow plant, has passed into Anglo-American ownership. Limestone is brought from the quarry, situated on the former Midland line between Derby and Manchester, to the lime-kilns at Hindlow, usually once a day and often twice. This traffic amounts to some 500,000 tonnes of stone a year, and dates from the late 1980s. In the mid 1990s, there was a distinct possibility that the traffic would be sent by road, but a substantial grant towards new wagons and loading facilities saved Buxton from being subjected to hundreds of lorry journeys per day passing through the town.

Lime is not the only mineral to be exported from the

Class 37s 37687 and 37677 arrives at Hindlow on 27th January 1990 with 7T81, one of the regular trains from Tunstead with limestone to feed the Hindlow lime kilns. (Paul Shannon)

area around of Buxton. In 1982, it was reported that BR was transporting barytes, a compound used in the drilling process, at the rate of 100 tonnes per day from Hindlow to Aberdeen for use in North Sea oil exploration.

In 1997, Dowlow Quarry began sending two trains of limestone per day to Ashburys, for use in the construction of the second Manchester Airport runway and the M63 (now M60) at Audenshaw Reservoir. This train still runs to Ashburys stone terminal, but only once a day. It currently uses the line from Stockport to get to the Dowlow branch (making it the first timetabled freight train to use the Stockport-Buxton line since the mid-1960s) but returns via Peak Forest and Chinley. This causes a problem – using a different route each way leads to an imbalance of tokens quite quickly, so they regularly have to be taken back to Buxton.

Dowlow also occasionally sends stone to Northenden roadstone terminal and to Cottam power station for the Flue Gas Desulphurization plant there. In recent years, it has also sent stone to Barham stone terminal in Suffolk.

Having been the preserve of class 37s for many years, most current services are hauled by class 66 locomotives, although class 60s are sometimes seen. During the possession of Dove Holes tunnel at Christmas 2011, an additional hand-worked crossover was installed at Buxton to allow easier movements from both the Dowlow and Peak Forest lines direct to Stockport. There was talk of keeping it as a permanent installation, but it now appears to have been taken out.

Needless to say, the remaining stretch of line south of Buxton has become something of a magnet for rail tours, ever anxious to seek out unusual stretches of line to carry passengers over, and on 21st September 1991, the Institute of Mining Engineers organised its "North West Railtour", which included a run to Hindlow behind 37706, returning to Buxton with 47479 leading. A few months later, on 30th November, two tours ran. Hertfordshire Railtours operated "The Peak Explorer" with 37425 heading the train from Buxton and 31420 leading the return trip, and "The Two Counties Explorer" was organised by Pathfinder Tours with 20013 and 20057 leading southbound and 47818 heading the return.

16th April 1994 saw the Branch Line Society run "The Caldon Peak" tour which included a run over the line from Buxton to Hindlow topped and tailed by 37407 (hauling southbound) and 37429 (hauling northbound). Class 56 locomotives provided the motive power for a rail tour on 25th January 1997, with 56081 heading the train to Hindlow and 56105 heading the return.

The 11½-mile stretch from Ashbourne to Hartington was opened for walkers and riders as part of the Tissington Trail in June 1971, and the remaining 1½ miles to Parsley Hay followed in May 1972. The Peak Park Planning Board had bought the former section in 1968, and demolished the wooden stations soon afterwards. 12,000 tons of quarry overburden were put onto the trackbed, which was seeded with grass in the spring of 1969. The Hartington to Parsley Hay section was bought by the Board in 1971.

In October 1981, the Tissington trail between Tissington and Alsop-en-le-Dale had to be closed to walkers so that an unsafe bridge could be demolished. This led a member of the Peak Park Planning Board, Professor John Tarn, to observe that the structures on the line were not so well built as on other railway lines. It is not clear on what basis he made this claim, but he remarked, "This trail has proved very expensive because we did not do our homework originally about the cost of retaining these structures". At a meeting of the Board's management committee in November of the same year, the former Chairman, Mr Norman Gratton, went so far as to say that if the Board had known how much it was going to have to spend on the High Peak and Tissington trails, they would not have been bought for leisure use. That might be seen now as particularly short-sighted. The trails are a wonderful asset to the county, giving people over 30 miles of relatively easy walking and cycling, and opening up a beautiful part of the country to many who might not otherwise venture out into the countryside.

The route therefore still caters for travellers, albeit under their own steam, but fare-paying passengers could have returned to the route in the mid-1980s when there was a proposal to run a horse bus along the trail. This would have had pneumatic tyres to minimise damage to the trail's surface, and as John Lambe, Chairman of the Peak Park Planning Board management committee wryly observed, "It will add a new aroma to those already available on the trail."

Rail tours still run over the remnants of the line south of Buxton, with Hertfordshire Rail Tours' "High Peak Railtour" visiting Hindlow on 21st April 2001 hauled by 66220 with 66084 on the other end leading the train back to Buxton. To bring the story right up to date, on 4th June 2011, Pathfinder Tours ran "The Peak District Explorer" between Buxton and Hindlow, 66126 leading southbound with 66174 heading the return. "The Limestone Cowboy", organised by UK Railtours on 20th August 2011, was also topped and tailed with 66121 leading towards Hindlow, and 66122 leading on the return to Buxton.

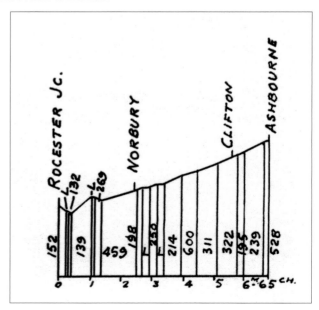

Chapter 6

The Line Described – Uttoxeter to Ashbourne

Uttoxeter, or "Utchetter" as it is known locally, is a market town in the heart of the rich agricultural country between Cannock Chase to the south and the Peak District to the north. After many years when the staple trades of the town were clock manufacture and tanning, other industries began to develop during the second half of the 19th century, which owed much to the coming of the North Staffordshire Railway. The foremost of these was the Leighton Iron Works of Messrs Bamfords and Sons, manufacturers of agricultural machinery, and the name of Bamford has been synonymous with Uttoxeter ever since. The other principal business at the turn of the 20th century was the brewery of Messrs Chas Bunting, Ltd.

In 1908, the NSR published a book called *Picturesque Staffordshire*, in which it was noted that before the railways arrived, Uttoxeter was well-served by mail coaches owing to its road connections with many important towns. In the early 19th century, the following coaches passed through the town:

- The "Light Post" from the White Hart to London every evening at 6.30pm, and to Liverpool every morning at 4.30am
- The "Express" from the White Hart to Manchester every day at 12noon, and to Birmingham every afternoon at 3.00pm
- The "Accommodation" from the White Hart to Derby every Tuesday, Thursday and Saturday at 11.30am, and to Newcastle-under-Lyme every Monday, Wednesday and Friday at 1.30pm
- The "Telegraph" from the Red Lion to Sheffield every Sunday, Tuesday and Thursday at 11.00am, and to Birmingham on the same days at 1.30pm
- The "Private Mail" from the Post Office for letters, parcels and passengers to Rugeley through Abbots Bromley every day at 6.00am, and returning the same day at 5.00pm.

At one time, there were three stations at Uttoxeter. Bridge Street, was opened by the NSR on 7th August 1848 to serve trains on the Stoke-on-Trent to Derby line, and when the Churnet Valley line opened on 13th July 1849, its Uttoxeter station was at Dove Bank. To save passengers the inconvenience of making their way between there and Bridge Street to change trains, Uttoxeter Junction station was built where the new line met the Stoke-Derby line, and opened on 11th September 1848.

On 30th October 1849, in a letter to the Board of Trade, the NSR reported on the accommodation for mineral traffic at Uttoxeter: "A line has been laid along the banks of the old canal to communicate with the Old Wharf for the purposes of the Lime and Coal Trade. It will also be valuable as a general accommodation. The works are not quite complete, but will be so in about a fortnight. Coal and Lime is now taken to the passenger station."

In March 1862, the Junction station was destroyed by fire and rebuilt. However, the layout at Uttoxeter was not very convenient for passengers travelling between Stoke and the Churnet Valley line, so under the North Staffordshire Railway Act of 1880, the "Uttoxeter Branch" was authorised to provide a chord (the West Curve) to connect the two lines and form a triangle. A new station would be built in the "V" of the new junction with the Stoke-Derby line, and the curve would join the Churnet Valley line just south of the site of Dove Bank station. The NSR wrote to the Board of Trade on 25th April 1881 to advise that construction was nearly finished, and following a similar letter on 18th May, Maj Gen Hutchinson was appointed to inspect the new line.

His report was dated 2nd June, and although he was happy about the new curve, he was concerned about the lack of any crossing facility for passengers at the new station. Having added a footbridge for this purpose, the railway informed the BoT that the station would be ready for

A view of Dove Bank station, which opened with the Churnet Valley line on 13th July 1849. This photograph was probably taken around the time of its closure in 1881 when the three stations at Uttoxeter were replaced by a single new one. We are looking towards Derby, and the original tall signal box is just visible beneath the awning on the left. Its replacement, Uttoxeter North, was a little further south. The locomotive (with a young boy sitting on one of its buffers!) is A class 2-4-0T No 6 dating from 1878.
(JR Hollick Archive Courtesy of the FLRS)

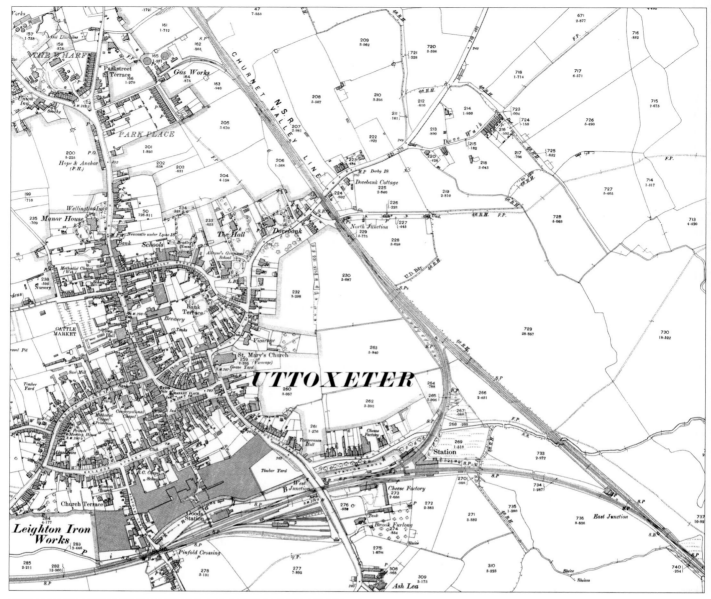

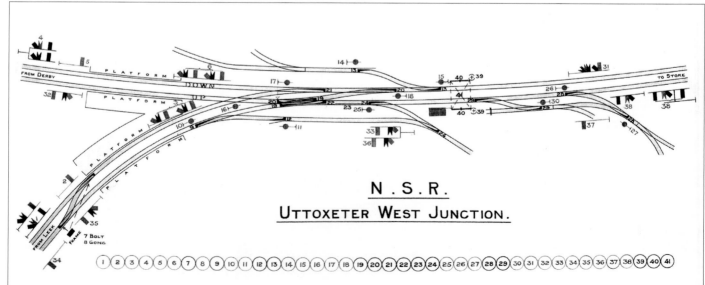

N . S . R .

UTTOXETER WEST JUNCTION.

inspection "on or before 17th September", and Hutchinson duly returned on the 30th. He noted that the new station "has been provided with ample accommodation, and is a handsome structure". It opened to traffic the following month.

This station was known from the outset simply as Uttoxeter, and as well as being better placed to serve trains from Stoke and Stafford going to the Churnet Valley, Ashbourne or Burton, it also catered for the extra traffic being generated by through workings on the GNR. The three previous stations (which had not been separately advertised in NSR publicity material) all closed when the new one opened.

The new station had four platforms connected by a footbridge. This was initially an open lattice one, but was later roofed, and even later, glazed. Unusually, it had two numbers – the span over the Churnet Valley line was numbered 1 as the first bridge on that line, whereas the span over the Derby-Stoke line was numbered 52 in sequence with the other bridges on that line. Platform 1 was used for main line departures to Stoke and Stafford, with platform 2 being used for trains in the other direction to Burton. On the West Curve, platform 3 was used by trains arriving from the Churnet Valley and Ashbourne lines, while platform 4 was used for departures on these lines. When there was both a Churnet Valley train and an Ashbourne train standing in platform 4, the latter stood at the head in order to depart first, the Churnet Valley train having the benefit of being underneath the awning. Another unusual feature was the signal within the junction, which carried the two down starting signals – one for each line skewed in relation to each other despite being mounted on the same post.

Barely a year after the new station had opened, on 6th October 1882, the Board of Trade received a letter from a Mr George Cooper, who owned a road called Brook Side (now Brookside Road) just north of the station. The NSR had built a new approach road to the station parallel with Brook Side, but separated from it by Picknal Brook, from which Cooper's road took its name. Cooper's letter noted that: "People walking from the town to the station in the dark see the station lights and naturally take the old road, and it now appears that several persons have fallen into the water, and last week a man fell in and was killed."

He considered that by constructing its road, the NSR had made Brook Side dangerous, and he demanded that a fence be erected between it and the brook at the railway company's expense. On 7th October, the BoT observed that they had no powers to assist Cooper, and on the 11th, the NSR wrote to the BoT to say that they had already fenced their road off from the brook, but that they would not fence Brookside as well. The following day, the BoT reiterated to Cooper that while they considered the NSR's response to be unsatisfactory, they had no powers to compel the company to erect another fence.

Not satisfied, Cooper wrote to the BoT on 23rd November pointing out that one fatal accident had already taken place, and that several people had fallen into the brook. The BoT wrote the next day to inform Cooper that one of its inspectors would take a look when he was next in the area. Quite why Major Marindin was in the area on 27th December is not known, but he visited the station, and reported that he believed Cooper had actually made the situation worse by building a retaining wall over which intending passengers were liable to fall. He made a number of recommendations, but restated the Board's inability to enforce any action by the NSR. Other than a note on 5th January acknowledging his report, there are no further references to this curious incident.

Potentially more serious was a collision that occurred on 11th October 1890, when a coal train coming from the Stoke direction ran into a number of vehicles standing at the Churnet Valley down platform. The coal train, having started from Harecastle with 4 wagons, had picked up 32 more at Chatterley, and was heading for Burton headed by NSR 0-6-0 No 86, a class F double-framed tender engine built by Nielson in 1865. It was very foggy and dark when the train left Chatterley at 7.00pm, and after passing Leigh station, the driver, Arthur Wardle, felt that his train was running away out of control. He screwed down the handbrake on the tender, put sand on the rails and whistled for the guard to apply his brake, but as he approached Pinfold distant signal, the speed remained at around 16 or 17 mph even though he had now reversed his engine as well.

Ahead of the runaway train, in the up main platform of Uttoxeter station, stood a GNR Stafford to Derby passenger train, and in the Churnet Valley down platform stood NSR 2-4-0 No 14 (built by Dübs in 1875) then an uncoupled MR milk van (No 144) and beyond that the 4-coach Ashbourne branch passenger train. At Uttoxeter West signal box, the signalman, William Beaman, was faced with a dilemma – should he allow the runaway to run into the back of the GNR passenger train, or should he divert it onto the Churnet Valley down line? He quickly chose the latter course and the coal train duly struck No 14 at around 15mph, pushing it into the MR milk van, and driving that in turn into the rear of the Ashbourne train.

Nineteen passengers on the train were injured, both locomotives were derailed and damaged, the milk van was demolished and pushed onto the platform, and four Ashbourne coaches were badly damaged (especially brake third No 33) with brake third No 28 being derailed. Wagons in the coal train that were derailed included MR 83382; Talk o' th' Hill Nos 674, 522 and 693; GI Eveson No 635; H Sowter No 20 and NSR Nos 3992, 5132 and 619.

The Board of Trade appointed Col Rich to investigate the accident, and he placed most of the blame on the guard of the coal train, Jonas Hayes for not applying his brake. It was alleged that he was asleep in his brake van, having been on duty (like the driver and fireman) for more than 12 hours. Supporting evidence came from various signalmen along the

Opposite page, top: The Ordnance Survey map shows the layout of the junction station and its environs at its zenith, but before the addition of the engine shed in 1901. (Reproduced from the 1899 Ordnance Survey map)

Opposite page, bottom: The signal box diagram for Uttoxeter West Junction dates from the North Staffordshire Railway era. (Collection Allan C Baker)

The aftermath of the October 1890 accident at Uttoxeter. C class 2-4-0 No 14, although badly damaged, was returned to service after undergoing repairs, and survived until 1919, by which time it had been transferred to the duplicate list as 14A. Brake third No 33 was probably the most badly damaged of all the passenger rolling stock involved, and in this view, the remains of the Midland Railway milk van can be seen between the carriage and the tender of No 14.
(JR Hollick Archive Courtesy of the FLRS)

route, who claimed that he could not be seen on the veranda of his vehicle applying the brake. Also found to be contributory factors were the lack of a brake on the engine and the inadequate weight of the brake van (8 ton 3 cwt). His recommendation was that all engines should have brakes, and that there should be at least one brake van weighing 10 tons for every 20 wagons in a train. The NSR subsequently built 10- and 20-ton brake vans, the latter being used on 40-wagon trains, the maximum length permitted.

Less than two years later, on 27th July 1892, another collision occurred at exactly the same place. At around 7.15 pm, an NSR Loop Line train arrived from Stoke with a milk van bound for Liverpool at its rear. This van was left on the down Churnet Valley line, whereupon the 6.10pm Macclesfield to Uttoxeter train arrived in the up Churnet Valley platform. Hauled by NSR 2-4-0 No 13 (sister engine to No 14 involved in the 1890 accident) the train had its usual five carriages, together with a saloon bound for Stoke and an additional third class carriage for Derby.

Shunter Gregory unhooked the locomotive and told the driver, Joseph Hughes, to collect the milk van and attach it to his train. He was then to take the whole train and put it in the

brewery siding off the down main line. Gregory's intentions (shouted to the same William Beaman as before in Uttoxeter West box) were that after putting the train in the brewery siding, the locomotive would leave the Derby carriage on the down Churnet Valley line, and return to the brewery siding to leave the saloon and milk van to be picked up by the 7.00pm Derby to Stoke train.

After overseeing these shunting movements, Gregory then ran over to the down Churnet platform to tell the driver of the Ashbourne train waiting there to "knock the third class carriage back into the New siding". As he was doing so, No 13 came over the through road from the down main line and crashed into the through carriage for Derby, injuring many of its 45 passengers. Fortunately, the Ashbourne train had not had time to set back as requested by Gregory.

The investigating officer found that Gregory had confused Beaman, who thought that Gregory had intended No 13 to put the Derby carriage into the New siding. He had therefore set the road to allow the locomotive to reach the down Churnet line. Meanwhile, driver Hughes thought that his part in the proceedings had ended, and knowing that the Ashbourne train would put the carriage in the siding, began to move his engine as if to proceed along the up main line to turn it on the triangle. Also criticised was "the dangerous and objectionable practice" of fly-shunting loaded passenger vehicles, and it was again noted that all the men concerned had worked a 12-hour day.

The "New" siding referred to by Gregory must refer to the one leading to the dock opposite the dairy that resulted in another visit by a Board of Trade inspector. The NSR having informed the BoT about the siding on 5th December 1892, Major Marindin was appointed to inspect the following day, and visited on the 21st December. He noted: "The points are worked from the Station Signal Cabin (*by which he must have meant Uttoxeter West*), which contains 39 working and 1 spare levers, and a gate wheel for working the gates of a level crossing."

His only request was that No 9 lever, which worked the new siding points, should be locked both ways with No 35, the lever working the starting signal to the Churnet Valley line. The NSR acted quickly, and confirmed that this request had been met on 30th December.

To the west of the station, Bridge Street crossed the line by a cast-iron girder bridge with brick parapets, although there was also a level crossing at this point, which gave access to The Farmers' and Cleveland Dairies Company Ltd. This was the location of Uttoxeter West signal box, an NSR type 1 design dating from 1881, which had a McKenzie and Holland 40-lever frame with a gate wheel, and was situated opposite the dairy on the same side of the tracks as a dock for milk traffic and horses. The site of the dairy was also used for a time as a brewery, and had its own siding to which access was gained from a spur which ran behind platform 1.

Further west, beyond the bridge, was the goods yard. This was built on the site of the erstwhile Bridge Street station, and in addition to numerous sidings on the down side, there was a goods shed on the up side. Other sidings were provided to serve the Anglo-American Oil Company (down side) and Bamford and Sons' Leighton Ironworks (on the up side, and reached by means of wagon turntables). The yard had a 5-ton capacity crane, a long loading dock, numerous cattle pens, a group of coal offices and a number-takers' cabin. Bamford's Leighton Ironworks covered an area of 10 acres and employed 400 people. At busy times, it was not unusual for 50 wagonloads of implements to be despatched in a day by rail to all parts of the world.

Beyond the yard towards Stoke was Pinfold Crossing signal box, a McKenzie and Holland type 1 structure of 1875, which had a 31-lever MCK&H frame with 5-inch centres and a gate wheel. In addition to the level crossing situated here, the box controlled the western end of the goods yard, and also the eastern end of the down reception sidings located further towards Stoke.

A further quarter of a mile west of Pinfold crossing, was Hockley crossing, an NSR type 2 structure dating from around 1872 where, on 18th March 1912, the NSR advised the Board of Trade that it was building a new connection to serve Bamford's works, which were growing and extending into what was to become known as their West Works or, more prosaically, "the Klondyke". This area of the works was not used in the winter due to a lack of heating, but in early spring, workers moved into this part of the factory to build up stocks of rakes and haymaking machinery. Because sales of this type of machinery represented such a large proportion of the company's turnover, the move each spring became known as "The Gold Rush to the Klondyke".

Lt Col Druitt was despatched to inspect the new connection on 10th May. He noted a new crossover and siding connection worked from Hockley Crossing signal cabin, in which a new frame had been provided containing 13 working levers and seven spares in addition to a gate wheel.

Engine stabling facilities were provided at Uttoxeter from the first half of the 19th century. In January 1849, a Mr Forsyth asked the Traffic and Finance Committee to sanction the conversion of "the existing engine shed at Uttoxeter…to a cheese store". This building stood to the west of Pinfold crossing, and its replacement was a single-road building that housed two locomotives and stood on the south side of the line between the crossing and Uttoxeter West Junction. The facilities of the second shed included a coaling platform at the rear and a turntable at the Junction station. This turntable was only 17ft in diameter, so it was replaced in 1873 by a 45ft turntable at Uttoxeter East Junction, which itself was moved to Stoke roundhouse when new curve was built in 1881 and the resulting triangle became available for engine turning.

A new engine shed was opened in early 1901 to the east of the new station within the triangle of lines. It was more extensive than the previous ones, and indeed was one of the larger sheds on the NSR outside Stoke, being built to accommodate 12 engines. No turntable was provided, but this was not the original intention, as the previous year, the Traffic and Finance Committee had approved a new shed "with turntable, coal shed, tank and carriage washing shed". The cost had been estimated at £8,000 but the winning tender, submitted by Messrs TR Yoxall, was for only £4,054. However, this related to the shed only, plans for the turntable and carriage shed being abandoned as costs rose. Before opening, an extra £250 was needed for the water supply, and the installation of a Worlaston water softening plant costing £550 was approved in June 1903. The coal shed, originally intended to be a substantial brick building with a crane, was built as a rather primitive and flimsy structure, which was little more than a simple canopy over the rails.

In practice, the shed housed eight or nine locomotives, mainly for local passenger work. There was smattering of ex-NSR locos up until early in 1935, but the ensuing years saw a standard passenger allocation of 2-6-2T and 2-6-4T locos until, by 1954, the allocation was half a dozen 4MT tanks plus a lone class 4F 0-6-0 provided for goods work. By the 1960s, there were 3F 0-6-0Ts and some BR Standard tanks, and an additional feature at this time was up to a dozen locos dumped in the sidings by the Picknal Brook awaiting their fate, including an ex-Lancashire & Yorkshire Railway 2-4-2T still in LMS livery.

In the 1920s, Uttoxeter shed was grouped under Stoke in

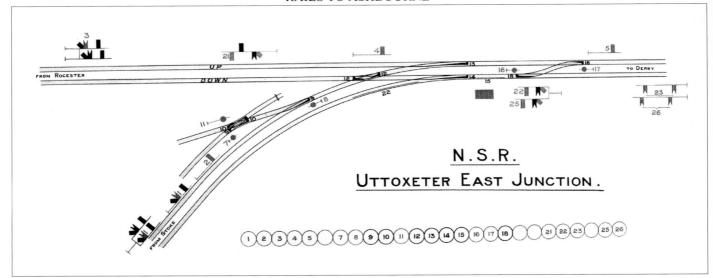

The NSR signal box diagrams for Uttoxeter East Junction showing the entrance to the engine shed (above) and Uttoxeter North Junction showing the Uttoxeter Gas Company's siding (opposite).
(Collection Allan C Baker)

Left: Uttoxeter shed in 1950. Lined up from left to right is Stanier 2-6-2T (the number is indistinct, but appears to be 40129), Fowler 2-6-4T in the middle and Stanier 2-6-4T on the right, the latter two being the "stock-in-trade" locomotives for Churnet Valley and Buxton line services.
(RK Blencowe)

the North Stafford Section of the LMS. In 1935, however, it was transferred to become a sub-shed of Crewe, and was given the code 5F, which it kept until final closure on 7th December 1964.

The signal box at Uttoxeter East was an NSR type 1 structure dating from 1877, and had a 26-lever frame. Between here and Uttoxeter North Junction (where there was another level crossing) seven sidings (called New Sidings) fanned out from the access road to the engine shed inside the triangle of tracks. These were provided to store wagons detached from through trains, or from trains that arrived during the night. Such wagons were then collected and worked by a daily "shed to yard" train. The same happened in reverse, with wagons being worked from the goods yard to the sidings to be made up into complete trains, or to be picked up piecemeal by trains running between Burton and the Churnet Valley line. Uttoxeter North signal box was originally another NSR type 1 design built in 1881 with 29 levers, but it was replaced (evidently to appease local

inhabitants who complained about the length of time Dove Bank crossing was closed to road traffic) in May 1908, 30 yards to the south, by a brick-built NSR type 2b box also with 29 levers. The new box was 971 yards away from Uttoxeter East and 826 yards from Uttoxeter West.

In 1899, coinciding with the opening of the Ashbourne to Buxton line, the NSR produced plans for a line at Uttoxeter that would have linked the West Curve north of the station with the Stoke-Derby line immediately to the east of the station. 350 yards long, it would have allowed for the building of a true triangular station, similar to that at Ambergate on the MR, but it was never built.

An list of early employees at the three original stations is given in *White's Directory of Staffordshire* for 1851 This shows Henry Workman (Inspector), Edward Browne (Agent), George Wood (Booking Clerk, Dove Bridge) and Edward Walter Stocker (Booking Clerk, Bridge Street). It is likely that with his Inspector status, Workman was in overall charge of all three stations. Ten years later, *Harrison, Harrod &*

N.S.R.
UTTOXETER NORTH JUNCTION.

FROM ROCESTER

UP

DOWN

TO DERBY

TO UTTOXETER STATION

① ② ③ ④ ⑤ ⑥ ⑦ ⑧ ⑩ ⑪ ⑫ ⑬ ⑭ ⑮ ⑯ ⑰ ⑱ ⑲ ⑳ ㉑ ㉒ ㉓ ㉔ ㉕ ㉖ ㉗ ㉙

Co's Directory & Gazetteer of Staffordshire gives Henry Norris as having responsibility for the three stations with Thomas Bould as Goods Agent. In 1877, Thomas Mellor became the Station Master at Uttoxeter, a post he held for over 30 years until around 1910. His successor according to Kelly's Directory for 1912 was John Birkin, but he himself was succeeded by Thomas Brown from 1915 until he retired in 1928.

The NSR facilities listed in the Railway Clearing House Handbook of Railway Stations for 1904 included the ability to handle goods, passengers and parcels, furniture vans, carriages, portable engines, machines on wheels, livestock, prize cattle vans and horse boxes – the number of which increased significantly when Uttoxeter Racecourse was opened on 3rd May 1907. These facilities also extended to LNWR traffic, but the GNR was listed as dealing with goods, passengers and parcels only. The only named siding recorded was that to serve Bamford's. Wilts United Dairies (United Dairies from 1917) had a milk-processing plant at Ingestre and another at Uttoxeter itself, which provided for local needs and also served London, with milk from both plants being sent away via the GNR. Traffic to Derby could be sent to the GNR station at Friargate by joining that railway at Egginton Junction, or access to Derby Midland station (referred to by the NSR as "Derby NSR") could be gained by continuing to Willington Junction and joining the MR there.

The NSR working timetable for July to September 1914 allowed for up to 70 goods trains to call at Uttoxeter on most weekdays from various different directions, although most of these must have been conditional, as returns show an actual number of about 25. The majority of these, of course, were through trains with wagons being detached and added as necessary. Only about four goods trains a day terminated at Uttoxeter, and only one of these was an express goods, this being the Crewe to Uttoxeter which arrived at 4.15am every day except Sunday and Monday.

One of the chief imports into the town was coal, which was required as a fuel, and for conversion into coal gas. On the north edge of the town was the Uttoxeter Gas Company, opened around 1880, which was served by Gas Works

Above: Uttoxeter North signal box seen in April 1959 looking towards Rocester. Uttoxeter gas works can just be discerned above the crossing gate. (HB Oliver/Author's Collection)

Siding, 300 yards north of Uttoxeter North Junction. On 29th January 1898, the NSR notified the Board of Trade that it had built a new connection to serve the gasworks. Lt Col Yorke was appointed to inspect the new connection, doing so on 21st March. He noted that the points and sidings were worked from Uttoxeter North Junction signal box, which had 28 levers, one spare and a gate wheel. He made no recommendations as a result of his inspection.

The gas company had its own private-owner goods wagons, and in addition to buying its coal directly from the pit, it also appears to have bought coal through a local coal merchant, Eckersley Bros. Both these companies' coal wagons could therefore be seen regularly, together with wagons owned by Derbyshire Co-operative Society, another coal merchant in the town, and wagons from the collieries themselves. Some of these were local such as Haden and New Haden (Cheadle), and Talk O'Th'Hill (Stoke-on-Trent), but others came from further away.

Another large user of coal was Bamford's, who had its own wagons for the purpose. They also required other raw materials such as lime, iron, pig iron, coke and sand, which would have been delivered in a mixture of private-owner and railway-owned wagons – sometimes NSR-owned, but equally likely to be from any of the other main-line companies.

These were the needs of the industries in the town, but there was also a huge range of general goods traffic such as stone, agricultural machinery, animal feedstuffs, grain, meat and other provisions. Other private-owner wagons known to have operated from Uttoxeter belonged to PC Brisbourne, Brisbourne and Neville and the NSR Employees Coal Association.

On 30th October 1945, the Ministry of War Transport reported that Major GPS Wilson of the Board of Trade had inspected a new down loop and two dead-end carriage sidings that had been constructed between Pinfold and Hockley crossings at an estimated cost of £9,450.

On 21st November of the same year, the Ministry reported that Major Wilson had inspected another new siding connection on 17th October. This was a dead-end siding of approximately 100 yards with a trailing connection into the down line of the Churnet Valley line to Rocester. This siding had been constructed in 1943 on behalf of the Ministry of Works and Planning to serve a general store of the Ministry of Food. The connection ("suitably trapped") was worked from the adjacent Uttoxeter North signal box which (as noted by Lt Col Yorke over 50 years earlier) had a frame of 28 working levers and one spare.

By the time the 1956 edition of the *RCH Handbook of*

Above: With the footbridge removed and awnings cut back, Uttoxeter station is already looking a shadow of its former self in this view taken on 26th June 1972. All services on the Churnet Valley line had ceased on 4th January 1965 with the withdrawal of the workmen's service, and the track had been lifted – cars can be seen parked on the former trackbed. Services over the Stoke to Derby line continue today, but nothing of these buildings remains today. (M Bott, JA Sommerfield Collection)

Railway Stations was published, there were few changes in the traffic handled, but the crane capacity was now 6 tons, and the number of named sidings had grown fourfold. Bamford's still had their siding, but others were listed for the Ministry of Agriculture Fisheries and Food, West Midlands Gas Board and United Dairies. In the 1962 *Appendix*, a siding had been added for Shell Mex & BP Ltd, but the Ministry of Agriculture and Gas Board sidings had closed. United Dairies also had a siding at Egginton by this date.

Uttoxeter's proximity to Derby Works made it a suitable destination for test runs, and one of the most unusual locomotives to be tested in the area was the diesel-hydraulic type 3 prototype DHP1. This was built by the Clayton Equipment Company of Hatton near Tutbury, and was a joint venture with Rolls-Royce and Lt Col FLR Fell, who had designed the 4-4-4-4 diesel-mechanical No 10100 in the early 1950s. The elusive DHP1 only ever made two runs with a train, both from Derby to Uttoxeter and Rocester and on up the Churnet Valley line. The first run, on 17th February 1964 consisted of seven passenger coaches, and the second, two days later, had a load of 12 unfitted open wagons and two brake vans weighing just over 200 tons. Apart from six light-engine movements, no other runs on a main line were made, and the locomotive was broken up in 1967.

Uttoxeter North Junction signal box closed on 30th January 1966, having spent the period since the Churnet Valley line closed just turning engines on the triangle – much to the frustration of motorists, as the gates needed to be closed to road traffic for this manoeuvre. Its MCK&H frame (reduced in size to 16 levers) found a new home at Shackerstone on the Battlefield Line, and its shell survived into the 1990s when the Uttoxeter bypass was built. Uttoxeter East signal box was closed on 19th January 1969, these closures bringing to an end the operation of the triangle at Uttoxeter (track at the former locomotive shed was removed around this time as well). The oil sidings at the Shell Mex & BP depot, formerly controlled by Uttoxeter East box, were subsequently worked by a ground frame off the main line, and the former Churnet Valley line platforms were converted into a car park to cater for demand on race days.

It was also reported at the end of 1968 that the layout at Pinfold Crossing had been simplified by the removal of a crossover from the down main and goods line to the up main and warehouse siding. Two of the sidings at Pinfold, formerly "double ended" were scotched, and control of entry to them was transferred to Uttoxeter West.

Uttoxeter station became unstaffed on 3rd May 1971, and was closed to goods traffic on 2nd July 1973, although private sidings remained open after that date. Uttoxeter West signal box lasted a little while longer (renamed Uttoxeter on the closure of East and North) closing on 18th November 1973, and Pinfold Crossing box and Hockley Crossing box lasted even longer, both closing on 25th January 1981.

These latter boxes were replaced on closure by a new box, opened two days later on the Stoke side of the road at Pinfold Crossing, called simply Uttoxeter. This is a standard BR (LMR) type 15 box with a second-hand 40-lever tappet frame, and was among the last three mechanical boxes to be opened in the country. By means of closed-circuit television cameras, this box controls the level crossing at Hockley, and also controlled Pinfold Street level crossing until it closed on 29th March 1998, the road having been blocked off before it crosses the line. It retains its lifting barriers, but only pedestrians use the crossing. After closure, the upper (timber) section of Hockley Crossing box was moved to Caverswall Road on the Foxfield Railway where it is still in use, and the crossing keeper's cottage survives as a private residence

Bamford's works have recently been flattened, and the station is a shadow of its former self, which is surprising considering that it serves an important national sporting venue. The remaining 1881 buildings were demolished in 1987 following a fire, and replaced by a "bus shelter". Echoing Maj Gen Hutchinson's inspection, there is currently no footbridge, passengers having to cross the line on the level under the control of a Network Rail employee stationed there for just that purpose. For a more comprehensive history of the railway at Uttoxeter, readers are strongly recommended to seek out the article written by Allan C Baker and Mike G Fell in issue 37 of *Railway Archive* (Lightmoor Press, December 2012).

Trains left Uttoxeter's sharply-curved Churnet Valley platforms to head north-west before turning north-east to reach Rocester, the first station on the Churnet Valley line, and the junction for Ashbourne. There were a number of gated level crossings on this stretch of line, one of which, at Spath, would be no more worthy of note than the others were it not for the fact that it was the first crossing in the country to be fitted with automatic lifting barriers.

Lifting barriers were not new to this country, some gates having been replaced with them in the early 1950s, but they were still manually operated. The Ministry of Transport therefore began to look at systems where the movement of the barriers was triggered by an approaching train. After a fact-finding tour of Holland, Belgium and France by officials from the MoT in 1956, Parliament passed an Act in 1957 authorising "safety arrangements at public level crossings such as automatically or remotely operated barriers".

On 15th April 1959, the London Midland Region of BR applied for permission to provide "an Automatically Operated Barrier Installation" at Spath in Staffordshire. The road (the B5030) mirrored the railway by running between Uttoxeter and Ashbourne via Rocester, and in preparation for the scheme, the LMR surveyed road use between 10th and 16th August 1958 and again between 6th and 11th October 1958. Motor vehicles crossing averaged around 1,500 a day, and there were also sundry bicycles, pedestrians and animals. A footnote to the survey noted that, "in the Summer, particularly at holiday times, road traffic is sometimes heavier than usual because of visitors to Alton Towers". Taking everything into account, including a T-junction just 100 yards along the road to the west of the crossing, the Ministry decided on 8th May 1959 that: "This appears to be an excellent crossing for an experiment with automatic half

Above: The original NSR signal box diagram for Spath Crossing. (Collection Allan C Baker)

Left: Spath Crossing in early 1961 just after the installation of the half-barriers. A signalman is still present in the box as it was not unusual to keep a signal box manned to monitor things during the initial couple of weeks of operation; the box's days are numbered, though. Could that be a BR official in the suit? (Nick Allsop)

barriers."

The installation of the barriers and control equipment manufactured by the Westinghouse Brake and Signal Company Ltd commenced in late November 1960 with authority for the crossing being given by the British Transport Commission (Churnet Valley Line) (Spath Crossing) Order 1960 of 19th December 1960. By Thursday 2nd February 1961, work had progressed enough for Col McMullen of the Railway Inspectorate to formally inspect it. A locomotive and saloon was provided for the inspection, and he granted permission for the crossing to be brought into use on the following Sunday, "subject to completion of the fencing and the road surface as well as attendance at the crossing until further notice".

The education of road users was paramount to the safety of the system, so BR embarked on a publicity campaign with leaflets being circulated to all local residents, schools receiving visits from BR officials, and much being published in the local media. A press conference was held at the crossing on the morning of Monday 6th February, and a 2-car DMU shuttled between Uttoxeter and Rocester to operate the crossing at various speeds. This snippet from the *Daily Mail* of 30th January is typical of the press coverage: "Robot Crossing – Britain's first train-controlled level crossing was tested yesterday at Spath, Staffordshire. Instead of gates, it has red and white poles which are automatically lowered across the road when a train trips an electric contact on the line."

The *Financial Times*, told its readers that, "the Installation has cost between £5,000 and £6,000, but it is estimated that after three years there will be a net saving of about £2,000 a year represented in the wages of the three signalmen who formerly looked after the gates and in maintenance".

Despite much attention being paid to this first installation of its kind, there were some teething troubles.

Top: A view across the tracks towards Bamford and Sons' Leighton Ironworks, probably taken around 1905 judging by the types of wagons in use. All the wagons appear to be either North Staffordshire or Midland Railway types, with the exception of the private owner wagons, many of which belong to Eckersley Bros, a local coal merchant. The only other discernible PO wagon reads "William ....ings", which can possibly be interpreted as William Jennings, a coal trader from Stafford, although it is not known for certain whether or not he had his own wagons. (Author's Collection)

Middle: This view is looking across the Stoke-Derby lines at Uttoxeter, probably some time in the second half of 1983. The junction for the Churnet Valley line has long since been removed, and the cars on the right are parked on the trackbed. Uttoxeter West signal box would have been on the opposite side of the tracks this side of the road overbridge in the distance. This bridge had replaced an earlier level crossing, which remained to serve the dairy whose building can be seen on the left. Evidence of this crossing can still be seen today. (Kestrel Collection)

Bottom: This view, taken on the same day as the previous photograph, is looking back towards the station from Station Road. Again, cars can be seen parked on the former Churnet Valley trackbed, as can the roof of the remaining building on platform 2 for Burton and Derby. (Kestrel Collection)

Above: Seen on 4th April 1979, the only platform building to survive after the closure of the Churnet Valley line was this one on the Burton and Derby platform. Stripped of the awning that shrouded it and its twin on the branch platform, it looks quite naked, and the presence of the modern waiting shelter only adds to a rather depressing scene. (Kestrel Collection)

Right: The lattice signal post at the west end of platform 1 once held a starter and a distant with repeaters for each due to the presence of the footbridge. By 14th August 1995, the elegant post only supported a single starting signal. (Kestrel Collection)

Below: The scene on 13th July 2012 records the minimal facilities now present at the station. The semaphore signal remains, but the lattice post has gone. (Author)

Top: Thankfully, the delightful cottages at the two minor road crossings between Uttoxeter and Rocester survive and have been adapted as private dwellings. They were almost identical in design, but the chief difference was that Crakemarsh, seen here on 13th July 2012, was blessed with more chimneys, with a consequent difference in the arrangement of its windows. It has recently been extended to the right and (not visible on this photograph) extensively to the rear. (Author)

Middle: Combridge Crossing cottage is seen on the same day, and survives in more original condition, although it too has been extended to the rear. Its single chimney has a window to its left, and it also has a window at the front instead of the large chimney breast evident at Crakemarsh. (Author)

Bottom: You really have to look very hard these days to see any evidence of a railway in Rocester, let alone all the infrastructure associated with a junction. This is the site of Ashbourne Road crossing on 13th July 2012 with no evidence of the crossing keeper's cottage remaining. Edes Farm Drive runs back along the trackbed of the Ashbourne branch on the right. (Author)

Top: The station building at Norbury and Ellaston has been added to frequently over the years, but never more so than after closure, such that it is now a very imposing building – especially when viewed from the other side of the mill stream. It is seen here on 14th August 1995. (Author)

Above left and right: The goods yard at Norbury was on the opposite side of Dove Street from the main station buildings, and has been subsumed into the nearby farmyard since closure. Two original railway buildings remain on the site, as shown here on 13th July 2012. The brick-built building almost certainly dates from the North Staffordshire Railway era, but the pre-cast concrete building dates from the BR era. These provender stores were designed for the storage of animal feed, and were leased to individual traders and national distributors; they could be found in station goods yards all over the country. The trackbed west of Norbury station has also been taken over by the farm and is used as an internal road to serve various fields. The buildings on this page are all on private property, and photographs were taken by kind permission of their owners. (Both, Author)

Above and right: A rather run-down Clifton station on 17th February 1980. Since the removal of the signal box, the station building has changed hands a number of times, and is now a well-kept private dwelling. (Both, Author)

Below: The siding to Mayfield Mill (almost a branch-line in its own right!) exists now as a road with bridges over the Henmore Brook and the River Dove, seen here on 13th July 2012. (Author)

Below right: Between Clifton station and Ashbourne, Green Lane was crossed on the level. No photos have been found of the scene before closure, and it is unlikely that there was anything other than an open ground frame here. Seen on 21st June 2013, the crossing keeper's cottage would seem to have been enlarged considerably from the original building. (Author)

Above: LNWR G2 0-8-0 49439 of Buxton shed is seen here outside Ashbourne No 1 box on 14th June 1962 with a northbound freight from Uttoxeter. The locomotive would be withdrawn at the end of the year. (Colour Rail)

Left and below left: Ashbourne good shed is seen here on 14th July 2012, and while the redevelopment of the old station site has opened up the area greatly this side of the goods shed itself is almost hidden. Nevertheless, it is still performing a useful function over 150 years after it was built. (Both, Author)

Below: This row of seven terraced houses (the eighth having been unsympathetically added more recently) was built by the North Staffordshire Railway and is seen here on 14th July 2012. (Author)

Above and left: Other than the goods shed, little remains to suggest that a railway ran through Ashbourne. At the opposite end of the station site, a bridge takes the trackbed, now a footpath, over the Henmore Brook, and a little further on is the Church Street overbridge, both seen here on 14th July 2012. Beyond here, the path passes through Ashbourne Tunnel and onwards along the LNWR route as the Tissington Trail.
(All, Author)

Below: The Station Hotel is a gem of late-Victorian Arts and Crafts architecture, and it is good to see that having undergone several name changes, it has now reverted to its original name, even though visitors might wonder where the station is. This photograph was also taken on 14th July 2012. (Author)

Publicity is everything. Both the North Staffordshire and the London & North Western railways recognised that most of their passenger traffic would be day-trippers seeking out the pleasures of the countryside, and that their lines (particularly after the opening of the LNWR line) were in a wonderful position to exploit the natural beauties of the borderlands of Derbyshire and Staffordshire.
(All Author's Collection except top-left, Nick Wheat Collection)

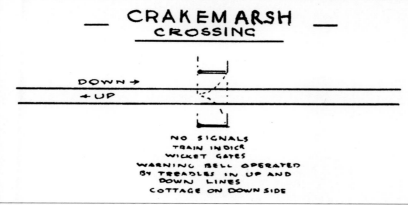

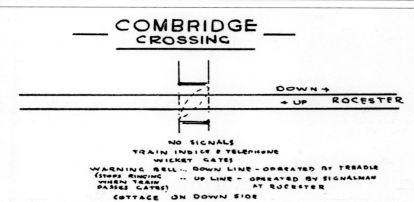

Peaks in traffic due to the proximity of Alton Towers, together with the presence of a T-junction just beyond the crossing, led to traffic tailing back over it. Anecdotal evidence also suggests that the "Barriers Failed" alarm in Uttoxeter North box had no switch to acknowledge it, so it rang and rang…! It is thought that this was rectified before the signalmen revolted! Any initial problems were relatively short-lived, however – the closure of the line saw to that, and in the intervening years, the road itself has been done away with thanks to road improvements in the area. (The author has been unable to verify reports that Spath signalbox survives at Etwall.)

Lessons were undoubtedly learned from this pioneer installation, but sadly, not enough to prevent the disaster that occurred at nearby Hixon on 6th January 1968, when a Scammell tractor drew a huge abnormal load onto a similar crossing. It was struck by a Manchester to Euston express resulting in the death of eight passengers and three railwaymen.

Two more roads were crossed on the level before Rocester was reached. First came Crakemarsh Crossing and this was followed by Combridge Crossing. The delightful crossing cottages still exist as private dwellings at both these locations.

Top: Crakemarsh Crossing after closure. (Birch Holland Collection)
(Layouts of Crakemarsh and Combridge crossings – John Swift/Signalling Record Society)

Opposite page, top: A 1953 view of the main station buildings at Rocester taken from the road, and showing off the distinctive Tudor-Gothic style of architecture used for the Churnet Valley line. The Station Master's house and signal box are behind the photographer. (Author's Collection)

Opposite page, bottom: This photograph was taken in the early 20th century. The awning replaced one more reminiscent of the roof of the down platform building in 1894, and the Gentlemen's First Class Waiting Room was added in 1903. (Collection Allan C Baker)

Top right: In the late 1950s, a new crossover was installed to simplify the junction and allow Buxton and Ashbourne passengers to use the up platform for both up and down trains. This was after timetabled passenger services had been withdrawn, of course, so was only of benefit to excursion passengers. The waiting shelter is visible on the narrow down platform, behind which is the loop that connected the yard with the siding for the brick and tile works. This required a separate gate across the road, visible in the photographs on pages 48 and 87. The building on the right is Simister's corn warehouse, originally built for the Uttoxeter Canal and later becoming the JCB social club. (Collection Allan C Baker)

Bottom right: Fairburn class 4 2-6-4T 42160 comes off the Ashbourne branch with an excursion on 7th October 1961. (Midland Railway Trust)

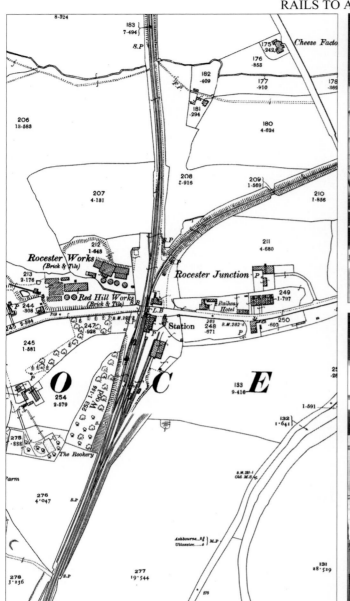

N.S.R.
ROCESTER YARD CABIN.

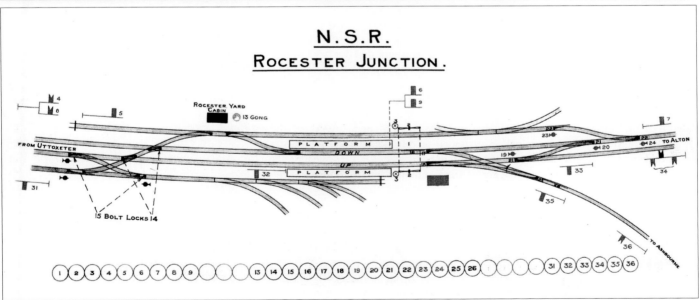

Opposite page, left: This map has been created by merging two sheets together, and a siding appears to have been added at some time to the south of the station although the full extent of it is not clear. (Reproduced from the 1899 Ordnance Survey map)

Opposite page, right: Two views of the interior of Rocester Junction signal box taken on 2nd April 1956.
(Both, Ian Scrimgeour/Signalling Record Society/Kidderminster Railway Museum)

This page, top: Rocester Junction signal box, built on to the Station Master's house, is seen here on 28th March 1965.
(FW Shuttleworth)

Opposite page, bottom and above: The signal box diagrams for the two Rocester signal boxes. (Collection Allan C Baker)

Rocester

About a mile above the spot where the Churnet joins the Dove – two rivers, whose courses flow through some of the prettiest scenery in Staffordshire – lies the quiet village of Rocester, midway between the two watercourses and near the south end of the Churnet Valley. It was at one time a Roman station, and in 1795 remains of Roman works, probably baths, fragments of pottery and copper coins were discovered in a field near the Church. Croxden Abbey, a most interesting old ruin, is within easy reach. It was founded by Bertram de Verdon in 1088. The remains, dating from the 13th century, are about 40 feet in height, and include a magnificent Gothic arch, the old guest house, etc. The heart of King John is said to have been interred here. (*Picturesque Staffordshire*, published by the North Staffordshire Railway, 1908)

The station at Rocester, dated from the opening of the Churnet Valley line on 13th July 1849, and had two platforms with a bay platform on the up line for local traffic to Uttoxeter. In common with the other stations on the line, the sandstone main buildings were on the up side, and were in a Tudor-Gothic style. On the down platform was a much smaller wooden waiting shelter, and between the station buildings and the junction for Ashbourne to the north, was a road crossing, which like Clifton further along the branch, had a turnstile for pedestrians. Also here was the signal box, 3m 1434yd from Uttoxeter North, with the Station Master's house joined to the rear of it.

Lighting was by oil lamps mounted on wooden posts, but in LMS (or BR) days, these were replaced by electric lamps mounted on Midland Railway cast-iron standards.

In addition to the usual passenger, milk and goods traffic, corn and timber was handled, and stone was brought from Hollington Quarries to the station, where it was cut prior to being transported all over the country. In a letter to the Board of Trade on 30th November 1849, the NSR reported on the accommodation for mineral traffic at Rocester: "Extensive accommodation provided at this place for Goods and Minerals. The trade just commenced."

The Ashbourne branch made a single track junction into the double track Churnet Valley main line, even after the building of the LNWR extension from Ashbourne to Buxton. However, coincidental with the opening of the new line, the NSR wrote to the Board of Trade on 30th June 1900 to advise them of alterations made at the Uttoxeter end of Rocester station, as a result of which, Lt Col Yorke was appointed to inspect. In the event, Maj Gen Hutchinson carried out the inspection, which was dated 11th September. He observed that there were new and altered connections with both main (Churnet Valley) lines on the up side of the station, which were worked from a yard frame containing 17 levers, of which 4 were spare. The frame was controlled by two interlocked levers in the Junction signal box, which he noted contained 36 levers, of which eight were spare, and a gate wheel for the level crossing.

His major recommendations were that the junction down home signals should be heightened and bracketed, that a down distant signal should be provided and the locking for the main line facing points should be lengthened. The NSR responded on 6th February the following year to report that all the alterations had been made as required.

The yard box (on the down side of the line and not a block post) closed on 18th June 1955 in connection with the remodelling work that saw the junction replaced by a single trailing lead and a facing crossover at the Uttoxeter end of the station. When the work had been completed Rocester station box was left with all of its 36 levers working.

The *RCH Handbook of Railway Stations* of 1904 showed that the station was equipped with a crane of 10 tons capacity. Private owner wagons operating from Rocester included CA Hartley trading as The Red Hill Band Brick and Pipe Works (by 1908), TB Dyer (by 1926) and TW Langton (by 1933). The 10-ton crane was still listed in the 1956 edition of the *RCH Handbook*, which also included an additional entry for the Red Hill (Staffs) Brick and Tile Company's siding, which had actually been added opposite the Ashbourne branch junction as far back as 1901.

The first Station Master at Rocester (at a salary of £52 per annum) was Mr Pendlebury, and he was assisted by 3 signalmen. A later incumbent was Thomas Dewsbury, who was well-known locally for having only one arm. He was in the post until at least 1911, and by 1917, Mr Maddock had taken over. An article in the *Staffordshire Sentinel* for Monday 24th June 1912 included the following progress report on its appeal for the North Staffordshire Infirmary:

The NS Infirmary – The "Sentinel" Shilling Fund – Today's Receipts

NS Railway Employees
Stoke Station, 4s 9d received
Rocester Station Employees, 9d received

Rocester Station Employees
Dear Sir,
Enclosed 9d the fourth and final contribution for the infirmary fund.
Yours &c,
A Booth
June 10th 1912

It is not clear who Mr Booth was.

From 19th November 1960, the signal box (along with others on the Churnet Valley line) came under the supervision of Kingsley & Froghall. The station remained open to passengers until 4th January 1965, but goods services had already been withdrawn with the closure of the Ashbourne line from 1st June 1964, so closure to passengers resulted in complete closure of the station. The site of the station and junction has now been completely subsumed by the JCB works (there is a family connection with Bamford's of Uttoxeter, but no business connection) although Station Road still exists as a clue to its former whereabouts.

Norbury and Ellaston

Almost immediately after leaving Rocester, the branch made road crossings on the level at Alton Road and Ashbourne Road, with a crossing of the River Churnet in between. Like the rest of the station site, Alton Road crossing has been swept away (as has the road itself), but the site of the crossing of Ashbourne Road can still be identified. Shortly after this, the line turned northwards to cross the River Dove by a bridge at Swinholm and enter Derbyshire for the first time.

A Traffic & Finance Committee minute (No 15080 of 21st April 1891) refers to the reconstruction of a bridge over the River Dove, 1 mile 32 chains from the junction at Rocester, and orders abutments to be made for a double line (and other works for a single line) at a cost of £2360. It seems to be referring to the river bridge at Swinholm, but the reason for the rebuilding is not clear as this was some years before any doubling would have been required as a result of the extension from Ashbourne to Buxton. The implication is that the existing bridge had simply reached the end of its life.

Some years later, the Directors' minutes for 23rd June 1908, refer to the reconstruction and widening of a bridge one mile 23 chains from the junction. The distance (9 chains less than the bridge referred to above) suggests

Above: Signalling diagrams for Ashbourne Road and Alton Road crossings at Rocester. (John Swift/ Signalling Record Society)

Left: As with Rocester, this is merged from two maps with a consequent slight discontinuity through the station. (Reproduced from the 1899 Ordnance Survey map)

that it relates to an occupation bridge before the river bridge is reached – possibly borne out by the approved cost of only £100 from the capital account.

The line now passed through George Elliot country, Roston (a mile south of Norbury) being the birthplace of her father, Robert Evans, and his brother. These two were Adam and Seth Bede in *Adam Bede*, Norborne was Norbury, while nearby Ellastone was represented by Hayslope in the novel. Oakbourne was Ashbourne, and the counties of Derbyshire and Staffordshire became Stonyshire and Loamshire, respectively. Many of the characters in the book were well-known individuals in the neighbourhood.

The single-platform station was opened as Norbury after the opening of the branch, according to the report of the line's opening in the *Derby Mercury*, which stated that "it is intended to erect a station"; it was the original passing place for trains on the single-track line between Rocester and Ashbourne. Perhaps because of confusion with the London, Brighton and South Coast Railway station of the same name, the NSR Traffic and Finance Committee on 16th July 1901 approved a proposal to rename it Norbury and Ellastone from November 1901. The spelling of Ellastone with the final "e" is how it has always been shown on Ordnance Survey maps, but it seems that the signage erected at the station always showed it as Ellaston without the "e". From 2nd April 1923, (perhaps to bring timetables in line with the spelling on the name boards), the final "e" was dropped, and the station was henceforth referred to as Norbury and Ellaston, which name it retained until closure.

White's Directory of Derbyshire, published in 1857, included details of the station: "Railway Conveyance – The North Staffordshire Line (Ashbourn branch) from whence there are 4 passenger trains each way daily to Rochester and Ashbourn." Samuel Vinney was listed as the Station Master at this time, but by 1860, he had been succeeded by William Uall (more likely, Udall). By 1871, William Berrington was in charge, and he was succeeded by Thomas Barker at some time between 1876 and 1881. *Kelly's Directory* for 1887 listed WT Webster, but in the 1891 edition, the Station Master was Joseph Grocott. John Maddocks was the incumbent by 1908, and was there at least until 1912, after which Albert Ibbs was listed for 1916. The 1922 and 1925

editions of the same Directory list Thomas Griffin, but both the 1936 and 1941 editions had no Station Master listed.

The principal traffic at the station, apart from passengers, was milk, cattle and timber, for which an 8-ton crane was provided. This is confirmed in the *RCH Handbook of Railway Stations* for 1904, but it had been removed by the time of the 1956 edition.

A peculiarity of the station was the uneven level of the platform, which was situated on the down side of the line. It was lengthened towards the road crossing in the autumn of 1900 to handle milk traffic, with the result that between the original platform and the extension (and in front of the station building) the platform dipped nearly to rail level. At the point where the platform dipped there was originally an outside ground frame resembling a signal box without a top. Dating from 1899, it was replaced in 1904 by a proper NSR type 2 signal box with 20 levers (1 spare) on the same site and 2m 806yd from Rocester station box. A McKenzie and Holland signal had both the down starting and up home signals mounted on an original slotted post.

Private owner wagons listed as operating from Norbury included Henshaw and Sons (at least from 1874 to 1880), Wm Holland (c1924) and EA Chell (by 1926).

Norbury station served several gentlemen's country residences, notably Norbury Hall, Doveleys, Calwich Abbey, Wootton Hall and Wootton Lodge. It is a measure of the importance of railway traffic in the 19th and early 20th centuries that canvassers from the LNWR, MR and GNR would visit the houses each summer to try to secure contracts to transport the households to Scotland for the August grouse-shooting season. Each house required saloons, servants' coaches, horse boxes and carriage trucks, and special trains and saloon traffic were common occurrences at Norbury.

One of these country houses, Doveleys, deserves mention here, as it was the home of one of the foremost Victorian pioneers of minimum gauge railways, Sir Arthur Percival Heywood. This landed aristocrat argued strongly that 15 inches was a viable gauge for a worthwhile railway, and proved his point by building a fine system at another family home, Duffield Bank (just north of Derby), and an even more extensive one at Eaton Hall, the Cheshire seat of the Duke of Westminster.

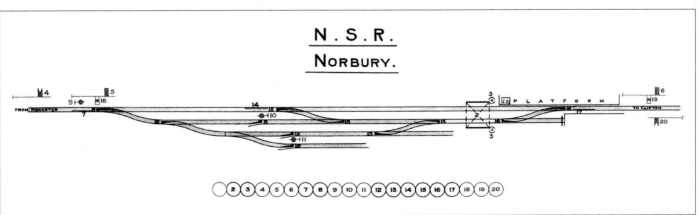

The NSR signal box diagram for Norbury. (Collection Allan C Baker)

Top: A view of Norbury and Ellaston taken in 1910, which bears comparison with the photograph on page 14. The most obvious change is the covered the lever frame, and just visible in the distance is the unusual combination of down starter and up home on the same post (see also page 93). (Collection Allan C Baker)
Bottom: In this 4th April 1954 view, further work has been done to the platform to reduce the number of different levels, but in less than seven months the station will lose it passenger service. (Pat Webb)

Top: Views towards Rocester are less common that those in the other direction, and here we see Stanier 2-6-4T 42667 on the last day of passenger services, 30th October 1964. (Midland Railway Trust)
Bottom: After closure, everything remains except the signal box, and a garage has been built. (Birch Holland Collection)

The unusual signal at Norbury with the down starter and up home signals (made from mahogany) fixed to the same McKenzie and Holland post - originally slotted, but by now, filled in. Photographed on 21st August 1950, the signal is a useful point of reference to show the position of the bowstring lattice girder bridge relative to the station.
(JR Hollick Archive Courtesy of the FLRS)

At Doveleys, two railways were built, the more robust 15-inch gauge line having been preceded by a 9-inch gauge line. Compared with the Duffield Bank and Eaton Hall systems, the railways at Doveleys are less well-known, and in truth, were never as grand as his two more-famous schemes. What little is known about them is recorded in Mark Smithers' excellent book *Sir Arthur Heywood and the Fifteen Inch Gauge Railway* (Plateway Press, 1995) and it is worth recording here that Sir Arthur had plans to extend his "Dove Bank Railway" to either Rocester or Norbury station.

If this seems a little far-fetched, it should be noted that Heywood's railways were not mere playthings for the idle rich. The system he had built at Eaton Hall was a true working railway with an interchange siding at Balderton, some three miles away on the Great Western Railway, and it is quite natural to think of him wishing to make a connection to the North Staffordshire Railway from Doveleys. The interesting thing here, though, was that in order to reach Norbury, he would have needed to bridge the River Dove, as the estate was on the opposite bank to the station.

Rocester was a more likely site for a connection, and there is even evidence of some earthworks to bear this out, but whichever direction he had chosen, he would have needed the co-operation of his neighbours to the north or to the south, and neither of them shared his enthusiasm for such a scheme. This all took place in the early years of the 20th century, and it is probably fair to say that the First World War scuppered any further progress. Nevertheless, a narrow-gauge railway along the lines of the Ravenglass and Eskdale Railway would have been an interesting addition to this corner of Staffordshire.

Just to the north of Norbury station, the line briefly returned to Staffordshire originally crossing the River Dove at an oblique angle by a timber viaduct described in the plans as "Timber gearing, 22 openings 12 feet Span each and 5ft High above ordinary Level of Water". The whole structure was supported by upwards of fifty piles driven into the bed of the river, but as a result of the opening of the LNWR between Ashbourne and Buxton, and the proposed doubling from Rocester, a new bridge was constructed. The Secretary of the company wrote to the Board of Trade on 23rd February 1903 saying:

Herewith I beg to enclose a Plan showing two temporary connections which have been laid in at Norbury for use during the reconstruction of the bridge over the River Dove, and shall be obliged by your Board sanctioning the use of these connections, subject to any requirements being carried out that your Inspecting Officer may order.

These connections were required for the delivery of materials to the site, and the letter was accompanied by a plan drawn at 2 chains to an inch, which is reproduced here:

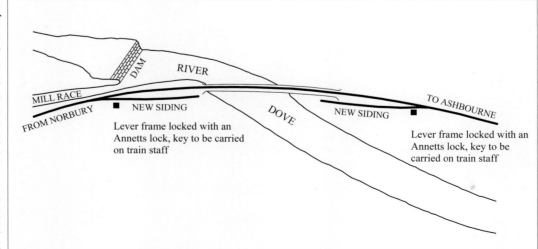

Top: The bridge over the River Dove at Norbury is seen here under construction in 1906. Eastwood, Swingler & Co secured the contract for the work as a result of a successful bridge replacement that they had undertaken near Hixon, which caused no interference to traffic on the line. The bridge at Norbury had been prefabricated and, according to contemporary reports, was hauled into position in just 18 minutes.
(Collection Allan C Baker)

Middle: Seen after completion, George James Crosbie-Dawson, Chief Engineer of the NSR is on the left, and on the right is his protégé, the Resident Engineer for the Ashbourne line, Freddie Barnwell. Despite appearances, the line remained single between Rocester and Clifton, and the additional line was probably only used during the construction of the bridge.
(Author's Collection)

Bottom: A photograph taken in around 1970 before the bridge was dismantled and sold for scrap. It is clear from this view that the single running line remained on the north (left) side of the bridge.
(Norbury Collection)

Opposite page: The reconstruction of next bridge over the River Dove at Knaveholme was a much less challenging exercise, with the new bridge being constructed alongside the original one. This photograph was taken in March 1914 and is looking towards Rocester. Whether or not the buildings were erected in connection with the rebuilding is not known.
(Norbury Collection)

The Board replied two days later that Lt Col Druitt would make the inspection, "as soon as he conveniently can". His report, dated 12th March, said:

I have inspected the new temporary connections... Each connection is worked from a ground frame containing 1 lever, which is controlled by an Annetts Key attached to the electric train staff for the section Norbury-Clifton. The interlocking and other arrangements being satisfactory, I can recommend the Board of Trade to sanction the use of the temporary connection in question.

The new bridge, designed by the NSR Chief Engineer, GJ Crosbie-Dawson, comprised a centre span of two bowstring lattice girders and, at each end, ordinary web girder spans. The central girders were 187ft 6in long (giving a span of 184ft over the river) and 25ft high, while the end girders measured 124ft 8in and 81ft 7in. The main girders rested on 13ft diameter wrought iron caissons, filled with cement and masonry, and sunk into the river bed to a depth much greater than planned due to the bed of the river being very soft. The structure had a total weight of about 670 tons, and required approximately 53,000 rivets. Contractors for the work were Eastwood, Swingler & Co, Victoria and Railway Ironworks of Derby, and it is believed that the new bridge was opened in 1906.

The building of the new bridge was recorded in a one-page article in the *Railway Magazine* of October 1907, which made mention of the original bridge, which was apparently subject to much disturbance due to trees and branches being washed against it in heavy floods. Being over 50 years old, it is hardly surprising that the NSR sought to replace it, notwithstanding the fact that it was only built for single track.

The abutments for the new bridge were built, and the caissons lowered, by the NSR's own men under the supervision of Mr Thomas Adams, the assistant engineer, and Mr Cawley, the bridge inspector. One might have thought that the work would have caused severe disruption to train services as the bridge was built on-site rather than the modern method of prefabricating and rolling into place. However, we learn from the *Railway Magazine* article that "the whole of the work was carried out without a hitch or interference to traffic, which circumstance does great credit to all concerned".

On 30th October 1906, a Traffic and Finance Committee minute noted: "Ashbourne Branch – doubling of line between Clifton and Norbury. Engineer instructed to negotiate for land and report." On 19th February 1907, a further minute reads: "Ashbourne Branch doubling of line Clifton and Norbury. Land required Harrison Estate, representatives offer to sell for £150 accepted." And on 6th August 1907, "Purchase of land from Capt Clowes, £55 approved on revenue account."

At Knaveholme, a little further towards Clifton at a point approximately 3 miles from the junction at Rocester, was another wooden bridge that brought the line back into Derbyshire for the final time. It is described in the plans as "Timber gearing, 9 openings 12 feet Span each and 8 feet above ordinary Level of Water". This smaller bridge was replaced by a steel structure (not on the same scale as its neighbour nearer Norbury), probably in 1914. Both bridges have since been removed, the bowstring girder bridge being dismantled for scrap in 1971.

The station had its fair share of little dramas, played out in relative obscurity over the years. One such was when a horse and trap collided with an Ashbourne-bound train. Quite how the two came together is not known, but the Norbury signalman saw the horse and trap in a dangerous position and tried to stop the train. He was unsuccessful, and the engine crashed into the trap, smashing it to pieces. The horse was slightly injured, but nothing is known about the fate of the driver.

On Tuesday 16th July 1912, the *Staffordshire Sentinel* carried the following report:

On Monday evening Mr E Sale, coroner for the Hundred of Appletree, held an inquiry at the railway station, Norbury, relative to the death of Michael Gordon, 36, an Irish harvester, whose body was found on the North Stafford line early on the previous morning. Mr W Thorley was foreman of the jury, and Detective Inspector Arms, of the North Stafford Railway Co's police, was in attendance. The first witness was Michael McCann, labourer at Mr Smith's, Wooton Park, who said deceased was his cousin, and had been employed by Mr WH Oldham, of Norbury, for the past six weeks. He had no relations in England, where he had lived for seventeen years. Witness last saw him alive on Sunday week, when Gordon remarked that he was saving money in order to go to America next spring. John O'Donnell, a young Irish labourer, in the employ of Mr Appleby, Roston, stated that he had known the deceased for the past three weeks, and on the night they met, witness and two others slept with Gordon at Mr Oldham's farm. Witness saw him again on Saturday night at Rocester, when with a friend they went to the Cross Keys, but the landlord refused to serve them, as it was closing time. They parted then, but witness and the friend met deceased later, and they all went in the direction of Roston, by way of the line as far as Swinholme Bridge, where witness and his friend left Gordon, who continued walking on the line in the direction of Norbury. Deceased was slightly under the influence of drink.

John Harrison, foreman platelayer, Roston deposed that he had occasionally seen deceased at Norbury. At about 9 o'clock on Sunday morning witness found the body four feet from the rails on the right hand side of the track coming from Rocester, about 60 yards from the 2¼ mile post from that village. That was about a mile from Swinholme Bridge, where anyone intending to go to Roston would leave the railway. Witness saw that the man was quite dead, and that his head was cut open on the left-hand side, and his face bruised. He at once reported the matter to the stationmaster at Norbury, who sent a message to Constable Arnold, and the body was afterwards removed to Mr Oldham's stables. Witness added that the last ordinary train to pass the place was about 9 o'clock, but on Saturday there was an extra train from Uttoxeter to Ashbourne, and passed the spot about 11.30. Deceased would probably not be aware of the train. PC Arnold, Roston, said the body was bruised, and there was a large wound on the left side of the head. The nose and mouth were covered with blood, and in witness's opinion the body must have been turned over several times. A partly-filled bottle of stout was in deceased's coat pocket, as well as £1 0s 4d in cash. The jury returned a verdict that Gordon was knocked down by a train and accidentally killed whilst trespassing on the railway.

Further details appeared in the paper the following day, but added that "A new train, starting from Uttoxeter at 11 p.m. for Ashbourne, had been put on for the first time that night". It was therefore, most unfortunate that Gordon, a native of County Mayo, was unaware of it.

The Directors' minutes for 28th July 1914 record the purchase of land and a cottage at Norbury for £450, but it is not clear what is being referred to.

Since closure, Norbury station has been converted into a private house, whose garden utilises part of the trackbed. Through the kindness of the current owner, the author has seen how the station building was added to possibly four or five times over its lifetime. The old signal box is still on-site, although not in its original position, and a prefabricated grain store and the weighbridge office remain in place on the other side of the road.

The line from Norbury continued quite close to the River Dove, and after passing Sides Mill it passed a siding that trailed back on the left to Simpson Bros' Mayfield cotton mill immediately before Clifton station was reached.

Clifton

Mayfield, situated about one-and-a-half miles from Ashbourne and half-a-mile from Clifton, is a favourite resort for tourists who are desirous of seeing Mayfield Cottage, where Tom Moore resided for about four years. During that time he wrote "Lalla Rookh" and other poems, amongst them one on Ashbourne Church bells. The poet came to Mayfield in 1813. During his stay, one of his children died and was buried in the Churchyard, where a tombstone may be seen over the grave. Within half-a-mile of the Church, the river Dove is crossed by the Hanging Bridge, an ancient stone structure of five arches. About one mile distant is Okeover Park, which has been in the possession of the Okeover family for many generations; it is over 200 acres in extent, and is well stocked with deer. The scenery of the surrounding country is exceptionally pretty, being thickly wooded, and hills and dales can be observed in every direction. (Picturesque Staffordshire, published by the North Staffordshire Railway, 1908.)

Situated on Watery Lane, the station was opened with the Ashbourne branch on 31st May 1852 as Clifton and Mayfield, but from 22nd August 1893 it became known as Clifton (Mayfield) – a stone in the retaining wall of Clifton Cottage garden opposite the station buildings bears the date 1893. In some NSR timetables it appeared as simply Clifton

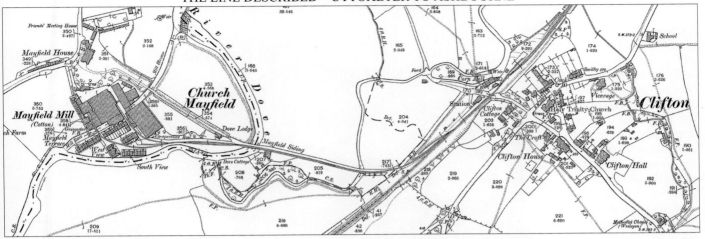

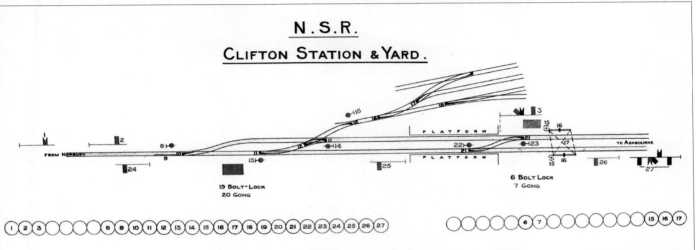

Top: The OS map of Clifton showing the siding to Mayfield Mill. (Reproduced from the 1899 Ordnance Survey map)

Above: The NSR signal box diagram for Clifton Yard and Station boxes. (Collection Allan C Baker)

or alternatively Clifton (for Dovedale), and in LMS days, it was sometimes referred to in timetables as Clifton for Mayfield. Originally built with a single platform, it comprised a large number of buildings, mainly made of brick, next to which was a level crossing overlooked by the bay window of the signal box. Beneath the signal box was a wicket gate for pedestrians in the form of a turnstile. The Station Master's house was built behind the station building and was attached to it.

A picture of the early signalling at Clifton is given in Lt Col Yorke's report to the Board of Trade during the doubling of the line to Ashbourne at the end of 1898. The road level crossing gained a temporary 5-lever ground frame in addition to Clifton station box which, apart from the unusual window, was a standard NSR type 2 box containing 17 levers; some rearrangment of the locking had been carried out in this box to control the junctions between the new and old lines. In his recommendations, Yorke asked for a slot to be added to the advanced starter, to be worked from the level crossing frame, and interlocked with the gates. He also he asked for a new stop signal to be fixed to the existing distant signal post on

the Ashbourne side of the crossing, and this too was to be interlocked with the gates.

On 30th June 1900, the NSR wrote to the BoT advising that all the doubling work had been completed, and another inspection ensued. The railway advised in its submission that the Clifton Yard signal cabin (3m 260yd from Norbury box) now operated all the goods yard points except those leading from the sidings to Mayfield Mill. The entrance to the sidings, instead of facing up trains, was now from the other direction trailing back from the new up line.

Operation of the crossing gates had reverted to the main Station signal box "bolt-locked from the Yard Cabin", and the turnstiles were controlled by a "free lever" (the addition of the new Yard signal box had freed up levers in the station box, rendering the temporary level crossing frame redundant). The accompanying plan showed two platforms that were 150 yards long with a waiting shed on the up platform, a 1½-ton yard crane and a dock for milk and horse and carriages.

On 5th July, the BoT advised the company that an additional waiting shed should be provided on the (original)

An early (c1890) view of Clifton taken before the doubling work was carried out, and showing the corn mill in the background that was served by a siding. The mill was the Down'ards goal for Ashbourne's annual Shrovetide football match between those born north of the Henmore Brook (the Up'ards) and those born south of it (the Down'ards). Although now demolished, a plaque on the site serves the same purpose these days. (JR Hollick Archive Courtesy of the FLRS)

down platform due to the station building being at the extreme end. It also noted that the crossover road was too near to the level crossing. The company replied the next day to point out that there was already a waiting room in the station building, and that the down platform was where it had always been, the only difference being that it had been lengthened. Nevertheless, it agreed to the BoT's wishes, saying that the Engineer would "of course put a small Waiting Shed on the Down platform as requested by you". It continued:

With reference to the Cross-over Road, this was put in the position shown to suit our Traffic Department, it is only required for Engines to run round their Trains and our Engines are only 47ft 7in long, whereas the space between the points and the Crossing is 70ft. Under these circumstances I presume we have your permission to use this subject to your Inspector's approval.

They received a favourable reply dated 12th July: "A waiting shed or shelter on that (down) platform is very desirable", and, "The cross-over road need not be objected to under the circumstances explained in your letter." After a final inspection dated 15th September, the BoT observed that the new up and down platforms each had waiting rooms together with "a bridge communicating between". The main building was also extended westwards around this time.

The demands on the Station signal box had reduced so much (being "retained only for working the gates") that it now only had three working levers, 12 spares and a gate-wheel. As mentioned previously, it was bolted by an interlocking lever in the new Yard box, which worked all points and signals, and had 27 levers, of which four were spare. The Board's only recommendation was that a lock should be added between levers 3 and 23, and the NSR confirmed on 7th November that this had been done.

Thereafter, the station had three platform faces, one each side of the two running lines, and a third (bay) platform,

serving the first of four sidings, the outermost one being provided to serve Mayfield Mill. No crane is listed in the *RCH Handbook of Stations* for 1904, but Mayfield siding is. It headed through a gate after leaving the branch, and ran approximately one-third of a mile to the mill, crossing over the River Dove into Staffordshire as it did so. Wagons to and from the mill were hauled by horses. The trackbed and bridge are still in use as an access road, and the alignment of the track into the station goods yard can still be seen. Other sidings served coal merchants, of which there were two – Tom Bagshaw (Bagshaw Bros) and Charles Abbot.

Milk trains from Ashbourne called at Clifton each evening, where vans full of 17-gallon churns were waiting to be picked up. These would have been brought to the station by 70 to 80 farmers from the surrounding area, who could also collect feedstuff for their cattle from the station.

Possibly the first Station Master was John Hodgkinson, as he is listed in the 1857 edition of *White's Directory*, but in the 1861 census, William Yeomans is listed. By 1876, he had been replaced by John Ford, and Frederick Ellerton appears in the 1881 edition of *Kelly's Directory*. On 30th April of that year, Ellerton was reported to have married Harriet Mountford, his position being given as Station Master at Clifton. The 1887 and 1891 editions list George William Rogers, and *Bulmer's Directory* for 1895 has Thomas F Elton, but in 1903, he was succeeded by Frederick Sherratt. A porter at this time was Mr Norris, and William Dunn was a porter-signalman. From the report of an accident at Ashbourne (see page 106) we also know that two platelayers were James Hollis and Joseph Massey. Mr Sherratt retired as Station Master in 1912, and was succeeded by William H Goodall. He was a leading member of the church choir, and also served as a churchwarden as did George Roe, who also worked on the railway. Goodall was still the Station Master according to the 1922 edition of *Kelly's*, but by the time of the 1925 edition, he had been succeeded by Samuel J Dean. Neither the 1936 nor the 1941 *Kelly's* lists a Station Master at all. Another local personality associated with the line was

Right: The siding to Mayfield Mill is seen here passing in front of Dove Lodge. A passing loop was provided on the siding , the turnout at the eastern end being visible here.
(Author's Collection)

Below: The remains of the unfortunate Mr Melbourne's lorry in its final resting place, having been propelled through the station by the 7.05am passenger train from Ashbourne.
(Author's Collection)

Mr Ridley, who drove the first engine to Clifton in 1852. He went on to become the oldest driver on the line, and died in 1900.

In 1903, an unfortunate accident befell the Station Master's house. A spark from a passing train is thought to have been blown through an open upstairs window starting a fire. Brigades were called out from Mayfield Mill and Bond's Mill, Ashbourne, and they managed to put it out, but not before considerable damage had been done to the bedroom. In the same year, the 4.20pm train one Tuesday was passing Sides Mill when a cow strayed onto the line and somehow got itself caught between the two coaches nearest the guards van. The unfortunate animal was carried along in this position for about 80 yards before it was run over and killed. One coach was derailed, but no passenger was hurt, although many were shaken. Until 1904, there was a telegraph office at the station, but this was closed, allegedly because there was not enough work to pay the wages of the messenger boy.

As if to reinforce the bucolic nature of the railway in this remote corner of Derbyshire, passengers were reputed to be able to descend from the train, pick some mushrooms for dinner, and get back on again without difficulty. A train was once witnessed stopping for the fireman to pick up a bundle of bean sticks, which were placed on the tender, before the train set off again!

The most serious accident to take place at Clifton was in August 1918, and was reported in the *Ashbourne Advertiser*:

A shocking accident, resulting in the death of one man and very serious injuries to another, occurred at the level crossing at Clifton. The collision happened between a motor lorry laden with milk, and the 7.05am passenger train from Ashbourne. The gates of the crossing were against traffic on the road, when a lorry, which belonged to the Ashbourne & District Co-op Milk Products Association, driven by Reginald Melbourne, approached down the steep and narrow road leading from the village. For some unexplained reason, it crashed through the gates, just at the instant the passenger train engine was passing the station. The engine, which was running tender first, caught the fore part of the lorry, carrying it along the line for some thirty yards before the train could be brought to a standstill. Mr Melbourne's assistant, Thomas Waring, was severely injured.

Mr Melbourne was killed instantly.

Above: Clifton Yard signal box, 16th April 1961. (HB Oliver/Author's Collection)

Left: Running "wrong line", Stanier 2-6-4T 42605 is heading a track-lifting train probably in the summer of 1964. (JR Hollick Archive Courtesy of the FLRS)

Opposite page, top: A fine overall view of Clifton station in 1953. (Author's Collection)

Opposite page, bottom: The removal of Station signal box with Blue Peter presenter, Simon Groom, standing on the low-loader. (Author's Collection)

After closure, the goods yard and station buildings continued to be used as a coal depot, and on 7th October 1983, the *Derby Evening Telegraph* reported that the empty shell of the station signal box was to be taken to Cheddleton Railway Museum for preservation. The signal box had been bought by Clifton couple Anne and Steve Liverman, and it was their wish that the box should go to "a good home". The story created a lot of interest locally, including a letter to the paper from Mrs Mary Heap, who related that her father, Fred Green, had been a porter-signalman at Clifton, where he had met her mother.

A further article appeared on 8th November, and on 15th November, the *Telegraph* carried a report of a visit to the box by the BBC programme, *Blue Peter*. Under a photograph of presenter Simon Groom (himself a Derbyshire-man), the article told how Mrs Kathleen Stevenson had been featured on the show. Her late husband, Fred, had also been a signalman at the station, and she was presented with a Blue Peter badge to mark her appearance. A final report on 10th December, confirmed that the box would be transported to Cheddleton in one piece on the following Wednesday (14th December).

A couple of years earlier, the same paper featured Clifton station in a "Know Your Place"

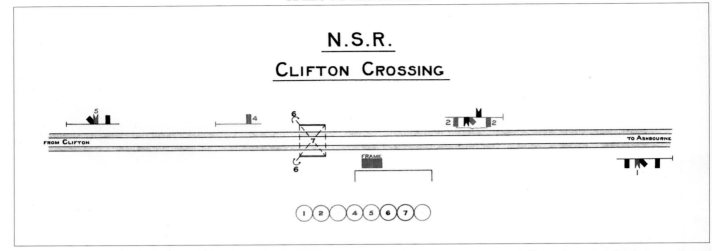

The signalling diagram for Clifton Crossing. Very little traffic can have used the road, especially as there is a ford across the Henmore Brook not far beyond the crossing. Nevertheless, it was considered sufficiently busy to be signalled and manned. (Collection Allan C Baker)

quiz, which gave rise to a flurry of letters including one from a Mrs Clarke, who had been born at the cottage next to the station. Mrs JE Ings had spent her childhood near the station, and recalled that it was a busy place with cheap excursions to Belle Vue (Manchester) on Saturday nights for two shillings return. Recollections of sitting round the waiting-room fire on winter nights were sent in by TW Holmes of Mayfield, and Mr KW Birch of Allestree told how his grandfather had been killed in 1903, when he was trapped by a runaway horse -drawn wagon at the sidings. Finally, another former signalman at Clifton, Mr W Blood, sent reminiscences about the Shrovetide football matches.

After spending nearly 20 years in storage in the car park at Cheddleton, in early 2001, the signal box was transferred to Consall where it has been completely restored as a major part of a most beautiful recreation of the station next to the Caldon Canal. In its current guise, it uses many parts of the lever frame that used to be in the signal box at Leigh, just west of Uttoxeter.

The station building at Clifton is now a private residence, and has changed hands many times since the station was closed, the asking price in October 2007 being £365,000. In the late 1980s, the earlier extension at the western end was demolished to make way for a warehouse, leaving the original building with a couple of later extensions added.

Immediately on leaving Clifton station, a siding served Clifton Corn Mill on the opposite side of Watery Lane. A little further on, the line crossed Green Lane at Clifton Crossing, which was manned, before reaching the outskirts of Ashbourne.

Ashbourne

The 1835 *Pigot and Co's Directory of Derbyshire* gives an interesting view of Ashbourne before the coming of the railway. All coaches called at the Green Man in St John's Street, the "Royal Mail" running from Manchester to London daily, and passing through Ashbourne at 2.45pm. On the same route, the "Telegraph" departed daily at 9.20am, and the "Defence" late at night at 12.45am. All coaches went through Derby, Loughborough, Leicester, Market Harborough, Northampton, Dunstable, Woburn, St Albans and Barnet. In the opposite direction, the "Royal Mail" and the "Defence" both departed at 10.00 every morning, and the "Telegraph" at 6.30 every evening. All northbound coaches went through Leek and Macclesfield on their way to Manchester.

The original NSR station building was at the bottom of School Lane, which, until the opening of the Buxton line, ran through to Clifton Road. The NSR station was made of brick and stone, to which an overall glass roof was added in 1877. The engine shed, built by 1880, was opposite Ashbourne No 1 signal box (1m 689yd from Clifton Yard box), and incorporated a large water tank supplied initially from an adjacent well. It officially closed on 14th November 1932, but survived for around another four years, and remained in use unofficially (at least for coaling and watering) until it was demolished. It originally stabled two engines, with another engine for the branch being kept at the first Uttoxeter shed. These were usually tank engines for the branch passenger service, but locomotives from LNWR workings were also serviced here. After closure, a single locomotive was provided, which worked from Uttoxeter shed. In a similar style was the goods shed, which became the last building to survive.

The Station Master's house was opposite the Railway Hotel, and shortly after the opening of the line, John Harris was listed as the Station Master in *White's Directory of Derbyshire* for 1857; it is possible that he was the first Station Master, and the fact that he is shown as living at "Compton in Clifton township" implies that the Station Master's house was not built at that time. According to the 1861 census, Francis Alison had taken over, with John Ridley succeeding him by 1870, John Marlow by 1876 and John

Reproduced from the 1899 Ordnance Survey map

Owen Jones by 1879.   The next Station Master was David Dean, whose retirement was marked by an article in the November 1909 edition of *Railway Magazine*:

A notable retirement from railway life is taking place in the resignation of Mr David Dean, joint London and North Western and North Staffordshire Railways' stationmaster at Ashbourne.   He began his career in 1858, when he entered the service of the North Staffordshire Railway at their canal wharf, Etruria, near Stoke-on-Trent.   He rapidly gained promotion acting in the navigation superintendent's office, cashier's department, and relief sections.   Thirty-six years

ago he was transferred from 'canal' to 'rails', and was appointed to the goods manager's office at Stoke.   He was next made Goods Agent at Burslem, and from there he went to Ford Green as Stationmaster and Goods Agent.   He took up his duties as Stationmaster at Ashbourne on January 1st, 1882, so that he has been intimately connected with the town for 27 years.

From 1st January 1877, Messrs Allsopp and Sons, brewers of Burton-upon-Trent, took out a seven-year lease on a couple of NSR buildings.   For £25 a year they rented the basement of the cheese warehouse belonging to the railway,

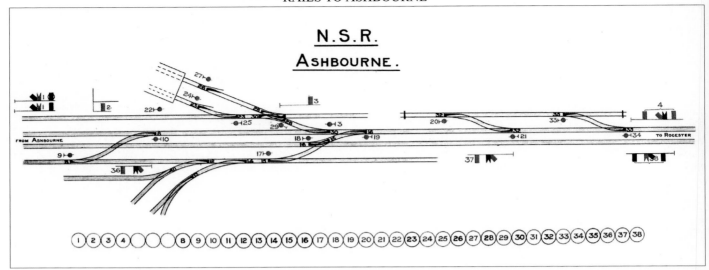

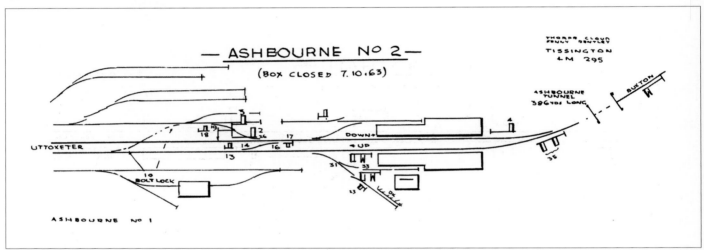

Above: Signal box diagrams for Ashbourne No 1 and No 2. (Collection Allan C Baker & John Swift/Signalling Record Society)

Opposite page, top: Ashbourne No 1 signal box seen on 16th April 1961. (HB Oliver/Author's Collection)

Opposite page, bottom: The engine shed photographed on 21st May 1936. (Collection Allan C Baker)

and for a further £10 a year they took over a building "used as a stable, being in the yard adjoining the railway together with a right of way to and from the premises". The total lease of £35 was to be paid twice-yearly in equal parts.

A further lease was granted on 25th March 1891 to Mr Frank Wright, a corn merchant of Ashbourne. This was for approximately 165 sq yd of land "together with a siding connection as may from time to time be agreed upon". The lease was for 21 years at £75 to be paid by equal quarterly instalments, and the company was to erect a warehouse to plans and specifications already agreed with the NSR. The cost of this was estimated to be £750, and a grain store was subsequently built in the south-east corner of the station site next to the stables and to the rear of the Station Master's house. It was served by a siding that was an extension of the one that ran through the goods shed, and subsequently, the Station Master's house became part of the offices of the company.

In November and December 1890, the *Derby Mercury* followed the trial of 30-year-old William Bromley Beresford, who for nine years was head goods clerk at Ashbourne. It seems that on a number of occasions, Beresford had pocketed monies paid to the NSR, but on the arrival of the company auditor on 23rd October he absconded to his mother's house at Stone where William Harris, the chief detective of the North Staffordshire Railway, arrested him. It was suggested that over a period of time he had misappropriated around £50, his annual salary at the time being £70, but although Beresford admitted the charge, he disputed the amount taken. He was tried on three specimen charges before Lord Chief Justice Coleridge at Derby Assizes on 9th December, and was sentenced a week later to three months with hard labour. Interestingly, the NSR appeared reluctant to press charges and recommended mercy. These and other mitigating circumstances resulted in a more lenient sentence than the judge would otherwise have imposed.

As at Clifton, we are indebted to Lt Col Yorke for a description of the signalling arrangements at Ashbourne around the time of the doubling in 1898. There was a 2-lever ground frame, with both levers locked from Ashbourne Station Yard (No 1) box, which had 16 levers, all in use. Again, the locking had been altered at the yard box as a result of the new works, and the ground frame was newly added. Yorke was not happy about the arrangements, and asked that the ground frame have its signal wire encased, and a longer locking bar be provided at the facing points. The yard box was to be altered so that levers 4 and 5 would be released by 13, and the normal position of No 14 points were to be from the left-hand (new) line of rails.

The opening of the line from Buxton necessitated the building of a new station at Ashbourne, in order to cope with the increased passenger, mineral and freight traffic that the new line brought. Although jointly owned by the two railways, it was built to a standard LNWR design with wooden buildings on wooden platforms. Ashbourne No 2 signal box (435yd from No 1 box) and all the station home and starting signals were also to a standard LNWR design, and the whole station was jointly worked by the two companies following a Joint Station Agreement dating from 30th June 1901. This resulted in unique insignia for the Station Master's uniform; the staff were employees of the NSR and wore that company's uniform, but the Station Master's hat bore the initials AJS for Ashbourne Joint Station. Tickets of the individual companies were issued, but station notices and the goods drays were inscribed "L.N.W.

& N.S. Joint Rlys". The station boasted a bookstall for WH Smith above which was a station clock made by W Potts & Sons of Leeds.

After the new joint station was built, the old station buildings remained in use as a goods yard and offices until well into the 20th century. To the east of the goods shed a terrace of seven houses was built fronting on to Station Street. These houses still stand (nos 58 to 70) and further to the east, in the angle formed by Station Street and Station Road, some land was eventually given over to allotments. In 1936, the LMS offered all this land for sale. The houses ("brick, slated, 3 bedrooms, outside WC and coalhouse in yard") were said to be bringing in gross rents amounting to £152 3s 6d per annum, and the four allotment gardens were being rented out at 14s 6d per annum. The LMS noted that it would wish to rent back one of the houses on a 21-year lease for one of its employees (it seems that by this time the earlier Station Master's house had gone, although it isn't known which employee is being referred to here).

The goods shed still stands (it was listed Grade II in February 1974) having been used for many years by Nestlé, who developed a large milk production facility alongside. The factory, built in 1911, was the company's main producer of canned milk products for UK and overseas markets, but in late 2002, its closure was announced due to a decline in the demand for products like Carnation evaporated milk and sweetened condensed milk; production ceased in June 2003. Plans for the development of the site were approved in December 2005.

The goods shed is built of white sandstone, with a slate roof. There are two roadside entrances, each of which has a large pedimented wooden canopy supported on brackets. There is a door of a similar type at the south-west end, and the windows on the north-west elevation have cast-iron glazing bars with some remnants of the original translucent glass still in place. A corn mill for JO Jones & Sons was later built at the south-east corner of the goods shed.

The short down bay was added some time after the new station was opened; it was too short to hold an arriving train (although it was signalled for such a purpose) so was used as a siding. In the early 1950s, it was resignalled as a siding, and the siding trap and stop-block were removed.

Just a few months after the opening of the new station and the line to Buxton, a serious accident occurred. On 1st January 1900 at 6.10pm, the 5.43pm passenger train from Rocester ran into an LNWR Walsall to Buxton goods train that was standing at the down main home signal of Ashbourne No 1 signal box. No passengers were injured, but the guard of the passenger train was slightly shaken.

The passenger train consisted of nine coaches – five owned by the NSR and four by the LNWR – and was hauled by class B 2-4-0T no 29, a Clare locomotive dating from 1883 and rebuilt in 1898. The goods train consisted of 22 empty goods wagons and a brake van, the six-coupled tender engine and two other wagons having been detached for shunting purposes. The engine and three coaches of the passenger train, together with eight wagons of the goods train, were damaged – four of the latter being derailed and turned over.

Lt Col Yorke was called upon to investigate the

Opposite and right: Two postcards produced in the first decade of the 20th century, which provide contrasting views of the station from opposite viewpoints. (Both Author's Collection)

accident, and wrote his report on 24th February 1900 after taking evidence from all the railway workers who had been involved in the accident. For the LNWR, driver Joseph Jenvey and brakesman John Seaton were interviewed, while the NSR traincrew was driver William Davies, fireman Steven Smith and guard George Goodall. Other players in the drama that unfolded were JH Durose (yardman employed by the Joint Companies at Ashbourne), Clement Bosson (signalman also of the Joint Companies), James Hollis (platelayer), William Dunn (porter-signalman at Clifton) and Thomas Brookes who was the brakesman of an NSR Ashbourne-Stoke goods train that was waiting for the passenger train to clear the road at Clifton.

The goods train, which was running nearly two hours late, arrived at the home signal of Ashbourne No 1 box at 5.57, where it stopped. The engine and two wagons were detached and sent into the yard for shunting, leaving the remainder of the train standing on the down main line. Signalman Bosson had not given the "Train out of section" signal to Clifton, but at 6.2, he received a "Train waiting" signal from William Dunn. Bosson notified this to Durose, who assured him that there was little shunting left to do, and that it would be quicker to finish and send the goods train away than to move it over to the up line out of the way. Bosson agreed, but just before the shunting was finished, the passenger train arrived and ran into the goods train at about 12mph.

The question was how the passenger train had been allowed to leave Clifton while the goods train was still occupying the section at Ashbourne. It had arrived at Clifton at 6.7, but although the home and starting signals were off, the distant and advanced starter were both at danger. Under normal circumstances, it would have been in order for the train to depart from Clifton and stop and wait at the advanced starter, but on this day it was particularly foggy, and rule 45D required that in such conditions, trains must be kept within sight of the signalman as far as practical. Furthermore, it

specifically forbade the practice of trains drawing past the starting signal towards the advanced starting signal, and yet this is exactly what the driver of the passenger train had done.

There still remained the question as to why, having done this, driver Davies took his train past the advanced starter at danger. He claimed that when he left Clifton he could not see it because of the fog, and that when he did see it, it was off. This was contradicted by Dunn, who maintained that it was at danger throughout (he also claimed in his defence that it was not foggy at Clifton at the time). Unluckily, perhaps, for Davies, an up train was waiting outside Clifton station, and brakesman Brookes was able to corroborate Dunn's evidence that the signal was at danger.

Yorke seems to have taken a fairly lenient view of Davies's error, however. He noted the difficult conditions that evening, and put great stress on the fact that because Dunn had let him leave Clifton under these conditions, it was reasonable for Davies to assume that the advanced starter was off, and that he had a clear run (even though the distant had been at danger). In view of this, and the fact that there was a specific regulation to cover the situation, he found Dunn to be more culpable than Davies.

It is quite possible that the fog was intermittently clearing and then reappearing, and indeed Dunn said in his evidence that he saw fogman Hollis going off duty at the time this was all happening. He might therefore have felt somewhat hard done by to be shouldering more of the blame than a driver who had passed a signal at danger. We do not know what happened to either of them subsequently, but it is very likely that both were disciplined in some way.

Yorke's report gives details of the rolling stock involved and the damaged sustained by the vehicles. The NSR engine received severe damage around its front end, and it was reported that its frames were bent. This damage did not prove to be terminal, however, since it survived to become 29A in the NSR duplicate list in 1921, eventually being withdrawn by the LMS in October 1932 as its No 1444. The

Above: A major employer in the town was Nestlé, whose creamery is seen sandwiched between Clifton Road and the railway in 1925. It closed in 2003 and was demolished in 2006.

Left: A continental vehicle at Ashbourne, possibly delivering equipment from the company's Switzerland headquarters, also in 1925.

Opposite page, top: A view from the railway side some time in the 1920s. Either side of the milk tanker are a 6-wheel milk van with sliding doors either side and a passenger full brake being used for milk churn traffic, both of LNWR origin.

(All courtesy of Derbyshire Local Studies Libraries and www.picturethepast.org.uk)

damaged carriages (all NSR) were 4-wheel brake third No 307 (built 1882), 6-wheel third class No 126 (built to diagram 12 in 1897) and 4-wheel third class No 61 (the body of which survived in use as a garden shed until 1970 when it was rescued by the Knotty Coach Trust for preservation at the Foxfield Railway), the first two suffering most from the accident. The damaged wagons in the LNWR train were Buxton Lime Company's No 160 and seven LNWR wagons – 37980, 61480, 1530, 61564, 33472, 11311 and brake van no 1556, which was presumably the first to be hit by the passenger train.

The signals in the yard, unlike those at the new station, were all of NSR origin (by the early 1930s, the yard intermediate outer home signals had been removed as redundant). The platforms were used as a milk dock and for loading cattle traffic, but around the middle of the 20th century, they were built on to provide a warehouse for Peake's.

A number of local companies had private owner wagons operating from the town (confirmed dates in brackets). These included Joseph Coates (by 1869), Thomas Smith (1871-74), John Twigge (1887-89), JO Jones & Sons (1894-1926) and

Simpson Bros Ltd, owners of Mayfield Mill (1903-19). JO Jones & Sons were millers and corn, manure and coal merchants (later also insurance agents) with premises at Clifton Road and the station yard. It is also believed that Ashbourne Gas Works had its own wagons.

Kelly's Directory for 1900 contains references to a cheese warehouse at the station (presumably the one previously leased by Allsopps the brewers, Agent: Tomas Bridden) and three coal merchants – Alfred Dakin, John Twigge and Henry Coates. Four years later, the *RCH Handbook of Stations* listed various facilities at Ashbourne, including a 10-ton crane in the yard.

On 13th May 1901, The LNWR informed the Board of Trade of a new bay line to the down or west side of the platforms at the south (NSR) end of the station, which connected with the down running line. Two days later it received confirmation that Lt Col Yorke had been appointed as inspector, although in the event, Lt Col Druitt submitted his report on 7th August. He wrote:

A new down bay line, signalled for arrival only, has been laid in, with facing points in the down main line. Some trailing points from a siding in the down main line have been removed and the siding now connects with the down bay line. The down platform has been lengthened about 48ft and made 3ft wider, and is 3ft above rail level. An overflow culvert under the line consisting of 4 brick arches of 6ft span in the square has been lengthened 17ft to carry the permanent way of the new down bay line. This culvert is of suitable construction and appears to be standing well. The signal box contains 30 working levers and 6 spaces, and the additional interlocking and other arrangements are correct.

The Station Hotel was opened in November 1901 by James Eadie Ltd of Burton-upon-Trent whose name still appears in stained glass over the main entrance. It was built by a Mr Kershaw, also of Burton, to the design of Messrs Wright and Thorpe, with interior furnishings being provided by Maples of London. The first manager was Edgar Dray, who had previously worked at several auspicious establishments, and brought a high standard of luxury to Ashbourne. After a number of changes of name following the closure of the line, it has now returned to its original title.

The first motor car in Ashbourne, a De Dion Bouton, was used by the engineer to the line, and was kept in the garage at Hulland House, which, together with The Mansion (the former residence of Dr Taylor, a friend of Dr Johnson), had to be bought by the LNWR as parts of their gardens were required for the new station. (Hulland House was included in the 1936 sale mentioned earlier, and was described as having "a frontage of 49 feet onto Church Street – brick, slated – a large house suitable for re-development – 10d per annum tithe rent, a big 4 bedroom house with 4 attic rooms, entrance hall and two reception rooms.")

Some development work took place in 1911, possibly in connection with the construction of the Nestlé factory, and in a letter to the Board of Trade dated 13th September of that year, the Secretary of the NSR requested its sanction to open

Top: An unusual view of Ashbourne station, looking towards the original terminus on 30th April 1962, and showing the juxtaposition of the old and new stations. (Collection Allan C Baker)
Bottom: Even more unusual is this view of the exterior of Ashbourne station directly opposite the Station Hotel, also taken in 1962. The small lay-by in the road where the vehicles are parked remains to this day. (BJ Miller)

Providing the corresponding view back to the footbridge compared to the photograph opposite, the 9.30am ex-Uttoxeter parcels train arrives at Ashbourne some time in the 1960s hauled by Fairburn 2-6-4T 42234. (Author's Collection)

a new siding. The BoT, responded on 16th September informing the NSR that Major Pringle would inspect the new works, but again it was Lt Col Druitt who actually performed the inspection. Some time then elapsed, as his report is dated 10th May 1912:

I have inspected the new works at Ashbourne on the North Staffordshire Railway. At this place, two new siding connections, with points trailing to the up line, have been laid in. These with the additional disc signals are worked from the old signal box, which now contains 35 working and 3 spare levers. The additional interlocking is correct, but trap points must be provided for each of the new sidings at the fouling point with the main line, as the existing traps are too far back. Subject to these being provided, I can recommend the Board of Trade to sanction the use of the above new works.

The NSR responded on 13th June to confirm that Druitt's recommendations had been carried out.

According to *Kelly's Directory* of 1922, in addition to JO Jones & Sons, there were two other coal merchants at the station – Kirkland & Perkins and Thomas Ridley. The Station Master at this time (most likely having taken over from David Dean at the end of 1909) was John Henry Collier, but by the time the 1925 edition was published, he had been superseded by John Frederick Barry, and Albert Smith had been added to the list of coal merchants.

The 1936 edition shows the Station Master to be George William Thornhill and he was still in office in 1941. There were quite a few changes to the list of merchants at the

station over this period, but JO Jones & Sons remained a constant presence. By 1936, and continuing in 1941, he had been joined by the Anglo-American Oil Co Ltd (who had a motor spirit depot in the yard), Shell-Mex & BP Ltd (oil merchants), and William Charteris, Derby Industrial Co-operative Society, Midland Supply Co and Ernest Victor Smith (coal merchants). Interestingly, *Kelly's* for these years omits a couple of coal merchants who appear in the *Nottingham, Leicester & Derby Trades Directory* for 1939-40 – the aforementioned Kirkland & Perkins and Yeomans & Son. This publication also lists the corn merchant, Frank Wright Ltd.

Thomas Ivor Jones became Station Master in 1948/49, replacing a Mr Roberts. He retired in 1955 due to ill-health, although it is possible that he might have simply stood down with a view to returning at some point in the future. A temporary Station Master was put in place, but if it was intended that Mr Jones should return, he was unable to do so, and he died in 1958.

It is appropriate at this point to look at the history of bus services around Ashbourne. According to the 1922 *Kelly's Directory*, the Trent Motor Traction Co Ltd ran buses to Derby via Osmaston, Shirley Lane End, Brailsford, Kirk Langley and Mackworth roughly two-hourly between 9am and 7pm; these services were augmented in the summer. J Harrison's motor buses ran hourly between Ashbourne and Mayfield from 12noon on Saturdays only.

Three years later, the Trent service to Derby had been joined by a similar one run by Henry D Bayliss, and the frequency had improved to roughly hourly between 7.45am and 8.15pm (again augmented in the summer). The Green

Man had joined Harrison Transport Co's service to Mayfield.

By 1936, Trent was the sole provider of the Derby service, again hourly, but operating between 6.30am and 9pm. It continued to provide extra buses during the summer months, and in addition, there was an alternative service via Cross o' the Hand. It also ran services to and from Burton-upon-Trent, Mayfield, Leek, Stanton, Uttoxeter and Waterhouses.

Mention has already been made of the ancient Ashbourne custom of Shrovetide football, a no-holds-barred game that takes place through the streets on Shrove Tuesday and Ash Wednesday. This ancient competition between the Up'ards (born north of the Henmore brook) and the Down'ards (born south of it) combines the minimum number of rules with the maximum number of players, and bears little relation to the game we see on Match of the Day every Saturday night. It is not surprising, therefore, that the game has been known to bring train services to a halt, and one such occurrence was noted in the *Railway Magazine* of April

1963. The afternoon Buxton to Ashbourne goods train was delayed at the mouth of Ashbourne tunnel on 27th February of that year, because the ball (and its attendant scrum of players) had found its way into the tunnel. The length of the hold-up was not recorded.

Goods facilities at Ashbourne were withdrawn from 1st June 1964, on the closure of the line to freight services (there had been little change in the facilities over the years, but the 1956 *RCH Handbook of Stations* recorded an 8-ton crane in the yard). The station continued to be listed as a "non-rail-connected depot" for parcels and goods until the beginning of February 1965, and as late as 1966-67, the *Nottingham, Leicester & Derby Trades Directory* still listed two merchants at the station – JO Jones & Sons and Frank Wright Ltd. The station site was cleared in 1973 to make way for the current buildings. A couple of bridges survive, one being the riveted steel bridge taking the line over Henmore Brook just north of the station, and the other taking Church Street over the railway.

A very clear view of Ashbourne station in its final days taken from the footbridge – probably in the summer of 1963. Considering how long ago passenger services had ceased the condition of the station is quite remarkable. (Henry Priestley/Kestrel Collection)

Chapter 7

The Line Described – Ashbourne to Buxton

Leaving Ashbourne, trains were faced with a 2¾-mile climb to Thorpe Cloud at a gradient of 1 in 59. The first feature on leaving the joint station was the bridge carrying Church Street over the line immediately followed by the tunnel through the red sandstone to north of the town which, like the rest of the line, was built for double track even though only a single line was ever laid (the line of rails was laid on the up side of the double-track formation). The southern portal of the tunnel was built in stone, whereas the other end was built of engineering brick. Its construction required the demolition of several houses and two public houses (the Old Bear and the Britannia) on Church Street.

When the line was converted into the Tissington Trail, the tunnel was originally used to provide access from Ashbourne. However, in 1980, the condition of the inside of the tunnel was giving BR cause for concern, so they refused the renewal of the Peak Park Planning Board's annual lease, and closed the tunnel. BR made it clear that the tunnel was not due to collapse, but that there was sufficient danger of pieces flaking off the roof to warrant their action on safety

grounds. It is possible that the deterioration of the tunnel was due to vibrations from above, as there was not much material between its roof and ground level. Indeed, it is said that the noise from heavy traffic could be heard reverberating inside the tunnel.

In November of the same year, a route for the Ashbourne relief road using the disused tunnel was approved by Derbyshire County Council's planning committee. Four alternative routes for the road had been considered, and at a public exhibition attended by 1,000 people, the popular choice was the £2-million scheme that utilised the old tunnel (an alternative route, requiring a new tunnel, had been costed at £7m). Later in the same month, the proposal was backed by Derbyshire Highways Committee, but nothing came of the scheme.

The tunnel survives however, and in 1998 was bought by Sustrans to form part of its National Cycle Network. An announcement in mid-1999 confirmed that Derbyshire County Council would spend several thousand pounds reopening the tunnel and extend the Tissington Trail into

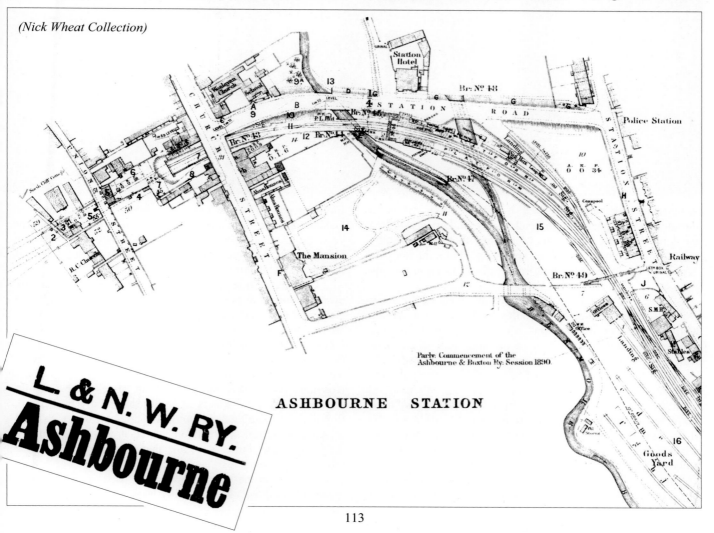

(Nick Wheat Collection)

ASHBOURNE STATION

Parlv Commencement of the
Ashbourne & Buxton Ry. Session 1890.

Left: Unseen for many years after closure, the interior of Ashbourne tunnel can now be inspected on foot (or by bicycle) to the accompaniment of railway sounds played through a system of loud-speakers. This view is looking north on 14th July 2012. (Author)

Below: Seven Arches viaduct looks very solid in this photograph taken around 1929. Events were to prove otherwise, however. (Author's Collection)

Ashbourne town centre, which it did in 2000. It is lit throughout, and hosts "Soundtrack" – a sound art installation by Jony Easterby and Mark Anderson that intermittently plays clanking noises, whistles, voices and slamming doors to evoke the atmosphere of the former railway to those passing through.

Shortly after leaving the tunnel, a seven-arch viaduct (No 39) carried the line over Bentley (or Bradbourne) Brook. Known as "Seven Arches" (not surprisingly) this brick-built viaduct was quite a landmark in the area, and when plans were being made to convert the line into the Tissington Trail, its future became the subject of heated debate. Initially, the Peak Park Planning Board announced its intention to demolish it due to the cost of maintenance. Defects had been found in the structure when it was inspected in 1978, but the Board later decided on a less-radical scheme that would have resulted in four arches being demolished, and the remaining arches being lowered in height by a third at a cost of some £104,000. West Derbyshire District Council disapproved of the scheme, and early in 1980 asked the Department of the

Environment to list the viaduct as being of architectural or historic interest. The attempt failed, and in February of that year, the Council reluctantly accepted the Planning Board's plans for the structure on condition that the rebuilding met certain aesthetic conditions.

Only two months later, fate intervened, as dramatic events unfolded at the viaduct. On 22nd April, as Mr Harold Gallagher was working on the bridge with a crane, five of the arches gave way and sent tons of rubble cascading into the brook; a sixth arch followed an hour later. The hapless Mr Gallagher's crane was on the viaduct at the time, and after he had jumped clear from his cab, he was taken to St Oswald's Hospital, Ashbourne, suffering from shock and a badly strained back. The waters of the brook rapidly backed up, flooding surrounding fields until workmen cleared a channel for the floodwater. The remains of the structure were highly dangerous, and there was talk that it would have to be removed by explosives.

Later examination of the bricks used in the viaduct revealed that those used internally were very poor, and could

Above: A class 4F 0-6-0 hauls its goods train northwards towards Seven Arches viaduct in the early 1950s. The post on which Ashbourne's (fixed) up distant signal is attached has been painted with black and white bands as a wartime visibility measure. (Eric Brown/Author's Collection)

be crushed by hand. Within a year, a new concrete bridge had been built to replace the viaduct, and the old trackbed landscaped to provide slopes down to the bridge on either side.

Thorpe Cloud

Thorpe Cloud station was the first out of Ashbourne, and although it served the village of Thorpe, it took the name of a hill about a mile away that overlooks Dovedale. Clearly the name was chosen with the tourist traffic in mind, and in some timetables it appeared as Thorpe Cloud (for Dovedale). The station was typically LNWR, being a single wooden platform with particularly spartan wooden buildings that lacked canopies.

According to the 1904 *RCH Handbook of Railway Stations*, the station had facilities

for passengers, goods and livestock, and by the 1956 edition, goods and passenger excursion traffic was handled, the station having closed to passengers along with the rest on the line on 1st November 1954. Final closure, again in common with the rest of the line, came on 7th October 1963, when the remaining goods traffic was withdrawn.

CE Davenport was appointed Station Master for the opening, but he was not there for long, being succeeded on 1st July 1900 by Thomas Alfred Hughes. His period of office ended on 15th July 1903 when he became Station Master at Cross Lane on the Liverpool and Manchester line. It is not clear whether there was a designated Station Master after this until Robert Jordan was appointed 25th August 1909. He was

(John Swift/Signalling Record Society)

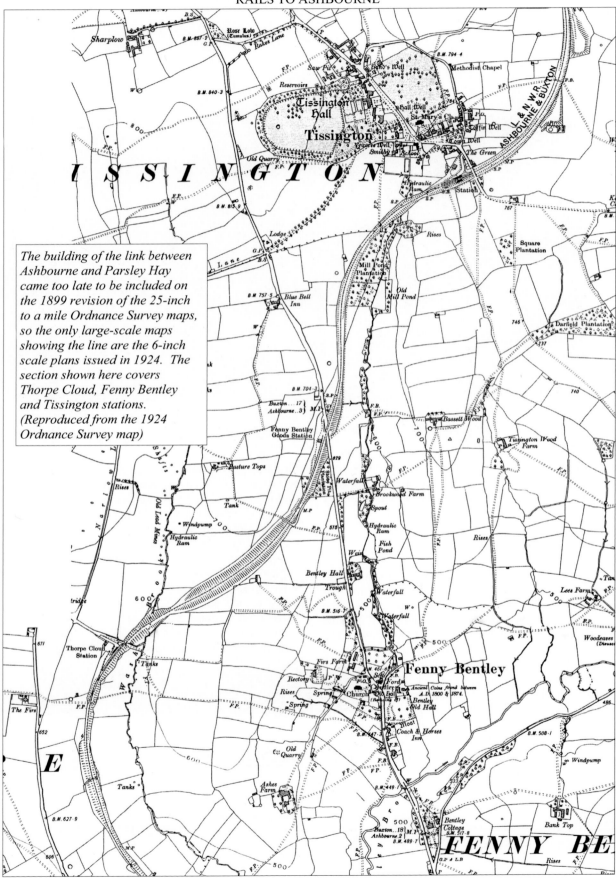

The building of the link between Ashbourne and Parsley Hay came too late to be included on the 1899 revision of the 25-inch to a mile Ordnance Survey maps, so the only large-scale maps showing the line are the 6-inch scale plans issued in 1924. The section shown here covers Thorpe Cloud, Fenny Bentley and Tissington stations. (Reproduced from the 1924 Ordnance Survey map)

Thorpe Cloud station caught the attention of Edwardian photographers as these pictures from around 1910 testify.
(Author's Collection and Glynn Waite Collection)

Top: Whether the photographer of this and the previous two pictures was the same person is not known – the bucolic charms of Thorpe Cloud station would provide quite a temptation to any photographer. This view would have been taken very soon after the line was completed, and could have been the work of the official LNWR photographer. Behind the station buildings is the Station Master's house, and beyond that can be seen the nearest buildings of Thorpe village. On the skyline is the distinctive shape of the 942ft high hill called Thorp Cloud, from which the station took its name. (Author's Collection)

Middle: Seen on 8th September 1964, we fast-forward towards the end of the station's life, the standardised wooden LNWR buildings conveying an ambience of impermanence. One cannot help wondering what would have replaced them had the line remained open. (Collection Allan C Baker)

Bottom: Providing a view in the opposite direction, this photograph was taken on 3rd August 1959. A loop, out of picture on the left, threw off a siding that ran behind the platform. (Author's Collection)

Opposite: The full extent of Woodeaves Canal is shown here (labelled "Mill Lade"). (Reproduced from the 1899 Ordnance Survey map)

still in office according to the 1922 edition of *Kelly's Directory*, but three years later C Morritt is listed, and by 1936, none is mentioned.

Freight traffic to and from Thorpe Cloud had to be worked by up trains, so that any traffic for the Buxton direction had to be worked first to Ashbourne. Similarly, traffic from the Ashbourne direction had to be worked to Alsop-en-le-Dale and forwarded from there on an up train. Wagons were not allowed to be brought onto the main line unless the locomotive was at the Ashbourne end of them.

Between 1934 and 1939, the LMS stabled a camping coach at Thorpe. These were old railway carriages containing two berths in each of three compartments, a dining room (converted from two former compartments) and a utility room for cooking and washing; paraffin was provided for cooking, heating and lighting. Most railway companies provided them, and with a rental of £6 per week, they provided affordable accommodation in a number of picturesque places up and down the country. Equipment included crockery, cutlery, glasses and bedding, all of which had to be checked each Saturday on "changeover day"; the bed linen arrived in a hamper from Derby Midland Station. After World War Two, camping coaches became popular again, but Thorpe Cloud only had one in 1954 and 1955.

Fenny Bentley

There was no let-up in the gradient, which continued at 1 in 59 between Thorpe Cloud station and the next, Fenny Bentley. Along the way, the line crossed a ridge from one valley to another, which caused much work for the contractors building the line, who had to remove 210,000 cubic yards of boulder clay before rails could be laid. It crossed the A515 for the first time here, and just south of the bridge was Fenny Bentley – never a passenger station, having only ever been open for goods traffic. It is no surprise, therefore, that successive editions of the *RCH Handbook of Stations* list it as such, the 1904 edition showing that the yard was equipped with a 5-ton crane. Traffic to and from Fenny Bentley had to be worked by up trains under the same arrangements as those in operation at Thorpe Cloud. Like the other stations on the line, it closed to goods (and therefore completely) on 7th October 1963.

Life must have been fairly quiet at this isolated outpost of the railway network – particularly as no passengers were catered for. One incident involved ex-LNWR class G2 0-8-0 49395 which experienced a "carry-over" (also known as priming) where water is taken into the cylinders with damaging results to its coupling rods. It was hauled to Uttoxeter where it was stored inside the shed with its bent rods in the tender.

An interesting, and largely undocumented, relic of early transport history was the nearby Woodeaves Canal, which remained completely isolated from the rest of the waterways network for the whole of its life. In 1784, a hosier by the name of John Cooper of Sandybrooke, together with John Matchitt, a grocer, and Philip Waterfield, a cotton-manufacturer, both of Derby, began building Tattersell Mill at Woodeaves. One of the earliest cotton mills in Derbyshire, it was originally powered by water brought from Bradbourne Brook by a 1¼-mile long mill leat, on land leased from Samuel Haslam under an agreement of August 1784. The three entrepreneurs were also granted permission to dig at Woodeaves Farm for any limestone that they might need to build the mill, and the leat was used as a canal to convey this in small boats.

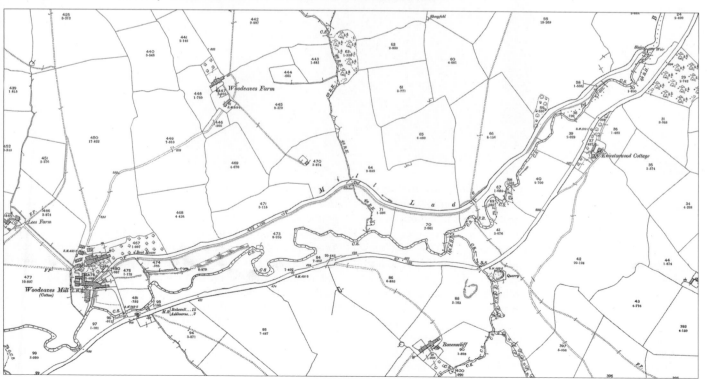

FENNY BENTLEY (N.B.P.)

TISSINGTON

← UP DOWN →

G F

Above: The very basic layout at Fenny Bentley which, like Thorpe Cloud, was not signalled. (John Swift/ Signalling Record Society)

Left: Not surprisingly, photographs of Fenny Bentley are very rare. No passengers alighted here, and public access must have been relatively infrequent. Just north of the station, the bridge over the Ashbourne-Buxton road was built wide enough for double track. The angled chrome strip separating the two-tone colour scheme shows the car to be a Wolseley 1500 rather than its Riley 1.5 equivalent, this photograph being taken 7th October 1963 – slightly later than the previous picture. (Both, HB Oliver/ Author's Collection)

Opposite: Class 4F 0-6-0 drifts towards Fenny Bentley on 17th May 1958. The bridge carried an access road to Pasture Tops (now Ashbourne Heights Caravan Park) and the points for the loop can be seen just beyond the engine. (Pat Webb)

In 1846, the mill was recorded as being powered by "a steam engine of 16 horses power, and employing 100 persons", and it is thought that the canal had fallen out of use by this time. Some of the workers lived in cottages in the mill yard, and others at Fenny Bentley. In 1895, it was reported that the mill was "fitted up with the best modern machinery, and contains 8,500 spindles. The special feature of the manufacture is cotton doubling for the lace and curtain thread manufactures of Nottingham and elsewhere". Until its closure, nearby cottages were lit by electricity generated at the mill and supplied to the residents free of charge (no pun intended...)

On 13th October 1899, the *Ashbourne News* contained a report of the Ashbourne Petty Sessions that had been held the previous Saturday. The Woodeaves Company, cotton spinners, were summonsed for employing two boys aged 14 and 16 at night, contrary to the Factory and Workshops Acts. The company said that the boys did not have to work as hard at night as if they had been employed in the day time, and would rather be on night work. No coercion had been used, and they had not been engaged in the mill during the day while they were doing night work. It was stated that the mill owners had kept 12 adult workers on all night regularly, but at the time the new railway was making it difficult to find enough men to carry on the night work. They therefore had to close the mill at night or employ the boys, and they had

chosen the latter course. The Bench did not think the boys had suffered very much as they had not been worked during the day as well, and imposed a fine of £1 in each case.

The mill ceased operating in 1908, and within a few years, most of the buildings had been demolished. However, the warehouse and engine house continued in use for various purposes, including that of a cheese factory. Stilton cheese was made between 1910 and 1930 by William Nuttall, brother of John Nuttall who made Stilton cheese at Hartington. The small portion that still remains is incorporated in a farm while the former manager's house is a private residence. Although the canal was shown on 1-inch Ordnance Survey maps until the early 1960s running roughly parallel to the brook, it is now not shown at all on the 1:50,000 series maps.

Immediately north of the station, the line crossed the A515 on a skew bridge. Bridge 29 was the largest single iron bridge on the line with a span of 91 feet, and to road users on the busy A-road, it had long been a hazard with its headroom of only 13ft 3in. This was demonstrated to tragic effect in June 2004 when a mother and son were killed when their car was in collision with a lorry that had swerved to avoid hitting the bridge. Work to remove it started on Friday 21st January 2005, and contractors spent the whole weekend using a 500-tonne crane to remove the structure. The 200-tonne wrought-iron bridge was replaced by a lighter steel bridge built by the Butterley Company and set at a height of 16ft 6in above the road. Derbyshire County Council spent £390,000 on the work.

Tissington

Still the line rose at 1 in 59 until Tissington station was reached. Tissington is an estate village with a picturesque blend of duck pond, trees, cottages, church, tearooms and an old hall, typifying the ideal model village. Tissington Hall is a fine Jacobean mansion, which has been the home of the Fitzherbert family for over 400 years, and the church dates back to Norman times, with much Norman work remaining inside, despite it having undergone a typical Victorian restoration in 1854.

By far the village's biggest claim to fame, however, is the well-dressing festival that takes place during the week of the Ascension. The five wells (with a sixth "children's well" added in more recent times) are dressed to depict various religious themes using natural materials such as flower petals and mosses pressed into clay and set in a wooden frame to form a colourful picture. The tradition is supposed to have originated as a thanksgiving for the constant supply of pure water to the village, and while many Derbyshire villages have well-dressing ceremonies, Tissington is probably the most famous.

The station, situated in a wooded cutting, had brick-built platforms as opposed to the timber platforms used elsewhere on the line. However, it had the usual LNWR wooden station buildings with the refinement of a canopy on each platform. The *RCH Handbook of Stations* for 1906 showed a wide range of traffic being handled, including goods, passengers and livestock, but no crane was listed. Following closure to

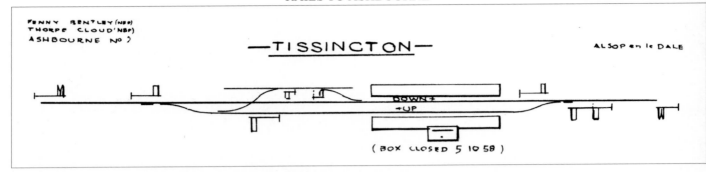

The signalling diagram (sadly un-numbered) for Tissington. (John Swift/Signalling Record Society)

both passengers and goods on 1st November 1954, there is no mention of the station in editions of the handbook after that date, although occasional excursions and emergency winter services were handled until final closure of the line in 1963.

At the opening, the Station Master was L Gould, who had formerly been at Parsley Hay, but on 1st December 1900 he was succeeded by Charles Arthur Nunn, who continued in the post until Henry Cope (listed in various editions of *Kelly's Directory* as "Harry Cope") was appointed on 1st September 1908. He was still listed in the 1925 edition, but those for 1936 and 1941 do not mention a Station Master at all, although it is believed that C Morritt had moved from Thorpe Cloud around this time.

During the First World War, some loaded wagons broke away at Tissington, and ran down the line through Ashbourne station and on to Norbury where they were deliberately derailed in a siding. The down midday London train was running from Uttoxeter to Norbury at the time, and had to be stopped and hurriedly reversed in case the derailment strategy was unsuccessful.

There would have been little development of the station over its relatively short existence, but on 21st February 1950, the Ministry of Transport was called upon to inspect a new facing connection to the loading dock siding in the down loop.

An early photograph of Tissington, probably taken around 1910 (the heyday of postcard views of local stations, it would seem). Perhaps the most remarkable thing about this view is the shear number of people employed at the station. The Station Master is likely to be Harry Cope. (Glynn Waite Collection)

Top: Fowler class 4 2-6-4T 42366 pauses at Tissington in 1953. (David Ibbotson)
Above: The corresponding view from the up platform on 19th June 1954. The obviously non-original masonry visible on the road bridge marks the location of a covered footbridge for the use of passengers. (Author's Collection)

Left: A view back towards Ashbourne giving a good view of the signal box in 1953. Little changed here between opening and closure. (David Ibbotson)

Below: Rails having been lifted, the station was falling into a bad state of repair by the time this photograph was taken. When the line was converted into a public bridleway, the buildings were swept away and the space between the platforms was filled in to create the car park. (Frank Sirett)

Opposite: The line hugged the contours as much as possible, but nevertheless, there was a gradient of 1 in 59 through the station for trains heading north. (Reproduced from the 1924 Ordnance Survey map)

Alsop-en-le-Dale

From Tissington, the line continued its relentless ascent over some particularly tortuous limestone country, which included difficult clay deposits due to geological faults in the area. Tissington Cutting was some ⅝ mile long and was followed by Newton Grange Cutting, both providing some respite on the near three-mile climb to Alsop-en-le-Dale station, the last half of which was at 1 in 71. At a distance of only two-thirds of a mile away, the station was perfectly situated to serve Dovedale.

Typically for stations on this line, it had wooden platforms and station buildings, and like Thorpe, it lacked canopies. For many years, perhaps in a desperate attempt to attract more custom, the station nameboard read Alsop-en-le-Dale for Alstonfield, although this name did not appear in timetables, which sometimes referred to Alsop-en-le-Dale (for Dovedale). Just to the north of the station, the line was crossed by an overbridge that carried the A515 on such a skew that at 110 feet long, it might have been better termed a tunnel.

The first Station Master was Henry Cope, and he remained until he took over Tissington on 1st September 1908. His successor was Arthur Bennett Broadbent, who was in charge until 16th June 1913, when he took over at Hurdlow.

Soon after the line was opened, the LNWR found it necessary to put in sidings approximately a mile north of the station to serve Alsop Moor quarry. On 5th April 1900, it informed the Board of Trade that its new work would be finished in four day's time. Lt Col Yorke was appointed to inspect, but in the event, Major Pringle was called upon to perform this duty. He visited the site on 23rd August and his report, dated 27th August, noted that all points were worked and locked from a ground frame in which there were five working levers and three spaces. The frame was unlocked by a key on the electric train staff. The company had stated that it only proposed to use the connection for up trains coming from the Buxton direction due to the gradient of 1 in 60, and based on this proviso, the installation was approved.

Access to the quarry involved crossing the main Ashbourne-Buxton road over a gated crossing. The Quarry Manager (Major Hubbertsy) lived at Alsop Hall, moving to Burbage Hall, Buxton some years

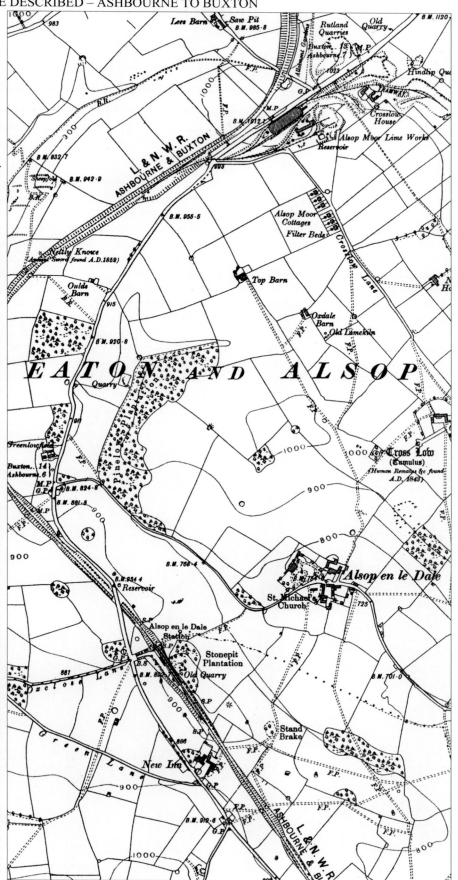

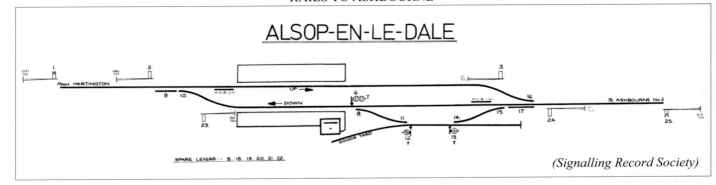

ALSOP-EN-LE-DALE

SPARE LEVERS :- 5. 18. 19. 20. 21. 22.

(Signalling Record Society)

later. At the quarry there was a large building containing about 20 kilns with a chimney about 275 feet high to provide the necessary draft. The lump lime produced went out by rail to several steelworks, including the Earl of Dudley's Round Oak Steel Works at Brierley Hill. Open wagons were covered with heavy canvas sheets which were dressed with a weather proof coating, and as these were expensive the quarry was charged if they were not returned promptly. It was the Alsop porter's job to check the sheet numbers, and quarry staff sometimes hid them under rubble or earth to avoid paying the demurrage charges!

Special arrangements governed the working of trains at Alsop Moor, the March 1937 edition of the *Appendix to the Working Timetable* having the following entry:

The tumbler points from the siding to the works are padlocked and the key is in possession of the Buxton Lime Firm's foreman, and unless he is in attendance no wagons must be placed in or taken out of the siding leading to the works. Wagons from and to the works must be placed in the loop, or on the running line, as the case may be, east of the high road, and must be attached or detached at one shunt. They must be marshalled next to the engine, and not uncoupled until they have been placed in the loop or running line and made secure. In consequence of the heavy gradients great care must be exercised by all concerned. Down trains must not call at the siding, and wagons on such trains must be worked to Hartington, and back from that station by the first available service.

Alsop-en-le-Dale in around 1910 with a healthy traffic in goods and milk evident. (Glynn Waite Collection)

Above: A view of Alsop-en-le-Dale station taken in June 1950 looking north. At the end of the platforms, the line passed over a footpath by a steel girder bridge, and beyond that it crossed the Ashbourne to Buxton road for the last time before reaching the outskirts of Buxton. Although referred to as a bridge (number 18) it could almost be argued that it constituted another tunnel on the line, as the skew angle of the road necessitated a length of over 100ft. The village of Alsop-en-le-Dale was to the east of the station, to which it was connected by the footpath. Passengers for down trains passed under the line and gained access to the platform by the approach road, while a flight of steps led to the up platform.

Middle: Taken from further back, but still facing north, the single siding can be seen branching off and running behind the signalbox. The bank of trees on the right screens Stonepit Plantation where there were the remains of an old quarry, abandoned before the arrival of the railway.

Right: A rare view of the rear of the down plaform buildings taken from the approach road.

(All, David Ibbotson)

Between 12th and 13th December 1901, a train of 6-wheel coaches became derailed by snow on Alsop Moor, and it took the efforts of 350 men to dig it out. The passengers were seemingly evacuated from the scene soon after the accident took place, but the driver and fireman stayed with the train, being supplied with food by local farmers.

The 1904 edition of the *RCH Handbook of Stations* shows that passengers, goods and livestock were handled, but there is no mention of a yard crane. Also listed was the quarry siding owned at that time by Hall and Boardman, who also had a brick yard and pipe works served by the MR at Swadlincote.

Charles Allen was Station Master from 1913 to 1938 and his son (also Charles) worked as a temporary porter at Alsop, Fenny Bentley, Thorpe and Tissington from 1930 to 1934. The Allen connection with the line goes back further than Charles, however, as the family moved from Ireland for the building of the line at the end of the 19th century.

The younger Charles recalled that in addition to his father there were two signalmen and two porters alternating for the early and late shifts. Excursion trains ran to Blackpool for the illuminations on Sundays in September and October (5 shillings return) and three times a year to Alton Towers (2 shillings including admission), and there was an occasional special through train to Glasgow around midnight on Fridays returning on Saturday night (25 shillings).

One regular passenger, known as Ma Pollit, kept a greengrocery and general store in Parwich. She had a horse and 2-wheeled cart, and went by train to Manchester once a week. While she was gone, the staff tethered her horse on a flat bit of embankment where it grazed all day, and then harnessed it ready for her return on the 6.35pm milk train from Buxton, loading up the goods she had purchased in Manchester.

Holidaymakers arrived to stay at the New Inns Hotel (now Newton House) and at Parwich Lees, and between 1934 and 1939 (as at Thorpe Cloud) a camping coach was stabled in the sidings – conveniently sited for access to the station toilets. Charles Allen remembered parties coming from London, Birmingham and Bristol, and all were greeted with a boiling kettle, a gallon can of water and any groceries they had ordered when they booked.

Passenger trains conveyed parcels, newspapers, mail and milk in churns, the milk being sent out on the 6.35pm train to arrive in London at 4.00am the following morning. Two large milk vans were left in the siding to be loaded throughout the day with about ninety 17-gallon churns. Boxes of cakes, chocolates and sundries arrived by train for the shops at Wetton, Alstonfield and Parwich, and in the Spring, boxes of day-old chicks arrived that had to be delivered on the same day. There was a sixpence delivery charge for those not collected, and Mr Allen remembered cycling as far as Hartington Moor to deliver some after getting home from work.

Newspapers arrived on the 8.10am train, and were collected by Esther Lees who cycled over from Parwich, leaving her cycle by the roadside near Alsop village, and walking up the footpath across the fields to save going round by the main road. Mail was also carried, and letters from the post boxes at Wetton, Alstonfield and Milldale were brought to the station in a large leather delivery bag by Miss Mycock. These were sealed at the station with sealing wax, and sent to Ashbourne Post Office on the milk train.

Two freight trains called at Alsop in each direction, handling coal, grain, beet pulp and animal feedstuff. All were dealt with in the single siding, which also served a small warehouse next to which was a weighbridge. Some of the freight was delivered by two railway lorries based in Ashbourne, and a railway parcel van (also from Ashbourne) delivered the parcels. A particularly busy time was when electrical installations were being installed in the area by Balfour Beatty.

Charles Allen recalled several occasions when snowploughs had to be called in to reach trains stranded in snowdrifts. On one occasion he had to go out in a snowstorm to relight the lamp in a distant signal. He had to walk ¾ mile in the snow, climb up the signal post ladder to the lamp, and then trek back to the station.

Neither the 1936 nor the 1941 editions of *Kelly's Directory* list a Station Master, but the former records the quarry being under the ownership of Buxton Lime Firms Co Ltd, and the latter, ICI Ltd (Lime Division). This ownership is confirmed in the 1956 *RCH Handbook*, which retained the listing for goods and livestock, but passenger facilities were only mentioned in relation to excursion traffic. The siding had been removed by the time the 1962 edition appeared, having closed in the late 1950s.

Disaster struck near Alsop on 13th May 1943, when Armstrong Whitworth Whitley Mk V EB338 of No 81 OTU crashed at 6.35pm while on a flight from Whitchurch Heath. Thirty minutes after take-off, the port engine failed, and although it was successfully restarted, it failed again. The pilot, FO Ernest Bull, attempted a forced landing, but struck a wall on the eastern side of the railway line before tearing up the track as it crossed the line, coming to rest in an adjoining field. The bomb-aimer, Sgt Gordon Belec of the Royal Canadian Air Force, was killed and the rest of the crew were all injured, but the accident could have been a lot worse as a train travelling towards Ashbourne had passed the site shortly before the crash.

Locomotives on Pinfold sidings (Uttoxeter) to Buxton turns exchanged crews at Alsop-en-le-Dale, with the engines being worked back the next day. This was the case up to 1962, and probably until the closure of the line.

On 18th January 1961, Nottingham High School took over the up platform buildings for use as a base for adventure training and academic studies such as geology, biology and geography. Subsequently, on 24th February, the *Derbyshire Advertiser* reported that about 30 schoolboys had given up their half-term holiday, and armed with scrubbing brushes, buckets and tools, were aiming to convert two waiting rooms, a booking office and another nearby building for their use. Around a year later, the platforms had become unsafe, with the result that excursion trains ceased to call at Alsop, which remained open for goods until the line closed on 7th October 1963.

Hartington

Beyond Alsop-en-le Dale, the line rose steadily at 1 in 60 until reaching a summit after about 2 miles, after which the line undulated mainly downwards for a further 2½ miles towards the next station, Hartington, which was approached by a brief uphill stretch at 1 in 100. This part of the line included one of the most expensive and troublesome earthworks, Coldeaton Cutting. Here, a 60ft deep cutting was carved out for a distance of three-quarters of a mile. 200 men worked on this cutting alone, excavating 314,000 cubic yards of stone with the aid of eight steam cranes and four locomotives to take away the spoil. Some of this was dumped onto a "spoil" bank in an area to the south and west of Hartington station, and a siding was opened here on 1st July 1901 to enable the spoil to be sent away to Crewe for use as a flux in steel-making.

Lt Col Yorke was appointed by the Board of Trade to inspect the new connection, but as often happened, the inspection was actually carried out by one of his colleagues – this time Lt Col Druitt, whose report is dated 7th August. He noted that the new connection was worked from the station signal box, which now contained 15 working levers and five spares. Also to the south of the station, a siding served Hartshead Quarry.

Hartington was the one of the larger settlements on the line between Ashbourne and Buxton, and as well as being a centre for milk production, it gave access to Beresford Dale – a northern extension of Dovedale. The former creamery in the village, often called the cheese factory, was founded by the Duke of Devonshire in the 1870s, and was one of the three sources of Stilton in the UK. It also produced its own Dovedale cheese and others such as Buxton Blue cheese before closing in 2009. Nearby, on the Staffordshire bank of the River Dove, was the famous fishing house of Charles Cotton, owner of Beresford Hall and friend of Izaak Walton, who celebrated fishing on the Dove in his book *The Compleat Angler*, published in 1653.

In anticipation of the opening of the line, the LNWR published a book called *Dovedale as it Will Be Seen from the North Western Company's New Railway*. It spoke in glowing terms about the district through which the line would pass:

Quite off the beaten track of the tourist and the tripper there is a picturesque locality in the heart of the Derbyshire Dales which at the present time is almost as primitive as it was when Izaak Walton and his good friend Charles Cotton used to go a-fishing in the River Dove. These worthies put up in the village of Hartington, from which the Duke of Devonshire takes his second title. It is so remote from the world that the nineteenth century, in the guise of a Rural Council, has only just disturbed it from its sleep.

This extremely sequestered spot lies as nearly as possible in the centre of England, surrounded by tracts of hills, swept by bracing breezes, where absolute quietude reigns, and within easy distance of the delightful dales of the Dove and the Manyfold (sic), with Beresford Dale to the west, and Lathkill Dale to the east. Hartington is such an exceptionally healthy

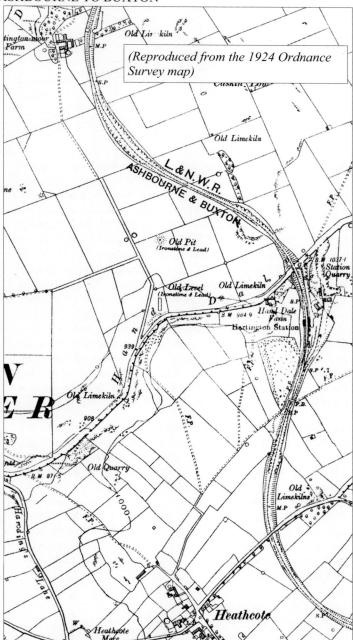

(Reproduced from the 1924 Ordnance Survey map)

place that, it is said, no doctor can get up a practice in it, and there is scarcely a death rate. Fortunately, the funerals are few, for when an interment takes place in the yard of the beautiful church the grave has to be blasted out of the solid rock. A certain number of favoured persons – anglers for the most part – have discovered this reposeful retreat, where in a fine fifteenth-century hall, now attached to a farm, board and lodging on most reasonable terms are obtainable, and modern rooms may be exchanged for large wainscoted apartments, with black oak furniture, timbered ceilings, ingle-nooks, window seats, and old-world comforts and luxuries, including, it is said, the romantic attraction of a lost secret passage, no one having in these days found the spring commanding the moving panel giving access, to the subterranean way.

HARTINGTON

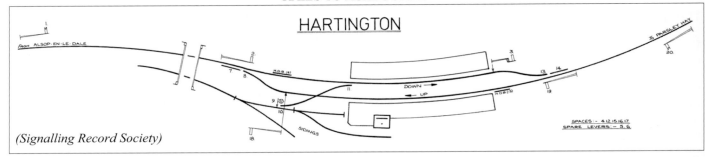

(Signalling Record Society)

But Hartington, with other little-known villages in the same country, is at last to be 'opened up' to traffic. The new railway which the London and North Western Company is completing, will bring strangers from London on the one hand, and Manchester on the other to explore this charming territory. In fact, the new link of thirteen and a half miles of line from Buxton to Ashbourne is an important one, for it will continue the Stockport and Buxton route, which is already extended nine miles southward to Parsley Hay, 1,107 feet above the sea level, to Ashbourne, whence a through connection will be obtained to London, via Burton, Nuneaton, and Rugby. A new and expeditious way will thus be provided for reaching Buxton, and the excursions from the centre, hitherto at the command only of well-to-do carriage folk, will be largely increased in variety, novelty, and beauty. Even now, by alighting at Hindlow Station, between Buxton and Parsley Hay, Chelmorton Church may be visited.

As at Tissington, Hartington station had wooden platforms and buildings with canopies, the approach from the village, 1½ miles down the hill from the station, having been cut through limestone. The 1904 *RCH Handbook* shows that there were facilities for most types of traffic including passengers, goods and livestock, and a 5-ton crane was available. The 1956 edition retained a similar listing, including the crane (removed by the time the 1962 edition), but the only passenger services were excursions and the emergency winter trains. An additional entry was for Hartington Quarry's siding, which ran through the yard to serve the quarry to the north-east of the station. This quarry closed in December 1966.

The first Station Master was John William Cope, who remained until 15th June 1903. After a very brief interregnum, George Fearn was appointed on 1st July the same year, remaining in the post until 1st January 1908,

after which Peter Hilton is listed in the 1908 edition of *Kelly's Directory*. His tenure was quite short, as George Edward Hartley became Station Master on 11th October 1909, lasting until 16th December 1912, to be followed by Ernest M Williams. He is known to have left the post on 22nd February 1916, and then there was a gap of a few months before C Mason was appointed on 21st August.

Kelly's Directory shows Arthur Bennett Broadbent as Station Master in both the 1922 and 1925 editions, presumably moving from Hurdlow. Also listed are T Berwick and Sons, railway wagon builders (although they were probably nearer to Buxton), Buxton Lime Firms (lime burners and stone merchants, Brierlow Quarry and Hindlow) and Dowlow Lime and Stone Co Ltd. (also at Hindlow). Neither the 1936 nor the 1941 editions list a Station Master, but both have entries for a number of firms operating at or near Hartington or Hindlow stations, all of which were on the stretch of line northwards to Buxton, and will be dealt with as we travel along the line.

The emergency winter service ceased on 7th October 1963, but goods services were handled until 6th July 1964, when only the private sidings remained; traffic to these ceased from 2nd October 1967. After closure, the signal box remained, and when the Tissington Trail was opened it found a new use as a base for trail wardens. The original 20-lever LNWR tumbler frame is still in full working order although it is not connected to anything.

Hartington is seen here on 1st April 1965 in surprisingly good shape after many years without a passenger service, and not long before complete closure.
(Collection Allan C Baker)

Above: Ex-GWR railcar W14W at Tissington with the Birmingham Locomotive Club railtour on 19ᵗʰ June 1954 as it waits to cross with a Buxton-bound passenger service. (Colour Rail)

Right: The gradient post at Tissington has now been repositioned against the down platform, so that it indicates the gradients the wrong way round, as seen here on 26ᵗʰ April 2013. (Author)

Below: On the last day of excursion traffic on 26ᵗʰ May 1963, the class 104 from Manchester Piccadilly is seen at Alsop-en-le-Dale on its way to Ashbourne.
(JW Sutherland, © Manchester Locomotive Society Collection)

Top: The "Leicestershire Rail Tour" of 8th September 1962 is seen at Hartington headed by Fowler class 4 2-6-4T 42343. Alongside it is an almost permanent resident at this time, the Wickham High-Speed Track Recording Unit, RDB999507. (JW Sutherland, © Manchester Locomotive Society Collection)

Bottom: Hartington Station looking south in 1967 with nature starting to take hold. (Richard Bird)

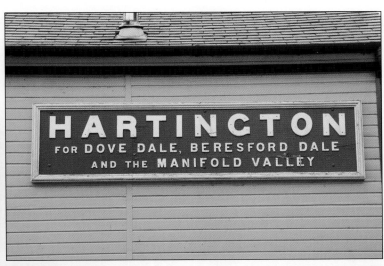

Above: Relics of the old line abound, not least at Hartington, where the signalbox, Hands Viaduct and a number of LNWR boundary posts survive. (All, Author)

Right: A snowy Parsley Hay is seen here in 1962. (Glynn Waite Collection)

133

Top: Parsley Hay is seen here on 30th September 1961 on the occasion of the second running of the SLS/MLS "High Peak Rail Tour". (Kestrel Collection)

Middle: A view in the opposite direction taken from the goods yard in August 1963. (John Thorn)

Bottom: Taken from the same direction, but with the photographer standing just to the right of the previous one, this 1967 view records the complete removal of the platforms and station buildings with the exception of the signalbox. (Richard Bird)

Opposite page, bottom left: A very rare colour view of Dowlow Halt in 1962. (Glynn Waite Collection)

Opposite page, bottom right: Seen here on 15th July 2012, Dowlow marks the northern end of the High Peak Trail, progress north through Hindlow to Buxton being impossible due to the continuing presence of the railway serving Hindlow Quarry. (Author)

Right: The original station building of the Cromford & High Peak Railway at Hurdlow is seen here on 26th April 2013. (Author)

Below: An aerial view looking towards Hurdlow with the bridge over the Pilsley road (see page 142) evident. (Richard Bird)

Below right: Ruston & Hornsby 0-4-0DH No 418793 "Dusty" seen here at Dowlow on 18th July 1984. (Howard Earl photograph, © Industrial Railway Society)

Above: Hindlow signalbox is seen here on 27th March 1978 following the realignment of some of the trackwork. (Neil Ferguson-Lee)

Left: The photographer has turned through 180 degrees to capture this view towards the dead-straight Hindlow tunnel. It is hard to believe that there was once a station here. (Neil Ferguson-Lee)

Below: Class 60 60020 is seen here at Hindlow with the 6H59 11.46am Peak Forest to Dowlow limestone working on 6th January 2009. (Paul Shannon)

Above: An expansive view of the line approaching Buxton at Harpur Hill taken on 27th March 1978, showing the bridge over Burlow Road and beyond that, Heathfield Nook Road. (Neil Ferguson-Lee)

Right: On 3rd March 1994, class 33 33116 "Hertfordshire Rail Tours" (numbered D6535) visited Derbyshire to film a training video. It is seen here crossing Heathfield Nook Road as it propels ex-NSE inspection saloon 975025 towards Hindlow. (Kestrel Collection)

Below: A composite shot showing the goods shed at Higher Buxton (known as Buxton South) taken from Peveril Road on 16th April 1978. (Neil Ferguson-Lee)

Above: Another view of the goods depot at Higher Buxton on 16th April 1978, still very much in use as a coal yard. (Neil Ferguson-Lee)

Left: Views of Buxton station in its later years taken on 27th May 1969 and, showing the old Ashbourne bay, 10th April 1976. (Both, Author)

Below: The station photographed on 15th July 2012. (Author)

Parsley Hay

The line rose more gently than previously (largely at 1 in 100 or 1 in 150) towards the next station, about 2 miles away, at Parsley Hay. The first station here had been opened by the C&HPR for goods in June 1833 and for passengers in July 1856. It was closed from December 1877, and after a temporary platform (dating from 1st June 1894) had been in use following the upgrading of the line from Buxton, the new LNWR station was brought into use at the opening of the Buxton to Ashbourne section on 4th August 1899. The new station was half a mile north of the junction with the C&HPR, and a little to the south of the site of the temporary station.

At 1107 feet above sea level, a 60ft deep cutting had to be dug for half a mile on the southern approach to the station, and artificial circular ponds known as meres were cut in the surrounding hillsides to catch dew and rain water to provide the water supply for the locomotives used by the contractors in the construction of the line.

The first known Station Master was J Brocklehurst, who was possibly installed at the time the temporary platform was opened in 1894, but is certainly known to have been there from 1st June 1897. He was followed by L Gould, appointed on 1st October 1898, who remained until he took over at Tissington on 1st August 1899. SC Beswick was then briefly in charge until 1st December 1899, followed by AG Whiting until 1st August 1901. After such rapid turnover in Station Masters, there was then a relatively stable period under Samuel Dearden (until 1st October 1907) and then John William Cope (formerly at Hartington) who stayed until at least 1925. The subsequent position is unclear, but OS Connolly is known to have been Station Master and Goods Agent in 1944.

In its article of October 1899, the *Railway Magazine* describes the line north from Parsley Hay to Buxton as "somewhat dreary and uninteresting", and Parsley Hay in particular as being "a very dreary-looking spot". However, its close proximity to Arbor Low, a Neolithic henge monument, was thought to give it an enormous attraction as a stopping-off point for "the antiquarian, and indeed, the public at large".

Not long after opening, on 14th February 1900, the LNWR wrote to the Board of Trade to inform them that by 17th February it expected to complete work on two connections with the main line ½ mile south of Parsley Hay. This was to serve a siding for the High Peak Silica Works of Messrs Wragg & Son. Lt Col Yorke was appointed to inspect, but Major Pringle inspected on 23rd August, and his report is dated 27th August. In it, he reported that all points were worked independently from two "dwarf frames", each of which contained two levers, the four points being locked by a key on the electric train staff. The gradient at this point was 1 in 150, and the company was prepared to use the

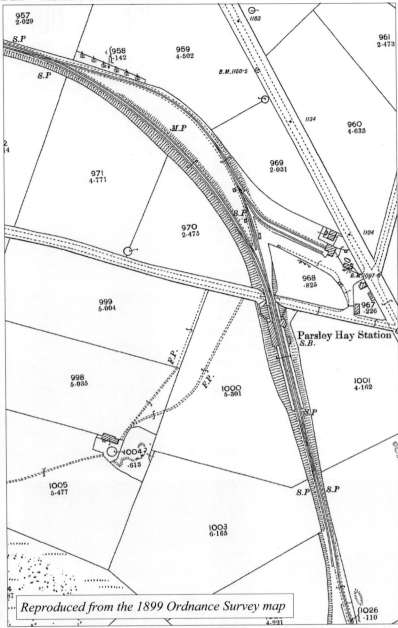

Reproduced from the 1899 Ordnance Survey map

connection only by special train from Buxton if this was considered necessary.

Pringle observed that "having in view the exposed situation of the connection's position, the proposal appears very desirable". The diagram accompanying the report shows the siding running north from a loop with up and down connections on the west side of the line, but a later map shows a connection facing down trains only. Throughout its life, down trains were not allowed to stop at the siding to attach or detach traffic. Wagons to the siding were to be worked to Parsley Hay and then moved to the siding on an up train.

The 1904 *RCH Handbook* recorded a 5-ton crane in the yard, which was apparently a feature through to the end. The only siding listed was the one for Wragg's, who also operated a brick works at Woodville and a pipe works at Swadlincote,

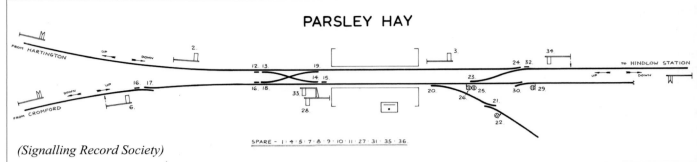

PARSLEY HAY

(Signalling Record Society)

SPARE - 1 . 4 . 5 . 7 . 8 . 9 . 10 . 11 . 27 . 31 . 35 . 36

Images of Parsley Hay showing (right) the view towards Buxton from the crossover a couple of years before closure, giving a vivid impression of just how isolated this outpost of the British railway empire was. Below is a view of the interior of Parsley Hay signalbox taken in 1967, the rugs over the lever frame giving an equally vivid impression of the biting wind that could blow up the signalman's trousers. This was possibly exacerbated by the removal of the platforms, which had at least provided an extra layer of timberwork (albeit not very airtight) to impede its progress. Below right is the view southwards on 7th April 1959 with the C&HPR diverging to the left and the Ashbourne line to the right. (Roger Hockney, Richard Bird and ER Morten)

and (in 1904 at least) were also operating the South Western Pottery at Parkstone near Poole, Dorset. By the time the 1956 and 1962 *RCH Handbooks* were published their Dorset interests had gone, but the works and siding at Parsley Hay remained.

The signal box had 36 levers of which 12 were spare, and it is said that the down starter had a shorter arm than usual because a normal length one had repeatedly been caught by the wind. While the line to Ashbourne closed for freight services from 1st June 1964, goods facilities lingered on at Parsley Hay until 6th July.

Hurdlow

The next two miles to Hurdlow station were virtually level, which must have come as a huge relief after the almost continuous 13½-mile climb from Ashbourne to Parsley Hay. There had been a station at Hurdlow since June 1833, and this was opened for passenger traffic over the C&HPR from July 1856. Between December 1877 and 1st June 1894 it was closed, but it reopened when the LNWR upgraded the line between Buxton and Ashbourne. When the line was extended to Ashbourne, a new station was built to the north of the road bridge, and comprised two platforms either side of the double track. The original C&HPR station had been on the south side of the bridge, on the down side of the line, and the white station building still exists.

The first Station Master was probably John William Cope (later of Hartington and Parsley Hay) who was installed by 1895 and stayed until 1st August 1899 with a brief period in August/September 1898 when he was at Dove Holes. During this time Henry Cope (later at Alsop and Tissington) took over. Samuel Dearden then arrived from Higher Buxton and stayed until he took over Parsley Hay exactly two years later. He was followed by JH Thorpe (until 5th September 1903), Charles Bowers (until 7th March 1904), George Edward Hartley (until 11th October 1909, exact arrival date not known) and Charles Allen (before taking over at Alsop).

Allen appears to have done a "job-swap" with Arthur Bennett Broadbent, who arrived at Hurdlow from Alsop on 16th June 1913. *Kelly's Directory* for 1916 shows him still at Hurdlow in 1916, but we know he then moved to Hartington, and the 1925 edition shows John Henry Lomas in charge.

The station was sometimes referred to in LNWR timetables as "Hurdlow for Longnor and Monyash", although this grand title is not thought to have been officially bestowed upon the station. Monyash, 1½ miles away, was a centre of

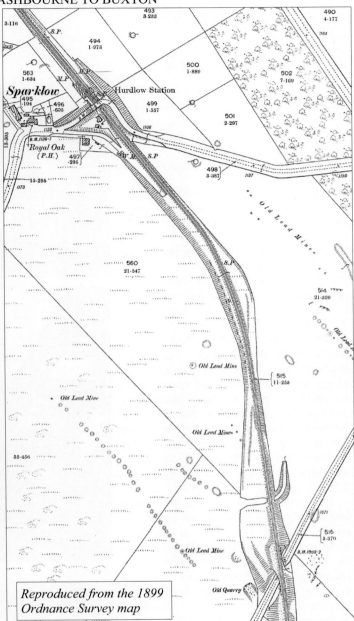

Reproduced from the 1899 Ordnance Survey map

the local lead mining industry, but by the time of the LNWR reopening, it was better known as a base for those wishing to explore the delights of Lathkill Dale; Longnor is 3 miles away. By referring to Hurdlow in this way, the LNWR can be forgiven for its worthy attempt to attract passengers to a

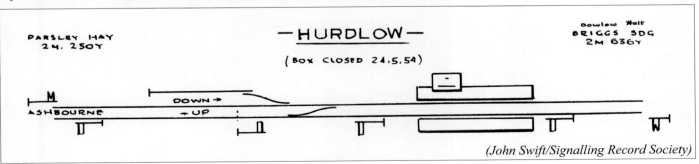

(John Swift/Signalling Record Society)

Top: Just before reaching Hurdlow station, a minor road to Pilsley had to be bridged, the contours demanding the impressive stone structure seen here in 1986. (David Ibbotson)

Middle: The earlier closure of Hurdlow station, compared to others on the line, resulted in a very dilapidated appearance when it was photographed on 3rd November 1956. (Author's Collection)

Bottom: By 1968, all the buildings and the footbridge had been removed to leave just the platforms. (Richard Bird)

station that was located in a particularly sparsely populated area.

The facilities were surprisingly generous for a station that was never likely to see much traffic, but each Easter Tuesday saw a huge influx of passengers arriving for the High Peak Hunt's annual point-to-point steeplechases. These were held on Flagg Moor near the village of Flagg, two miles away, and special trains for spectators were run from Manchester, Stockport and Buxton, and from Stoke via Ashbourne (continuing through to Buxton for servicing). They all arrived between 11.54am and 12.30pm, with the return workings leaving between 4.25 and 5.55pm.

The station was closed to passengers and goods earlier than the rest of the line on 15th August 1949, but on Saturdays there were three unadvertised services laid on for local railway employees to go shopping. In the summer of 1953, for example, there were two trains in the Buxton direction. One was the 7.50am ex-Ashbourne and the other was the 4.25pm, which set down only; they arrived at Hurdlow at 8.34am and 5.06pm respectively. In the other direction, the 10.25 ex-Buxton called at 10.43am.

Dowlow Halt

Dowlow Halt was at the highest point of the line at 1,260ft above sea level, and was reached after around 2 miles climbing at 1 in 60 from Hurdlow. The 17½ miles from Ashbourne had been on an almost continuous uphill gradient, but from here, the line would fall all the way to Buxton.

The halt was opened in 1920 for the use of quarry workers only. By an

Dowlow Halt, seen here in the early 1960s. Because it was not opened to the public until 1929, by which time the LMS had taken over, the nameboard was provided to a North Staffordshire Railway pattern by the District Office at Stoke. The Dowlow Lime & Stone Company's works can be seen to the right. (Author's Collection)

agreement made on 23rd January 1920 between the LNWR and the Dowlow Lime and Stone Co Ltd (for which the lime company was required to pay the costs of the Solicitor for preparing the agreement – 3 guineas including stamp duty) the railway company agreed to construct two platforms at the expense of the quarry company, who were to provide the materials for the platform walls and coping (except, for some reason, the mortar). They were also to provide the necessary lighting, and would do all the excavation needed for the foundations of the platform walls under the supervision of the railway company.

The costs were calculated to be £275, which covered all the work to be carried out by the railway, including supplying the mortar, constructing the coping and walls, erecting fencing and building a level crossing. On completion of the work the LNWR were to maintain the halt, for which the quarry company would pay £4 every half-year. There was also a clause that guaranteed the LNWR a sum of £150 a year from sales of workmen's tickets, for if sales failed to reach that amount, the quarry company were obliged to make up the difference. The services that would stop at the halt were listed as:

6.0am   from Buxton (milk empties train)
7.30am   from Buxton
4.10pm   from Ashbourne (except Saturdays)
11.5am   from Ashbourne (Saturdays only)

Within a couple of years, Mr Nicholson, the Station Master at Hindlow proposed that the halt be opened to the general public, but the District Superintendent at Manchester

wrote to him on 6th June 1922: "As you are aware this Halt has been opened for the use of the Workpeople employed at the Dowlow Quarry only, and it is not intended that it should be used by the general public."

However, the idea would not go away, and on 13th September 1929 the District Control Office at Rowsley wrote to the Chief General Superintendent at Derby:

I consider the time has arrived when this station should be open for all trains. At the present time about 150 passengers use the Halt daily and with the erection of 36 new houses by The Buxton Lime Firms Company within a quarter of a mile of the Halt additional traffic is bound to be brought to rail. At the moment there is no bus competition. The Halt was originally put down to oblige The Dowlow Lime and Stone Company and...the understanding locally is that it is now the property of the Railway Company. Will you please say if this is so and deal with the question of the Halt being made a permanent Station. I am asking for additional staff to cope with shunting arrangements at Brigg's Sidings, a matter of five minutes walk away and it is probable these could be utilised also for duty at the Halt.

In a separate letter, dated the same day, Rowsley noted:

At Dowlow Halt the ticket collecting should be performed by Guards of the respective trains but at the moment...there is no proper check on the passengers. The Buxton Lime Firms Old Briggs Siding and The Dowlow Lime and Stone Company are enlarging their plants and...a good deal of additional engine time is being incurred in consequence.

A picture of "the opposition", but who could resist this delightful photograph of a new, unregistered Seddon 30 tipper lorry probably photographed outside Seddon's works in Oldham before delivery to the Dowlow Lime & Stone Company. (Author's Collection)

Quite apart from the Dowlow Halt question we must have some assistance at Briggs Sidings with the Freight trains as at the moment the Guard is left entirely to do all there is to do in connection with this large volume of traffic. I recommend that we immediately appoint two Grade 2 porters to work late and early turn alternately to assist Guards in shunting operations and to assist with Passenger trains at the Halt. The additional appointments would reduce engine power to the extent of eight or ten hours per week which at 15/- per hour would effect an economy of £6 weekly.

On 25th October, the Chief General Superintendent wrote to Nicholson: "I am reconsidering the question of additional Number-taker and will advise you in due course what is decided. In the mean-time it is being arranged for Dowlow Halt to be opened to the public and commencing Monday, November 4th the full service of passenger trains will call at Dowlow Halt. To cover these additional trains I shall be glad to know that you can make satisfactory arrangements accordingly." It duly opened to the public on the proposed date, but never offered goods facilities.

There were two sets of sidings, both on the down side of the line to the north of the Halt, the nearest being the Dowlow Lime & Stone Co's sidings. Originally the Dowlow Lime Company, it later became part of Steetley Minerals, then Redland and then Lafarge Aggregates; it is still in production.

A little further away was Buxton Lime Firms' Briggs Siding, so named because the original quarry owners were Messrs R Briggs. Like many others in the area, however, the business was taken over by Buxton Lime Firms Co Ltd, which dated from 1891 when no less than thirteen independent quarry companies, owning seventeen quarries between them, were merged together. The new conglomerate

was able to vastly increase production by modernising their processes, and working conditions were improved at the same time. It is now owned by Tarmac Ltd, part of the Anglo American conglomerate.

On 20th April 1939, presumably as a result of a request for information, the Hindlow Station Master wrote to Rowsley Control: "The arrangements at the Dowlow Crossing are as follows. During work hours: The gates are operated by the Dowlow Lime & Stone Coy's Weighman. After work hours: The gates are locked, and in case they are required to be open during the night, the key is left with one of the firm's employees residing in Dowlow Cottages, and he is responsible for the proper working of the gates during this period."

This exchange presaged an accident on 28th March 1940 when a train hit a lorry at the level crossing. As a result, the LMS asked the quarry company to pay for a telephone so that lorry drivers could find out whether a train was due before they crossed. On 10th May 1940, the quarry company replied to say that after "long and careful consideration" they had come to the conclusion that a telephone would contribute "practically nothing to increasing the safety of crossing users".

TE Argile, in the Chief Commercial Manager's Dept at LMS HQ, Watford wrote to JM Kirkwood, District Goods & Passenger Manager at Derby on 25th May:

The Chief Operating Manager...does not accept the Dowlow Company's view that the provision of a telephone would not contribute towards the safe working of the crossing. It is pointed out that the man appointed by the firm to attend to the crossing does not devote the whole of his time to the duty as he has also to deal with the weighing of the firm's traffic, and even at those times when he does attend to the gates, he would know by using the telephone whether or not a train was approaching the crossing.

If the firm had all lorry drivers acquainted of the fact that the telephone had to be used to ascertain whether or not trains were approaching the crossing it is a reasonable view that this would tend to safer working. Notice Boards with suitable wording might also be fixed. Apparently the driver of the lorry involved in the incident which occurred on the 28th March had no idea that a train was approaching.

I do feel, therefore, that the necessity for provision of a telephone as protection at this crossing has been adequately demonstrated and, in a final effort to get the Dowlow Company to agree to pay the cost of installing the proposed telephone, I shall be glad if you will have the firm interviewed and, if they still decline to bear the whole cost, I am agreeable to their being told that the Railway Company are prepared to share the expense with them on a 50-50 basis. Owing to the increase in the price of materials, however, it should be explained to the Dowlow Company that the estimate of £36 for the installation of the telephone originally submitted will now be higher.

The quarry company were not to be persuaded though, and on 12th July, Mr Edgar, Hindlow Station Master, wrote to Kirkwood:

I have had this matter over with the firm but regret to say without success. It is not the cost of installation that they are concerned about, but they do not consider a telephone would overcome the risk of accidents. They point out that if the telephone was installed in their weigh office, drivers coming into the works late at night would not have access to it on account of the office being closed, and if it was placed outside in a cupboard or similar compartment, it would be likely to be tampered with by people using the footpath or by youths during the time the works are closed. Another objection is the long section between Parsley and the crossing on the Down Line which in normal running takes a train 15 minutes to traverse. The firm state that if a driver asked the signalman the position of the line and was informed that a train had just left Parsley Hay, he would not wait at the crossing until the train had passed. Also road traffic would be held up unnecessarily in cases where a train is a long time in section.

The firm have considered the provision of a telephone at the crossing very seriously, but do not consider that it will meet the case. If they were dealing with their own motors only they could make satisfactory arrangements, but many other motors including tradesmen's vans use the crossing, and some of these at nights after the works are closed and at weekends. I consider a bell worked by treadle is the only solution.

On the matter of using a bell, Argile wrote to Kirkwood on 15th December: "…the question of installing a bell operated by treadles was investigated three years ago when…the firm definitely declined to entertain the proposal owing to the high cost involved. The arrangements at this place have been under notice for about seven years and Mr Royle tells me that, in view of the crossing being registered for review of occupation level crossings generally when normal conditions apply, he has decided that the case be laid aside for the duration of the War."

On 26th November 1941, Rowsley Control wrote to the Hindlow Station Master (now Mr Peake):

The Chief Engineer has raised the question as to the liability for the maintenance of the shelter which was erected on the Down platform at this halt in 1924. The halt was constructed in 1920 at the cost of the Dowlow Lime and Stone Company for the use of their workpeople, the arrangement being covered by an agreement dated 23rd January 1923 (sic). This document makes the firm liable for the lighting of the platforms, the guarantee of the receipts on workmen's tickets of £150, and for the annual payment of £8 in respect of maintenance of the platforms and crossings. About 1930 the Railway Company decided make this halt a public one (and) under an agreement dated 22nd November 1930 the traders were relieved of the liability for maintaining the minimum revenue and lighting of the platforms. They are still paying the £8 per annum for the maintenance of the platforms and crossing. I shall be glad to know if you have any information as to the conditions under which and by whom the shelter was provided.

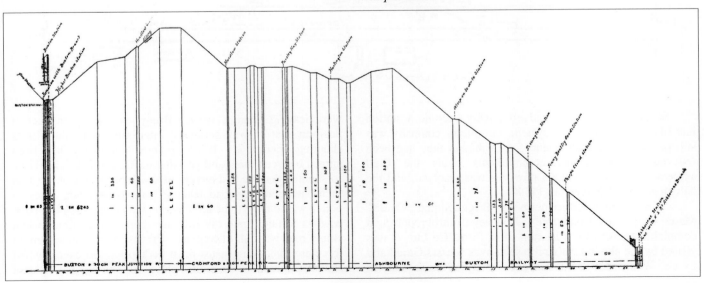

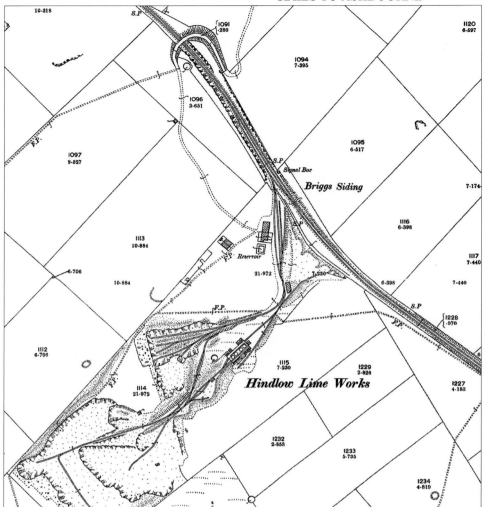

Left: Briggs Siding was sandwiched between Dowlow Halt (which had not been built when this map was prepared) and an occupation bridge. Even at the turn of the 20th century, the lime works had been developed to a large extent, and further expansion took place in the 1930s, and the late 1990s. (Reproduced from the 1899 Ordnance Survey map)

Below: The signalling diagram for Briggs Siding signalbox – the nameboard did not say "Sidings". (John Swift/Signalling Record Society)

Opposite page: Seen in 1986, before the remodelling of the late 1990s, the up and down main lines are snaking southwards with the sidings branching off to the right. Barely visible is a signal post opposite the siding, beyond which was the site of the signalbox. The hopper wagons standing on the former down line did not move for many years, and were eventually scrapped in-situ around 1997/8. Dowlow Halt was situated beyond the wagons next to the later works in the distance. (Neil Ferguson-Lee)

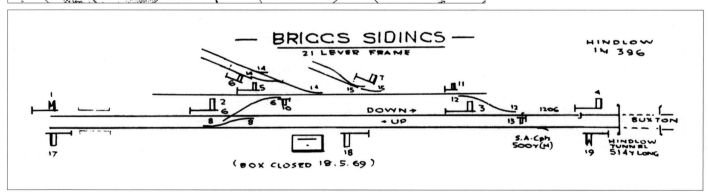

So although the halt had effectively become a station just like any other on the system, the quarry company was still paying for its maintenance, even though they had been relieved of their other commitments under the 1920 agreement! It is not known how this was resolved, and the halt closed on 1st November 1954.

As mentioned, further north was Briggs Siding. On 28th March 1925, Nicholson wrote to Rowsley Control reporting a complaint received from Buxton Lime Firms Co Ltd: "I was visited by the above firm's representatives Messrs Gould and Lyons, Wednesday last when complaint was made that we were leaving wagons in our Briggs Sdg Loop in such a position that it was seriously interfering with the firm's shunting operations. It was pointed out that it had been agreed between them and you that traffic for away should be so shunted that we had merely to attach but if this object was to be attained, the road leading from Briggs Sdg gates to points would have to be left clear to enable them to push back wagons through gate towards our loop at such times when empty road was full of wagons. The instructions at present in force are that siding gates must be kept closed except when shunting operations are taking place with our engines. Please

say if you agree to firm's application."

It is not known how this was resolved, but on 19th July 1929, Rowsley wrote to Nicholson advising him that Buxton Lime Firms were proposing to build sidings to serve a new crusher plant. It is possible that these were the subject of a visit by Lt Col EP Anderson, as he inspected new works at Briggs Siding on behalf of the Board of Trade on 11th May 1932. A new trailing connection had been laid into the down line, and points and signals were worked from Briggs Siding signal box, which was reported as having 18 working levers and two spares. A track circuit was provided in the rear of the down starting signal and was indicated separately in the box.

Wartime lighting restrictions resulted in a fatal accident in 1941, which prompted Mr Peake to write to Rowsley on 24th November. The Buxton Police Inspector and a representative of ICI had called on him two days previously to say that some "restricted" lighting was to be installed at Briggs Siding. This would require a switch in Briggs Siding signal box operated by the signalman. The reply was dated 26th November:

The question of providing restricted lighting was agreed with the ICI following upon the fatal accident which occurred at Briggs last Winter when Goods Guard Spry was killed. The suggestion has been agreed with the various departments of the Company, and all that is necessary now is for the ICI to intimate to the LMS Company when they propose to carry out

this work so that the Signal and Telegraph Dept can be advised in order to give them the opportunity to agree with the Contractors where the switch should be placed in the Box.

The letter was endorsed: "To S&T Dept, 28th July 1942. Lighting installed and switch placed in Cabin. Do you require to inspect same to see if it meets our requirements so far as your Dept is concerned. Lighting has been tested and is now awaiting to be passed by Police and ICI have taken up on this point."

Presumably as a result of the relaxing of restrictions after the war, Peake wrote to Rowsley on 4th December 1945 to tell them that ICI had added more lights to the existing ones. They had disconnected them from the switch in the signal box, and they were now switched on by the company. One wonders why this had not always been the case.

Hindlow

After leaving Briggs Siding, the line descended at 1 in 60 through the 514-yard long Hindlow Tunnel, and then crossed a road on a bridge before emerging at Hindlow station. The original Cromford & High Peak line crossed the new line above the north portal of this tunnel before curving north to run parallel with the new line.

The original C&HPR station was opened here in June 1833 and was served by the road that the new line crossed.

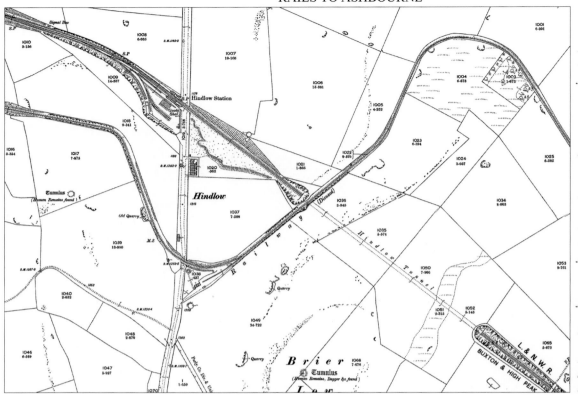

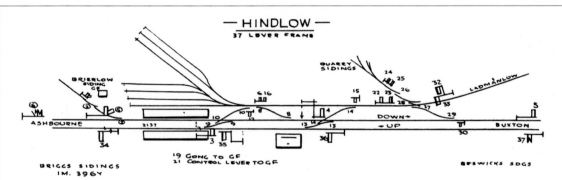

Top: Where the Cromford & High Peak Railway (shown as "disused") largely followed the contours at this point, the new line was driven through Hindlow Tunnel. The C&HPR station was south of the new station where the old line cross the road on the level. In time, much of the land between the two lines was filled with Spencer & Co's Brierlow Lime Works. (Reproduced from the 1899 Ordnance Survey map)

Middle: The Hindlow signalbox diagram dating from the 1950s. (John Swift/ Signalling Record Society)

Bottom: A fine overall view of Hindlow probably taken in the 1950s, and showing well the huge bank of spoil fed by tramways that used the old C&HPR line. (Kestrel Collection)

Opposite: Hindlow on 10th October 1965 looking towards the tunnel, and clearly illustrating the development that has taken place to the south of the line. By now the large kilns bore the name Beswick's Lime Works even though the original Beswick's Works were two miles further north. (Roger Hockney)

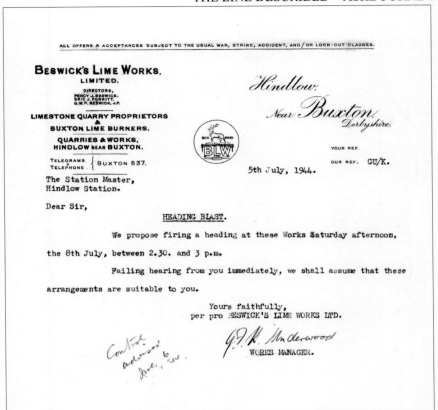

ALL OFFERS & ACCEPTANCES SUBJECT TO THE USUAL WAR, STRIKE, ACCIDENT, AND/OR LOCK-OUT CLAUSES.

BESWICK'S LIME WORKS,
LIMITED.

DIRECTORS,
PERCY J. BESWICK.
ERIC J. PORRITT.
G.W.P. BESWICK, J.P.

LIMESTONE QUARRY PROPRIETORS
&
BUXTON LIME BURNERS.

QUARRIES & WORKS,
HINDLOW NEAR BUXTON.

TELEGRAMS
&
TELEPHONE. } BUXTON 537.

Hindlow.
Near Buxton,
Derbyshire.

YOUR REF.

OUR REF. GU/K.

5th July, 1944.

The Station Master,
Hindlow Station.

Dear Sir,

HEADING BLAST.

We propose firing a heading at these Works Saturday afternoon,

the 8th July, between 2.30. and 3 p.m.

Failing hearing from you immediately, we shall assume that these

arrangements are suitable to you.

Yours faithfully,
per pro BESWICK'S LIME WORKS LTD.

WORKS MANAGER.

Above: Blasting at Beswick's Lime Works, Hindlow, was governed by an agreement between the company and the railway which, amongst other things required the railway to be given 24 hours notice of any blasting in writing.

This station was closed in December 1877, and the passenger station on the new line was opened by the LNWR on 1st June 1894 with access provided by steps up from the road. While there was not much potential for traffic in the immediate area, the station was convenient for Chelmorton, the highest parish in Derbyshire, with the church of St John the Baptist standing at 1,209 ft above sea-level. The new station was similar to others on the line such as Parsley Hay, with a wooden building on each of two wooden platforms.

The earliest Station Master who can be identified with any certainty is John S Holmes, who was certainly there at the time of the 1901 census. On 1st December 1903, Thomas Alfred Hughes took over, leaving the post on 17th January 1914. There was then a period with no identifiable incumbent until 3rd August 1914 when Henry J Pullen was appointed. On 25th June 1921, the *High Peak News* carried an article about Arthur Aldridge, who had been presented with an illuminated address on the occasion of his leaving Hindlow for a new post at Farnworth. It was reported that, "in less than two years, he had thrown himself into the life of all the neighbouring villages to such an extent that they could ill-afford to lose him". Mrs Aldridge received "a beautiful umbrella". *Kelly's Directory* for 1922 showed that

Above: A close view of the northern portal of Hindlow Tunnel taken around 1951. The formation of the original Cromford & High Peak line ran across the top of the portal as it wound its circuitous way down from Hurdlow to Ladmanlow. (David Ibbotson)

Left: Guard Arthur Millward stands at Spencer's Siding ground frame, situated between the station and the tunnel, in August 1966. (Colin Betts/Signalling Record Society/Kidderminster Railway Museum)

Opposite: Ryan and Somerville's Works, Hindlow, on a wintry 2nd February 1954 with 4wD Ruston & Hornsby No 221650 dating from 1944 just visible at the end of the siding in the distance. (Courtesy of Derbyshire Local Studies Libraries and www.picturethepast.org.uk)

Aldridge was replaced by John Stanley Nicholson, and the correspondence mentioned previously regarding the collision between a train and a lorry at Dowlow in 1940 identifies Mr Edgar as Station Master. By 1941, however, S Peake was being shown as Station Master and Goods Agent. As seen from previous paragraphs, the Station Master at Hindlow was also responsible for Dowlow Halt.

The large lime works nearby was named Brierlow Lime Works by it original owners, W Spencer & Co, but Buxton Lime Firms inevitably took over, and renamed the installation Beswick's Lime Works on 28th March 1933, even though the original Beswick's works was over two miles north at Harpur Hill, and was served by Beswick's Sidings. Rail access was provided on the down side of the line, immediately south of the station, and was known as Buxton Lime Firms' Spencer's Siding, a 6-lever ground frame controlling operations. This ground frame was removed in 1973 when a programme of rationalisation was carried out in the area, and control passed to Hindlow signal box. Jn Wright, a coal merchant, also operated from the yard at Hindlow.

After the station closed to passengers from 1st November 1954, goods facilities remained until 7th September 1964, but traffic continued to serve the private quarry sidings in the area until 2nd October 1967. The station was dismantled on and around 20th December 1966.

Hindlow signal box was built to an LNWR type 4 design, and opened with the line in 1892. It had a 27-lever LNWR tumbler frame, which was extended to 37 levers in 1928. It closed on 30th June 1982, when the electric token section was extended from Buxton signal box to Brigg's Siding ground frame. On closure, it was offered to the Peak Railway Society, who were busy gathering materials for their planned reopening of the line from Matlock to Buxton, and having purchased it from BR for £5, they demolished it over three weekends in 1983, storing the parts at Buxton. With no immediate use for the salvaged parts, and with Peak Rail vacating the site at Buxton, all was eventually scrapped or simply burned.

Just north of the station on the down side of the line, and also connected to the Harpur Hill line at High Peak Junction, was a siding to Ryan, Somerville & Co Ltd's lime works. On 28th January 1929 the company wrote to the LMS District Estate Office at Derby regarding the proposed site of new quarry workings, and on 21st February the following year they asked the LMS Manchester District Estate Office for permission to cut through the disused C&HPR line to a depth of approximately 20ft below the 2ft that had been agreed to in an agreement dated 17th May 1928. Evidently the LMS agreed to this.

The Board of Trade's list of Reports on New Works for 1932, includes an entry dated 17th May, reflecting a visit by Lt Col EP Anderson on 11th May to inspect a new trailing connection that had been made on the down line to serve the works. This connection crossed the single line from Harpur Hill with a double slip, and was "trapped into a short dead-end on the north side of the latter line". Points and signals were worked from Hindlow signal box which was confirmed as having 35 working levers and two spares. The down main line starter was said to be fully visible from the signal box, as was the whole of the intervening length of track.

A note in the March 1937 *Appendix to the Working Timetable* reflected the severity of the gradient at this point: "Trainmen must satisfy themselves before starting from Hindlow on the down main line or from the single line, that sufficient hand brakes have been applied."

Judging from surviving correspondence, relations between Ryan, Somerville and the LMS were often strained. In 1936 Ryan, Somerville complained about the unsatisfactory condition of the wagons supplied for their use, and suggested that they charge the LMS for cleaning them unless they could be supplied with "vehicles in a suitable condition for the loading of their traffic". At around the same time, the LMS replaced some of the signalling in the area, and requested a contribution from Ryan, Somerville, as set out in previous agreements. Ryan, Somerville declined.

Further friction occurred a few years later when Ryan, Somerville purchased a diesel engine for shunting, and started using it on the LMS line. The LMS did eventually give permission for these movements, but then Ryan, Somerville requested a reduction of charges by the LMS on the basis that they were now doing shunting work that the railway company had previously done! While this argument rumbled on, Mr Ryan had another complaint – this time regarding the number of coal wagons being delivered to their works. A figure of 9 or 10 per day had been agreed, but sometimes there were as many as 22 and on other days there were none. Given that "there was a War on", it does seem as though Ryan, Somerville often found it difficult to "keep calm and carry on"!

On 26th August 1947, LS Kettle at Derby wrote to the Goods Agent at Hindlow to inform him that 18 levers and quadrants needed to be renewed at Hindlow signal box. This letter was endorsed on 27th August: "The work has been completed". It is not known whether BR troubled Ryan, Somerville for a contribution, but in June 1950, they had occasion to write to Ryan, Somerville about the large amount of hydrated lime blowing about in the air. Nearly a year later, in May 1951, Ryan, Somerville replied that the situation was no worse than it had been for the previous 17 years, but that it had added a "canopy" to prevent lime dust getting into the open air "as much as possible". BR noted that this had made only a slight difference.

A letter from CP Millard a Divisional Manager at Manchester to Mr FA Taylor, the Hindlow Station Master on 3rd June 1965 requested information about the number of lever movements required each day at Hindlow. Quite why it was needed is not clear, but the information he received was:
Total number of lever movements made at the ground frame: 15 (3 times).
Total number of lever movements made in Hindlow station box to operate the ground frame: 12 (3 times).
Total number of lever movements for the signal box as a whole: 82.

High Peak Junction (not to be confused with the junction of the same name on the Midland main line at Cromford) was where the LNWR's "Buxton & High Peak Junction Line No 2" (also known as the Hillhead branch) was opened on 27th June 1892 to connect with the old C&HP line at Harpur Hill. This junction allowed trains to avoid using the original C&HP route from Dowlow, by providing a link from the new line to what remained of the C&HP line. As a result, the section of the C&HPR between Dowlow and Hindlow closed on the same day.

During the First World War, the Ministry of Munitions had stores, sidings and a "trench testing range" at Harpur Hill, and on 5th December 1916, the LNWR wrote to the Board of Trade regarding a request by the Ministry to provide

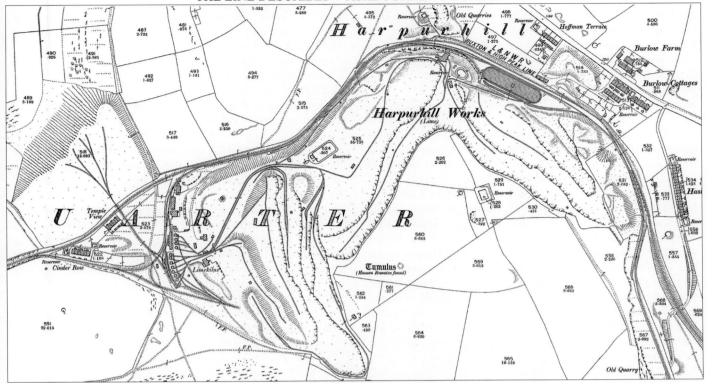

Opposite page, top: High Peak Junction where the Hillhead branch left the main Ashbourne-Buxton line. (Reproduced from the 1899 Ordnance Survey map)

Above: The network of lines at Harpur Hill. (Reproduced from the 1899 Ordnance Survey map)

a passenger service from Hindlow for workers employed at its premises, "but as these points are beyond the limit where passenger trains are authorised, I shall be glad if it could be arranged to give authority for the company to perform the services required".

The BoT replied on 6th December that it had no objection to the proposal, and that a platform at the terminus would be desirable. It would also "be glad to learn what method it is proposed to adopt for working the traffic". There is no further correspondence on the matter, but one assumes that with sufficient weight from the Ministry, and at a time of National emergency, the service was provided as requested.

The link served the Hillhead quarries, and became especially useful again during the Second World War, when an underground bomb store was built for the RAF in one of the quarries. A network of rail-connected tunnels was formed by building a series of arches in the quarry, which were then covered with a 40ft deep overlay of rock and soil.

In anticipation of the depot opening in mid-1940, the District Goods and Passenger Manager's Office at Derby wrote to Mr Edgar at Hindlow on 11th April to pass on a request from Wing Commander Whellock that LMS engines working in the depot siding be fitted with spark arrestors. This was such an obvious precaution that one almost wonders why it had to be spelt out by the RAF, and some 4½ years later, the effects of a careless spark at a munitions store (although not railway related) were demonstrated to tragic

effect when a massive explosion occurred at RAF Fauld, not far from Uttoxeter.

The LMS was responsible for keeping the four siding roads clear of snow in winter, but it was pointed out to the RAF's Resident Engineer in a letter dated 13th January 1941 that "the snowplough will put the snow from the track to the 6 foot…we cannot supply labour for keeping the 6 foot clear, and this will be a matter for you to deal with by your own staff". Another letter, dated 1st October 1942, records the rent paid to the LMS: "The Air Ministry have agreed to pay £250 per annum for the rental of the Sidings… Of this amount £100 is in respect of maintenance and renewals and £150 rental."

After a similar depot at Llanberis partially collapsed in January 1942, RAF Harpur Hill was closed as a precaution against a similar failure, and on 20th June 1946, the District Operating Superintendent at Manchester wrote to Mr Peake at Hindlow: "Will you please note it has now been agreed with the Air Ministry that the Department's use of the Railway Company's sidings at Ladmanlow (*amended from Harpur Hill*) should be regarded as having ceased as from 31st December, 1945." Despite this, Harpur Hill was subsequently reinforced and reopened, so that the District Goods and Passenger Manager's Office at Derby wrote on 26th April 1948 to say that the sidings were to become permanent Air Ministry installations, and the following entries were to be made in the *Handbook of Stations*:

Air Ministry No 28 Maintenance Unit, Harpur Hill, Hindlow.
Full name of siding: *Air Ministry Siding.*
Parent station and position: *Harpur Hill. Harpur Hill Ladmanlow.*
County in which the facility is situated: *Derbyshire.*
Railway Section serving the siding: *LM Region, LNW Section.*

The decision to continue activities at Harpur Hill was justified by the outbreak of the Korean War in June 1950, and from that time an element of 28MU was stationed at Ashbourne airfield and its satellite at Darley Moor. Munitions would be moved from Harpur Hill to Ashbourne for storage and maintenance – many of them having deteriorated whilst in store. This was done amidst much security by special train to Ashbourne where the bombs would be put on trailers and hauled by Leyland Hippos up the hill to the airfield. The refurbished ordnance was then transported to Woolwich Arsenal, again by train, which entailed the Leyland Hippos and trailers gingerly winding their way back to the railway station. The end of the Korean War in July 1953 signalled the end to these activities, and both airfields at Ashbourne closed the following year.

RAF Harpur Hill closed in 1960, the tunnels finding new uses, first as a mushroom farm, and later as cold storage for cheese. Together with a warehouse for bonded wine and spirits, the whole storage facility was eventually bought by the hauliers Christian Salvesen, who adapted the entrance as a loading dock. More recently, it was sold to the French haulier Norbert Dentressangle. The rail link together with the sidings at Harpur Hill was closed on 19th September 1973.

The quarry sidings served by the original C&HPR line at Harpur Hill were all owned by Buxton Lime Firms and comprised (in order from Hindlow northwards):

Dalby's Siding (on the remains of the C&HP line back towards Hindlow)
Hoffman Kiln (down side)
Crusher Siding (up side)
Chatter Siding (up side)
Old Kiln Siding (down side)
Central Stores & Wagon Repair (up side)
Cinder Row (down side)

Also at Harpur Hill, on a site that had been acquired by the Government in 1924, the Board of Trade ran an "Experimental Station for the purpose of Mining Research". By an agreement dated 21st August 1925 between the LMS and the BoT, the railway company extended an existing siding to serve the research station at a cost of £120 for which the BoT was liable. Mining research might have been the publicly-stated purpose of the station, but a later note reflects an additional use by referring to the opening of the "Ministry of Munitions Experimental Station, Harpur Hill" on 14th June 1927.

In 1932, history repeated itself when the Ministry of Mines requested that passenger trains be operated to Harpur

Right: The Hoffmann Kiln at Harpur Hill, as shown on the map on the previous page. A fire in the centre if the building burned continuously, and was directed around the building with heat passing into the surrounding rooms in turn. These rooms were filled with batches of lime ahead of the fire, and emptied after the fire had done its work, thus turning what was essentially a batch process into a continuous one. (Author's Collection)

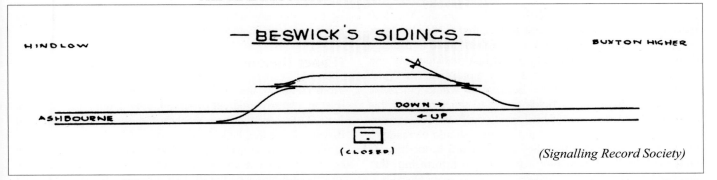

Hill. This time, the answer was not to be so sympathetic. At a meeting held on 18th February, the LMS District Engineer, Mr Rose stated that the line from Hindlow to Harpur Hill was not passed for the working of passenger trains, and said that expensive alterations would be needed. Furthermore, there was no station at Harpur Hill, and if passenger trains were allowed to run over the line, a new platform would be necessary. He was of the view that trains between Buxton and Harpur Hill would take more time than the buses would by road, due to it being a longer route, with a reversal necessary at Hindlow and a heavy gradient of 1 in 41 for 1 mile between Hindlow and Harpur Hill.

Mr Beadle for the Ministry informed the LMS that they would have to bear any expense in providing a new platform so, not surprisingly, the conclusion was that passengers should be taken by road from Buxton to Harpur Hill by North Western Road Car Co buses. The LMS was particularly keen to make such an arrangement with an associated bus company "to avoid private owners securing the business", and agreed that its Commercial Department would come up with an inclusive fare by rail and road, or alternatively make arrangements to perform the journey by road throughout.

In 1947, the facility became the Government's Safety in Mines Research Establishment (SMRE). This was part of the Ministry of Fuel and Power, and still exists. Since November 2004 has been the home of a unified Health and Safety Laboratory, an agency of the Health and Safety Executive. Part of the work of the laboratory is the investigation of explosions on trains, for which purpose it has built a section of railway track on which, somewhat bizarrely, are stabled some old London Underground carriages.

Continuing along the branch, next came Old Harpur (goods), then the Grin branch, and finally Ladmanlow Yard before the point at which the old line towards Whaley Bridge had been abandoned. However, the line from just north of Old Harpur to Ladmanlow was itself closed on 2nd August 1954 with the closure of Ladmanlow Yard, and the branch was further cut back to Harpur Hill from 2nd February 1966 leaving the SMRE with no rail connection. Grin Quarry was (unusually) not owned by Buxton Lime Firms, but by the Clay Cross Co, whose own engines would venture onto BR metals to collect empty wagons and deposit full ones.

Due to the climb northwards from Ashbourne, a banking engine was available if needed for trains bound for the Hillhead branch. When one was used, the leading engine would remain on the main line at Harpur Hill Staff Point while the banking engine propelled the train along the branch to the quarries. Any loaded train waiting to depart would be propelled back towards Hindlow by the erstwhile banking engine, which would then return to the quarries to resume shunting duties. The engine that had been left on the main line would take the train to Hindlow.

The section between Hindlow and Harpur Hill was worked by staff and ticket, and in the situation described above the loco remaining on the main line would have brought the staff from Hindlow, and would give it up at the Harpur Hill cabin (the Staff Point). The banking engine, having worked at the quarries would bring it back to Hindlow as the last loco leaving the section, while the loaded stone train would be regarded as an intermediate movement for which a ticket would be issued.

Outward traffic of limestone was largely ballast, but also included shipments to East Anglia where it was used in the production of sugar from sugar beet (known as "sugarstone"). Inward traffic included bituminous materials from Ellesmere Port which came in tank wagons and was mixed with limestone in the manufacture of tarmacadam. Before it could be removed from the tankers, it had to be steam-heated to make it less viscous.

Finally, before the line reached Higher Buxton was the aforementioned Buxton Lime Firms' Beswick's Sidings on the down side as the line passed by Staden Grange. The sidings were controlled between 1915 and 1949 by a signalbox of the same name on the opposite side of the line.

From at least the mid-1940s, a ticket agency was run by Miss S Wain of Old Row, Harpur Hill. On 10th December 1957, it was reported that Miss Wain was recently deceased, and that the agency was being carried on by her brother, Mr Walter Wain of the same address, who had actually been running the business on behalf of his sister for many years. His takeover was formally confirmed in a letter from the District Passenger Manager at Manchester on 8th January 1958, but the new arrangement was not to last long, as the Hindlow Station Master was informed on 18th September 1958 that Mr Wain was leaving the district. There was evidently some discussion about whether or not to appoint a successor, but in the 12 months from September 1957, Mr Wain had sold just less than £65 worth of tickets and it was decided that on the termination of his agency on 31st October 1958, no successor would be appointed.

This is presumably the same Mr Wain who had been the subject of a letter dated 27th July 1949 from the Manchester

District Goods Manager's Office to the Goods Agent at Buxton. The Cartage Assistant had visited a Mr Critchlow on his farm to investigate his complaint that a package delivered by the railway had been left in a roadside barn and not discovered for several weeks. The motorman, Mr Wain, stated that he had left it there because he would otherwise have had to drive across fields to get to the farm, and this involved him getting out of his lorry to open and close gates. Mr Critchlow did not insist that deliveries should be made to the farm, but suggested that they could be left in the barn as long as the railway sent him a postcard to inform him that this had been done!

The letter is endorsed with an instruction to tell Driver Wain that this arrangement was now in force, and to ask him to request the Leading Clerk to send the postcards. Wain admitted that he routinely left packages in the barn and would

sign the delivery note himself, but there is no indication of him being reprimanded for this.

Higher Buxton

From Hindlow, the line is still in use and descends more or less on a steady gradient of 1in 60, apart from a mile or so at 1 in 330. As the line reaches the southern outskirts of Buxton, it crosses Duke's Drive on a 176-yard long viaduct of the same name made up of 13 arches and with a maximum height of 94ft 6in above the road through Sherbrook Dale. Shortly after crossing the viaduct it reaches the site of Higher Buxton station, opened by the LNWR on 1st June 1894.

Barely half a mile from the terminus at Buxton, this station largely owed its existence to the presence of the goods yard on the down side of the line. Just two wooden platforms

---

London Midland and Scottish Railway Company.

Instructions to Signalmen at Station Box, Higher Buxton.

The Absolute Block Telegraph Regulations apply on the Up and Down Lines.

BLOCK TELEGRAPH REGULATIONS.

Regulation 3—When the section in advance is clear, the Is line clear signal for trains on the Up Line must be forwarded on receipt.

Regulation 4—No train or engine must be allowed to leave the sidings for right away on the Main Line until the Is line clear signal has been acknowledged by the box in advance.

OTHER INSTRUCTIONS.

Shunting to Opposite Line—Trains must only be shunted from the up Main Line to the down Main Line when there is an engine at the Buxton end of the train.

TRAINS WAITING ACCEPTANCE DURING FOG OR FALLING SNOW.
Down Line.

A Down stopping passenger train or other train marked to do work at the station may be allowed to draw forward to the platform to do its work after the signalman has been informed by the person in charge of the station that the Starting signal is at danger.

It will be the duty of the Station Master or person in charge to see that the signalman is informed when a Down stopping train has gone forward past the Starting signal, and the Train out of section signal must not be given to the box in rear, nor the Starting signal replaced to Danger, until this advice is received.

Rules 79 and 80 of the Book of Rules and Regulations and Block Telegraph Regulation 4, Clause (e)—When the Down Starting Signal becomes obscured by Fog or Falling Snow, the Signalman must arrange for the Fogsignalmen to take duty at their appointed places.

BY ORDER
of the
CHIEF GENERAL SUPERINTENDENT.

September, 1929.

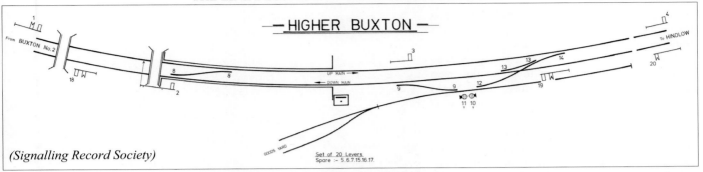

— HIGHER BUXTON —

(Signalling Record Society)

Right: Higher Buxton station taken in 1948. The white building on the right was used for a time as offices for the Dowlow Lime and Stone Co. (Stations UK)

Below: Stanier class 3 2-6-2T 40088 heads an up passenger working through Higher Buxton station on 30th March 1951, the day before the last passenger services ran. (ER Morten)

Opposite: Instructions to signalmen at Higher Buxton Station signalbox. (Author's Collection)

were provided with wooden buildings upon them, and with a journey time of less than 3 minutes to Buxton (third class single, 3d in 1941) it was not much used by passengers, who found it just as convenient to go to the main station. It is surprising, therefore, that it lasted as long as it did, only closing to passengers on 2nd April 1951.

There was a large, brick-built, goods shed in the yard (known from LMS days as Buxton South to distinguish it from the MR yard) together with a 1ton 10cwt crane, and in 1890, the *Buxton Advertiser* noted:

Messrs Neill and Sons, the well-known builders and contractors of Manchester, have obtained the contract for the erection of the goods shed at Higher Buxton in connection with the new station on the Buxton and Ashbourne line. Operations will almost immediately be commenced for the removal to Higher Buxton of the material that is between the Buxton excursion platform and St Anne's stables. Orders have been given for at once proceeding with the construction of a flying junction and marshalling sidings beyond the present signal box at Buxton Station.

The widening and improvement of the High Peak Railway from Hurdlow to Parsley Hay, a distance of 2 miles, is to be forthwith taken in hand. The line from Buxton to Briggs' Limeworks on Sterndale Moor, a mile and a half past Hurdlow, will be opened on May 1st next. The permanent way from Buxton to Hindlow is now being rapidly laid. In fact a single line is in working order and communication can be obtained between these places.

The earliest known Station Master is thought to be William Walker, although he is listed in the 1900 edition of *Kelly's Directory* as Goods Agent at Buxton. More certainty can be ascribed to Henry Duckworth taking over on 15th February 1900, and remaining in the post until 20th November 1906. On the 10th of the following month, Frederick Warhurst was appointed and was at Higher Buxton until 17th September 1908.

In order to reduce working expenses, and to provide more convenient facilities for the public, the LNWR and the MR signed an agreement on 30th July 1908 that provided for closer working

Right: The southern approaches to Buxton. (Reproduced from the 1899 Ordnance Survey map)

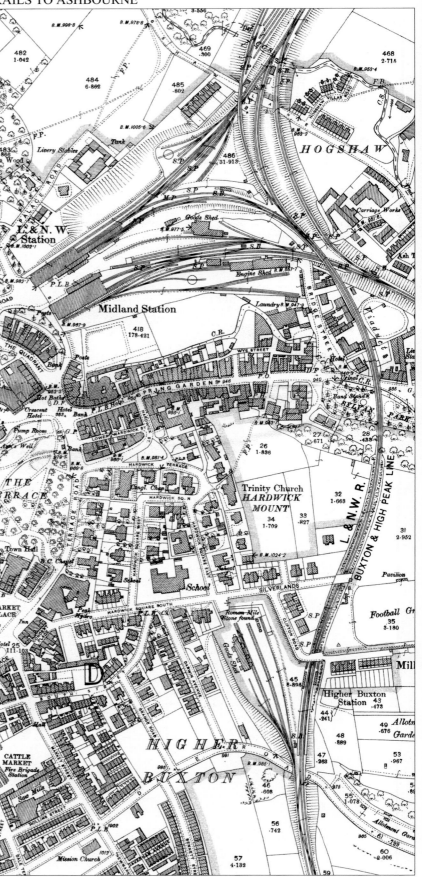

arrangements at locations served by both companies. Lasting for 99 years, and backdated to the first of the month, the agreement allowed for reductions in staff so that the MR Station Master & Goods Agent at Buxton (at that time, Samuel Pitt) became responsible for both stations in the town, and also Higher Buxton.

Pitt had been appointed to Buxton (MR) on 1st October 1907 and held the post until 14th July 1919 when he was succeeded by Samuel Hart. He remained until 18th July 1929 after which A Marston took over, but the exact dates of his arrival (and departure) are not known.

Kelly's Directory for 1936 listed the following merchants in the yard:

Bagshaw, Ewart (coal)
The Clay Cross Co Ltd (coal)
JB & A Moss (coal)
R Nall & Son (coal)
JW & S Slack (coal)
EP Youds & Son (cattle food)

Mycock & Tibbles were trading as R Nall & Son, and had taken over JH Buxton's site on 1st September 1927; in addition to their coal-stacking grounds, they also had a garage in the yard. By 1941, JB & A Moss had gone, but even by the late 1960s, there were still three coal merchants working out of the yard – JH Buxton (evidently still in business), R Nall & Son and H Rains & Son.

A letter from the District Estate Surveyor at Manchester to the Buxton Station Master dated 2nd February 1966 set out the amount of land leased by two tenants. JH Buxton were leasing 2,060 sq yd on land adjacent to Silverlands and Clifton Road for £50 per annum for an office and workshop, and partly for storage of coal and building materials. On land at the rear of Darwin Avenue, Messrs B&S Meredith leased 432 sq yd for £20 per annum as the site of a garage and a shed for cutting up firewood and partly for storage of firewood bags and coal.

Around November 1967, JA Rigley took over Nall's (Mycock & Tibble's) part of the yard, but within 4 months, it had reverted to its former tenant. An internal BR letter dated 14th April 1969 merely confirms the continued presence of H Rains & Son. The yard continued to receive coal until the early 1980s, and is thought to have closed around 1987.

Beyond Higher Buxton, entry to Buxton itself involved the construction of a substantial cutting at Mill Cliff followed by Spring Gardens (or Hogshaw Lane) viaduct immediately before the station. This is 353 yards long, and consists of 15 stone arches with an additional girder section where the line crossed the MR branch from Miller's Dale.

Above: Troops leaving the station at Buxton, possibly having just returned from the Front at the end of World War One.
(Courtesy of The Board Collection and www.picturethepast.org.uk)

Above: An undated aerial view of Buxton, although it would no doubt be possible to find an approximate date by close study of the buildings. The LNWR and Midland stations are seen top-right, and combine with the Crescent, the Devonshire Dome and the Palace Hotel to produce an elegant and well-balanced townscape. (Author's Collection)

Buxton

Leaving aside the existence of prehistoric man in the area, Buxton's more-recent history goes back to the Roman occupation, when the discovery of warm springs led to the growth of a spa town, known to its founders as Aquae Arnemetiae. In later years, it attracted such notable visitors as Mary Queen of Scots, and became part of the great estate owned by the Duke of Devonshire. Successive Dukes attempted to generate the kind of patronage enjoyed by Bath and Cheltenham, but its relative isolation mitigated against it. The coming of the railways changed this, and in the latter half of the 19th century, its population trebled to cater for the wealthy visitors who came to take the waters. Nevertheless, as far as railway connections were concerned, Buxton was very much "on a limb", its only chance of being on a main line (the proposed Manchester, Buxton, Matlock and Midlands Junction Railway) having been largely scuppered by the LNWR.

Buxton's earliest train service (the rudimentary one over the Cromford & High Peak Railway) has already been described on page 15, and a coach left the Cheshire Cheese at 2.15pm to connect with the passenger train that left Ladmanlow at 2.30. At the same time, there were several passenger coaches daily (some seasonal) to Macclesfield, Manchester and Sheffield.

The LNWR station at Buxton opened on 15th June 1863, with the arrival of the Stockport, Disley and Whaley Bridge Railway, which had been beaten to the town by the MR two weeks earlier. For two companies that were not known to see eye-to-eye on most matters, there appears to have been a remarkable degree of co-operation about the construction of the two stations, but this was due to the Duke of Devonshire being in a position to "bang heads together"! During the three years prior to the opening, several plans for the buildings were submitted to the Duke, but there was no agreement until Sir Joseph Paxton was consulted. As a result of his involvement, the two buildings provided a unified and imposing sight in deference to the reputation of Buxton as a watering place for the Nobility and the Gentry.

Regrettably, such good taste has been sadly lacking by more recent "decision makers". In contrast to the fine vista that graced the town for over 100 years, the MR station has long been demolished, and the LNWR station presents a very run-down appearance with the loss of its twin – and its overall roof.

The arrival of the railway had an immediate impact on the town. Daily papers were delivered regularly, and coal found it way more easily to the town. Bigger and better hotels opened to serve visitors arriving to take the waters, for instance, the imposing Palace Hotel, which occupies a prominent position on a hill overlooking the station. Opened in 1868, its exterior was designed by another servant of the

Duke of Devonshire, Henry Currey.

The local paper reported a disturbing incident on 3rd March 1882:

The Buxton Police have just received information of a diabolical attempt to upset a train on the LNWR at Buxton. It appears that a few days ago a goods train coming along the line at the junction of the two railway systems ran into a sleeper that lay across the metals. The engine with the assistance of the cleaners in front of the wheels, instead of being thrown off, carried the obstruction a distance of considerably more than one hundred yards before it pulled up. It was then removed, and the authorities telegraphed to, who sent down an inspector to inquire into the matter. No arrest has at present been made.

The station saw some development over the years following its opening. The exterior canopy, for example, was a later addition when the Ashbourne platform was built, as was the brick-built accommodation such as the ladies waiting room and the urinals, which were of standard LNWR design. In 1894, in preparation for the introduction of passenger services to Parsley Hay (and later Ashbourne) the main platform was extended considerably, with a new face (known as the bay) to serve Ashbourne line trains on the south side of the station where there were carriage sidings. The final stage of the station's development was the addition of the excursion platform on the north side, which appears to date from just after the opening of the line to Ashbourne. Ultimately, this became platform 1, while the extended platform faces became platform 2 (Manchester) and platform 3 (Ashbourne)

In the 19th century, the LNWR station at Buxton had a succession of Station Masters, the first two being appointed before the station was opened:

Clement Mitchell (29th May 1858 – 31st October 1861)
W Appleton (1st November 1861 – 1st November 1863)
Hugh Berry (1st December 1863 – 16th December 1864)
Ammon Schofield (1st December 1864 – 31st October 1871)
H Graham (1st November 1871 – 1st September 1873)
John A Chippindall (1st August 1873 – 9th November 1878)
Robert Lane (1st November 1878 – 24th March 1890)
Arthur Moore (1st March 1890 – 1st October 1894)
J Nicholson (1st October 1894 – 8th June 1896)
Ralph Sampson (1st June 1896 – 1st November 1903)
Thomas Wynne (1st November 1903 – 1st July 1904)
S Ratcliffe (1st July 1904 – 14th September 1905)
William Telfer (18th September 1905 – 1st November 1908 when the MR Station Master & Goods Agent at Buxton, Samuel Pitt, took over under the arrangements described on page 155).

In the 1900 edition of *Kelly's Directory*, the traders listed as operating at the station or in the yard were William Chapman (Colliery Agent, LNWR yard), WH Smith & Son (Newsagents, MR & LNWR stations) and James Kirkland (Coal Merchant, MR & LNWR yards). It was noted that

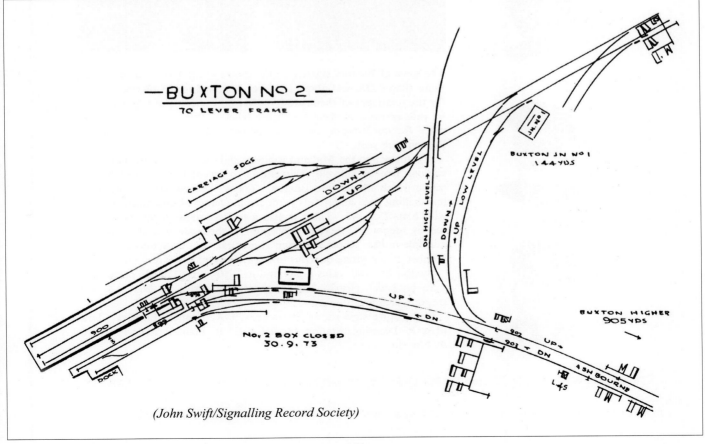

(John Swift/Signalling Record Society)

Spotlight on
BUXTON

The town of Buxton, situated in the centre of the Peak National Park more than 1,000 feet above sea level, is famed for its thermal waters for the treatment of rheumatics. Constant streams of visitors arrive by rail, *en route* in their search for relief. It is also a very popular place for conferences and large numbers of delegates descend on Buxton each year.

A century ago the Midland Railway and the L & N W R built their stations side by side, in their efforts to secure the lucrative tourist traffic which flowed into Buxton. Today the two terminal stations, marshalling yard and goods yard, are in charge of one Stationmaster with a staff of 146. There is also a modern diesel maintenance and fueling depot at Buxton servicing 15 three-car and five two-car multiple units. A branch from High Peak and Ashbourne serves a number of limestone quarries in the vicinity of Buxton.

Buxton has 100 trains a day and in 1960 about 178,000 passengers were booked. Nearly 200,000 passengers arrive at Buxton's two stations each year.

Our picture strip shows Stationmaster A. Laidler, Enquiry Clerk Miss P. Leeming, Station Inspector C. P. Plant, Passenger Guard A. Norton.

In November 1961, Buxton featured in British Railways' London Midland Region Magazine. (Author's Collection)

there were "Omnibuses to meet all trains, from the Shakespeare stables, Spring Gardens; Mrs Annie Barson, proprietress. Also, omnibuses run daily from Eagle Hotel, Higher Buxton, calling at Grove Hotel for 'Duke of York', Burbage, every hour." In 1910, *Bradshaw* listed over 35 routes to Buxton from places as diverse as Edinburgh and Folkestone, but the Second World War put an end to all through services.

On 2nd January 1919, Edward Eastwood (Railway Wagon Works, Chesterfield) applied for a lease on a site at Buxton for wagon repairs. Because of the 1908 agreement between the LNWR and MR, the application was made to the latter company, who informed its partner the same day. The LNWR duly entered into an agreement on the 15th of the month for 20 sq yd to be leased to Eastwood's for a cabin "to be placed well up to the fence so as to leave a clear cartway" for storing wagon repairing materials. Despite the Midland's involvement, the LNWR owned the land, and its lease with Eastwood's began on 1st March – nevertheless, it was left to the MR to collect the rent. One wonders to what extent the agreement actually resulted in savings, since there must have been a lot of financial toing and froing between the two companies.

Things progressed slowly, and it wasn't until 14th September 1920 that the Midland informed the LNWR that Eastwood's cabin had been erected. On 25th April 1936, Eastwood's wrote to the LMS to say that it was considering moving the cabin to a more convenient position in the cripple sidings, the move taking place a couple of months later. The cabin moved again in 1947 to a slightly larger site formerly occupied by a company called Wagon Repairs Ltd, and in March 1948 the company applied to erect a second cabin on a neighbouring site recently vacated by Central Wagon Co. Its two cabins would be 18ft apart, and they further proposed to cover the space between with a corrugated iron roof and back to protect stored timber.

Eastwood's now leased a total of 45 sq yd at Buxton, but from 1st November 1956 the whole facility was transferred to the Derbyshire Carriage & Wagon Co Ltd of Chesterfield, who almost immediately cancelled the lease for the second cabin.

In *Kelly's Directory* for 1922 and 1925, WH Smith had an outlet at the MR station, and there were two coal merchants operating: Kirkland & Perkin (MR & LNWR yards) and Day & Ferguson (LNWR yard and also Harpur Hill and Ladmanlow). Omnibuses now met all trains from the hydros, hotels and Wye Garage, Spring Gardens. Also, the North Western Road Car Co ran frequent motor bus services from the Market Place, Higher Buxton and The Crescent to the outskirts of the town, and from Stockport and Cheadle (later Matlock Bath, Glossop, Leek, Macclesfield, Altrincham and, significantly, Ashbourne) to Buxton several times a day.

Under the LMS, the two stations were naturally worked as one, the ex-LNWR platforms being numbered 1, 2 and 3, and the ex-MR platforms becoming numbers 4, 5 and 6. Road competition was now making its presence felt with

North Western running regular bus services to Ashbourne, Matlock Bath, Chesterfield, Derby, Bakewell, Hanley, Sheffield, Glossop, Leek, Macclesfield, Cheadle, Stockport, Altrincham and Manchester.

North Western (as they were always known) had been formed in April 1923 when the British Automobile Traction Co Ltd (part of the transport holding group, British Electric Traction Co Ltd) went into partnership with the other major early 20th century transport conglomerate, Thomas Tilling. BAT had run a service to Macclesfield from 1914, and in 1920 began town services from a garage at Burbage, also adding routes to Ashbourne, Leek and Stockport. The new North Western company began with 54 vehicles, and in 1926, replaced its Burbage garage with new premises in Charles Street, Stockport that had previously been a grinding mill.

In 1961, after being split into three operating divisions (Northern, Central and Southern) an office and a new depot with 43 vehicles were opened in Buxton Market Place. As far as stage carriage services were concerned, the company went out of existence in 1972, when the parts that had not been subsumed into the South East Lancashire and North East Cheshire (SELNEC) Passenger Transport Executive were divided between Crosville (Cheshire) and Trent (Derbyshire). Thereafter, North Western existed only as a coach operating company, losing its identity completely on 6th February 1974 when it became National Travel (North West) Ltd.

In November 1967, the curve between Buxton No 2 Junction and platform 3 was lifted, and the area was given over to industrial development. By this time, the only coal merchant listed in Buxton (according to the *Nottingham Leicester & Derby Trades Directory*) was JR Lomas, and even he was shown to be on Bridge Street, not at the station. Buxton No 2 signal box was responsible for movements in and out of the station from the Ashbourne line, and an LMS structure replaced the original LNWR box in 1933. The later box had a Railway Executive Committee (REC) 70-lever frame, but was closed in 1968 following the singling of the remaining line to Briggs Siding. Thenceforward, all movements in the Buxton area were controlled from Buxton No 1 box, an original LNWR structure (now fitted with new uPVC windows) with a 60-lever LNWR tumbler frame dating from 1894. Only 45 levers (Nos 4 to 48) are retained for current use.

Nowadays, the two platforms are used by the 25-mile service to and from Stockport and Manchester Piccadilly operated by Northern Rail. This is worked by DMUs and is basically an hourly service, augmented by extra trains at peak times. A number of buildings remain, but the days are long gone when the DMU sets were serviced at Buxton's own motive power depot alongside the locomotives used on the limestone trains.

There had been a small shed at Buxton since the earliest LNWR times (it even sported a Driver Buxton!) This was only able to hold four tender engines, and was on the site of the later diesel depot to the north of the line near the station. In 1892, this was replaced by a much larger 6-road shed built

Right: Buxton MPD on 18th August 1970.
(Kestrel Collection)

to a standard LNWR pattern with north lights on the south side of the line to Stockport and further away from the station. Originally a sub-shed of Longsight, Manchester, it was responsible for the sheds on the Cromford & High Peak Railway, and the new location allowed for several sidings to be provided at the same time.

Because of its position, and the type of traffic emanating from the area, the shed largely looked after freight engines, but from the early 1930s, a stud of 2-6-4Ts was looked after for the Manchester-Buxton-Ashbourne services. When the small two-road ex-MR shed closed in August 1935, its locos and men transferred to the ex-LNWR shed. The new diesel shed, and the subsequent usurping of steam resulted in the closing of the steam shed on 4th March 1968.

Journey's End, at least as far as this book is concerned. For the passengers in this train, the journey is about to begin as the crew of Stanier class 4 2-6-4T 42667 awaits the right-away for their journey south. The train is the 10.25am departure, and the date is 25th October 1954, just a few days before the withdrawal of timetabled passenger services. (ER Morten)

Industrial Locomotives Used at Locations Along the Route

Compiled from a number of sources, this attempts to list industrial locomotives operated by the various companies along the route of the line. I doubt whether it would ever be possible to compile a definitive list, and this certainly does not claim to be one. Locomotives are all standard gauge, except where noted, and are listed in order of build date within each operator's listing.

Air Ministry No 28 Maintenance Unit, Harpur Hill

No 183 4wD Ruston & Hornsby No 198321 built 1940. New to 28MU Harpur Hill. Disposal – *see note*.

No 184 4wD Ruston & Hornsby No 198322 built 1940. New to 28MU Harpur Hill. Disposal – *see note*.

No 185 4wD Ruston & Hornsby No 198323 built 1940. New to 28MU Harpur Hill. Disposal – *see note*.

No 186 4wD Ruston & Hornsby No 198324 built 1940. New to 28MU Harpur Hill. To Air Ministry Llanberis circa May 1942, but returned by March 1943. To Air Ministry, Altrincham circa February 1944.

No 236 4wD Ruston & Hornsby No 210477 built 1941. New to Air Ministry, Quedgeley, Gloucestershire before transfer to 28MU Harpur Hill. Disposal – *see note*.

No 192 4wD 2ft gauge Ruston & Hornsby No 200515 built 1940. New to 28MU Harpur Hill.

No 196 4wD 2ft gauge Ruston & Hornsby No 198286 built 1940. New to 28MU Harpur Hill, thence to Air Ministry, Burtonwood in 1958, thence to Sir William Arrol, Dalmarnock in 1959.

No 197 4wD 2ft gauge Ruston & Hornsby No 198287 built 1940. New to 28MU Harpur Hill, thence to Air Ministry, Burtonwood in 1957.

No 198 4wD 2ft gauge Ruston & Hornsby No 198288 built 1940. New to 28MU Harpur Hill.

No 202 4wD 2ft gauge Ruston & Hornsby No 200800 built 1940. New to 28MU Harpur Hill, thence to Air Ministry, Burtonwood in 1956.

No 203 4wD 2ft gauge Ruston & Hornsby No 200801 built 1940. New to 28MU Harpur Hill.

No 224 4wD 2ft gauge Ruston & Hornsby No 203019 built 1940. New to 28MU Harpur Hill, thence to Air Ministry, Pulham, Norfolk circa 1950.

No 228 4wD 2ft gauge Ruston & Hornsby No 203028 built 1941. New to 28MU Harpur Hill.

No 231 4wD 2ft gauge Ruston & Hornsby No 203031 built 1941. New to 28MU Harpur Hill.

No 232 4wD 2ft gauge Ruston & Hornsby No 203032 built 1941. New to 28MU Harpur Hill, thence to Air Ministry, Burtonwood in 1956.

Note: 183, 184, 185 and 236 to Air Ministry, Burtonwood (3) and another Air Ministry (1) site in 1961, but individual identities not known.

Beswick's Limeworks Ltd, Hindlow (Subsidiary of Staveley Coal & Iron Co Ltd)

4wP Crossley built 1925. New to Beswick's.

Lizzie 0-4-0D Hudswell Clarke No D559 built 1930. New to Beswick's.

Mary 0-4-0D Hudswell Clarke No D577 built 1932. New to Beswick's.

2ft gauge 4wP Crossley built 1925. New to Beswick's.

2ft gauge 4wD Hudswell Clarke No 558 built 1930. New to Beswick's.

No 3 2ft gauge 4wD Hudswell Clarke No 564 built 1930. New to Beswick's.

2ft gauge 4wD Hudswell Clarke No 589 built 1930. New to Beswick's.

2ft gauge 4wD Hudswell Clarke No 590 built 1936. New to Beswick's.

2ft gauge 4wD Ruston & Hornsby. Bought second-hand in 1957 (original owner not known).

Buxton Lime Firms Co Ltd (Later ICI Ltd or Clay Cross Co Ltd, Grin Limestone Quarry)

0-4-0TG Sentinel vertical boiler No 6310. Ex-Ford paper Co Ltd, Sunderland. To Grin Limestone Quarry. Scrapped circa March 1933.

No 5 0-6-0ST Manning Wardle No 488 built 1874. New to Logan & Hemingway, Newport, as *Maindee 7*. To WH Hutchinson, Newport, but returned to Logan & Hemingway in 1890, thence to RH Longbottom & Co Ltd, Wakefield before being sold to Buxton Lime Firms Co Ltd, Grin Limestone Quarry, Ladmanlow.

0-6-0ST Manning Wardle No 1744 built 1909. New to Walter Scott & Middleton, Morriston as *Loughor*. To Buxton Lime Firms Co Ltd, Great Rocks Quarry before being transferred to Grin Limestone Quarry, Ladmanlow as *Michael*.

RS12 4wP Sentinel No 460 built 1916. New to Tunstead Limeworks, thence to Alsop Moor Limeworks, thence to Harpur Hill Hydrating Plant, and thence to Tunstead Limeworks.

RS3 0-6-0ST Manning Wardle No 1971 built 1918. New to Alsop Moor Limeworks, thence to Long Sidings Works. To TW Twigg, Matlock in 1932 before being sold to Constable's Matlock Quarries Ltd, Cawdor Quarry. Scrapped in 1956.

RS10 4wP Sentinel No 1256 built 1918. Ex- Honeywell Bros. To Alsop Moor Limeworks, thence to Harpur Hill Hydrating Plant, and thence to Hindlow Limeworks before returning to Harpur Hill.

RS4 0-4-0ST Avonside No 1843 built 1919. New to Grin Limestone Quarry, thence to Clay Cross Co Ltd, Great Rocks, circa 1922. Known to have been at Hindlow Limeworks at some time thereafter.

RS9 4wP Sentinel No 2024 built 1921. New to Alsop Moor Limeworks, thence to Cowdale Limeworks. To Hindlow Limeworks in April 1956 and to Tunstead Limeworks in April 1957.

RS15 0-4-0ST Avonside No 1931 built 1924. New to Buxton Lime Firms Co Ltd, Tunstead, thence to Hindlow Limeworks.

RS20 4wP Fowler No 17725 built 1927. New to Alsop Moor Limeworks, thence to Harpur Hill Hydrating Plant by January 1952.

RS2 4wD Ruston & Hornsby No 408495 built 1957. New to Hindlow Limeworks.

RS11 2ft gauge 4wP Sentinel No 1255 built 1918. Ex-War Department. To Alsop Moor Limeworks, thence to Hindlow Limeworks by November 1931.

RS14 2ft 2½in gauge 4wP Sentinel No 1259 built 1918. To Hoffman's Limeworks, Harpur Hill from unknown previous owner, thence to Raynes Quarry, Denbighshire in February 1931.

RS17 2ft gauge 4wP Sentinel No 1301 built 1918. Ex-War Department, thence to Hindlow Limeworks. To Raynes Quarry, Denbighshire in September 1930.

RS13 2ft gauge 4wD (ex-petrol) Sentinel No 1308 built 1918. Ex-War Department, thence to Henry Bergeret & Cie, and thence to Hindlow Limeworks circa 1924. To Tunstead by March 1933, but returned to Hindlow by September 1937.

RS26 2ft gauge 4wP Sentinel No 1649 built 1918. Ex-War Department, thence to Hindlow Limeworks.

RS19 2ft gauge 4wP Sentinel No 1706 built 1918. New to Brunner Mond Ltd, thence to Alsop Moor Limeworks, and thence to Tunstead Limeworks by August 1934.

RS79 2ft gauge 4wD Sentinel built 1918. Ex-Cowdale Quarry, thence to Hindlow Limeworks.

RS22 2ft gauge 4wD (petrol until 1942) Sentinel No 4562 built 1928. New to Hindlow Limeworks, thence to Tunstead by November 1932, and thence to Cowdale Limeworks. Scrapped in 1953.

RS23 2ft gauge 4wP Fowler No 17958 built 1929. New to Hindlow Limeworks. Rebuilt as RS77 in May 1941 and transferred to Tunstead.

RS32 2ft gauge 4wD Fowler No 19883 built 1932. New to Hindlow Limeworks.

RS36 2ft gauge 4wD Sentinel No 5643 built 1933. New to Hindlow Limeworks, thence to Buxton Central Works.

RS37 2ft gauge 4wD Sentinel No 5644 built 1933. New to Hindlow Limeworks.

RS41 2ft gauge 4wD Sentinel No 5652 built 1933. Ex-Buxton Central Works, thence to Hindlow Limeworks.

RS43 2ft gauge 4wD Sentinel No 5654 built 1934. New to Hindlow Limeworks, thence to Bungay in 1949.

RS45 2ft gauge 4wD Sentinel No 5656 built 1934. New to Hindlow Limeworks, thence to Bungay in 1949.

RS48 2ft gauge 4wD Sentinel No 5675 built 1935. New to Hindlow Limeworks, thence to Bungay in 1949.

RS47 2ft gauge 4wD Sentinel No 5676 built 1935. Ex-Smalldale, thence to Hindlow Limeworks.

RS50 2ft gauge 4wD Sentinel No 5678 built 1935. New to Hindlow Limeworks, thence to Bungay in 1949.

RS51 2ft gauge 4wD Sentinel No 5679 built 1935. New to Hindlow Limeworks. Scrapped in December 1953.

RS52 2ft gauge 4wD Sentinel No 5683 built 1935. Ex-Tunstead, thence to Hindlow Limeworks.

RS57 2ft gauge 4wD Sentinel No 5691 built 1936. New to Alsop Moor Limeworks, thence to Hindlow Limeworks. Scrapped circa 1959.

RS62 2ft gauge 4wD Sentinel No 5694 built 1937. Ex-Tunstead, thence to Hindlow Limeworks. Scrapped in April 1957.

RS63 2ft gauge 4wD Sentinel No 5695 built 1937. Ex-Tunstead, thence to Hindlow Limeworks. Scrapped circa 1959.

RS61 2ft gauge 4wD Sentinel No 7801 built 1937. Ex-Cowdale, thence to Hindlow Limeworks. Scrapped in November 1957.

RS65 2ft gauge 4wD Sentinel No 7802 built 1937. Ex-Tunstead, thence to Hindlow Limeworks.

RS66 2ft gauge 4wD Sentinel No 7803 built 1937. Ex-Tunstead, thence to Hindlow Limeworks. Scrapped circa 1959.

RS69 2ft gauge 4wD Sentinel No 7806 built 1937. Ex-Tunstead, thence to Hindlow Limeworks. Scrapped in November 1957.

RS70 2ft gauge 4wD Sentinel No 7807 built 1937. Ex-Tunstead, thence to Hindlow Limeworks by December 1951.

RS71 2ft gauge 4wD Sentinel No 7808 built 1937. Ex-Tunstead, thence to Hindlow Limeworks, and thence to Buxton Central Works circa 1957.

RS72 2ft gauge 4wD Sentinel No 7809 built 1937. New to Hindlow Limeworks, thence to Buxton Central Works in 1957.

RS73 2ft gauge 4wD Sentinel No 7810 built 1937. New to Hindlow Limeworks.

RS74 2ft gauge 4wD Sentinel No 7811 built 1938. Ex-Tunstead, thence to Hindlow Limeworks. Scrapped circa 1959.

RS75 2ft gauge 4wD Sentinel No 7812 built 1939. New to Hindlow Limeworks. Scrapped October 1960.

RS76 2ft gauge 4wD Sentinel No 7813 built 1939. New to Hindlow Limeworks.

RS77 *See RS23 of 1929.*

RS82 2ft gauge 4wD Sentinel No 7814 built 1940. Ex-Tunstead, thence to Hindlow Limeworks before returning to Tunstead.

RS84 2ft gauge 4wD Sentinel No 7816 built 1941. Ex-Cowdale Quarry, thence to Hindlow Limeworks circa 1956. Scrapped December 1958.

Dowlow Lime & Stone Co Ltd

Heathcote 0-4-0ST Hudswell Clarke No 455 built 1896. New to Naylor Bros (*qv*) at a cost of £670, thence to Dowlow Lime & Stone Co. Scrapped by TW Ward in July 1952.

Cynthia 0-4-0ST Hawthorne Leslie No 3204 built 1916. Ex-Royal Arsenal, Woolwich. Scrapped in 1959.

Heathcote 4wD Ruston & Hornsby No 299108 built 1951. New to Dowlow Lime & Stone.

Cynthia 4wD Ruston & Hornsby No 412431 built 1957. New to Dowlow Lime & Stone.

Dusty 0-4-0DH Ruston & Hornsby No 418793 built 1958. Prototype of a variation on R&H standard 165DS class, and used as a "demonstrator" before returning to factory in 1958 to be re-engined. Sold to British Gypsum, Newark, thence to Dowlow in 1976. Purchased for preservation in 1991, going to the Bulmers Railway Centre in Hereford, thence to the South Devon Railway in 1993, where it has been used as yard pilot.

No 1 2ft 3in gauge 4wD Ruston & Hornsby No 171901 built 1934. New to Dowlow Lime & Stone.

No 2 2ft 3in gauge 4wD Ruston & Hornsby No 172340 built 1935. New to Dowlow Lime & Stone.

No 3 2ft 3in gauge 4wD Ruston & Hornsby No 192888 built 1939. New to Dowlow Lime & Stone.

Hartington Quarries Ltd, Station Quarries

2ft gauge 4wP Simplex No 7710. Ex-Derbyshire Stone, Hopton Quarry. To Leighton Buzzard Light Railway Ltd.

2ft gauge 4wP Simplex No 7933. Ex-Sir Alfred McAlpine & Sons Ltd, Ellesmere Port. To Leighton Buzzard Light Railway Ltd.

Hartshead Quarries Ltd, Heathcote Quarry, Hartington

2ft gauge 4wP Hibberd No 1807. Scrapped in June 1957

2ft gauge 4wP Simplex No 1087. Ex-War Department.

2ft gauge 4wD Simplex No 2054 built 1920. Ex-Derbyshire Silica Firebrick Co Ltd, Friden. Scrapped on site by Hawkins of Chesterfield in 1960.

Hillhead Quarries Ltd (Subsidiary of Hillhead Hughes Ltd)

4wD (ex-petrol) Simplex No 4184. New to Hillhead Quarries.

0-4-0D Hudswell Clarke No D643 built 1947. New to Hillhead Quarries.

2ft gauge 4wD (ex-petrol) Simplex No 1155. Ex-War Department.

2ft gauge 4wD Simplex No 5711. To R Briggs & Sons Ltd, Chatburn, Lancs.

2ft gauge 4wD Simplex No 5805. Ex-Hughes Bros (Derbyshire Granite Ltd).

2ft gauge 4wD Ruston & Hornsby No 166033 built 1933. New to Hillhead Quarries. To Hoare Bros, Tavistock.

2ft gauge 4wD Ruston & Hornsby No 181827 built 1936. New to Hillhead Quarries.

2ft gauge 4wD Ruston & Hornsby No 189960 built 1939. New to Hillhead Quarries. To R Briggs & Sons Ltd, Chatburn, Lancs.

2ft gauge 4wD Ruston & Hornsby No 235656 built 1946. New to Hillhead Quarries.

Ministry of Power, Safety in Mines Research Department, Harpur Hill

Nippy 3ft 6in gauge 4wD FC Hibberd No 2014.

T Ryan, Somerville & Co Ltd, Hindlow

4wD Ruston & Hornsby No 221650 built 1944. New to Ryan, Somerville.

No 1 3ft 6in gauge 4wD Ruston & Hornsby No 221638 built 1943. New to Ryan, Somerville.

No 2 3ft 6in gauge 4wD Ruston & Hornsby No 221637 built 1943. New to Ryan, Somerville.

No 3 3ft 6in gauge 4wD Ruston & Hornsby No 221636 built 1943. New to Ryan, Somerville.

No 4 3ft 6in gauge 4wD Ruston & Hornsby No 221635 built 1943. New to Ryan, Somerville.

2ft gauge 4wD FC Hibberd No 2525. Ex-Butterley Co Ltd, Butterley.

2ft gauge 4wD FC Hibberd No 2765.

No 6 2ft gauge 4wD FC Hibberd No 2770.

2ft gauge 4wD FC Hibberd No 2808.

No 1 2ft gauge 4wD FC Hibberd.

No 2 2ft gauge 4wD FC Hibberd.

No 3 2ft gauge 4wD FC Hibberd.

No 4 2ft gauge 4wD FC Hibberd. Ex-War Department.

No 4 2ft gauge 4wD FC Hibberd. (*Different loco from above.*)

No 5 2ft gauge 4wD FC Hibberd.

Appendix B

Locomotives Used by Naylor Bros on the Ashbourne to Buxton Contract

In terms of the length of time Naylor Bros were engaged on the construction of the line, this was by far their largest undertaking. In the years that they were involved (1888-1905) Naylor's were also engaged on a number of other works. The information given is based on lists produced by David Cole and FD Smith, and I also acknowledge the assistance of Allan C Baker. Why some locomotives received local names and others didn't is not known. Locomotives are listed in order of build date.

Jumbo 0-4-0ST Hunslet Engine Co No 190 built 1878. New to Awsworth Iron Co. To S Taylor, Runcorn, after use by Naylor's.

0-6-0ST Manning Wardle No 1134 built 1890. New to Logan & Hemingway, Beighton, as their No 11. Sold to Jackson & Co, Stowmarket after use by Naylor's, thence to Weston, Cleveland & Portishead Railway as their No 2 "Portishead", before passing to Wm Cowlin for use on Portishead Power Station contract.

Thurnscoe 0-6-0ST Manning Wardle No 1143 built 1890. New to Logan & Hemingway, Beighton, as their No 12. Sold by Naylor's, 1916.

0-6-0ST Manning Wardle No 1193 built 1890. New to Logan & Hemingway, Beighton, as their No 18. Sold to A Braithwaite after use by Naylor's.

0-6-0ST Manning Wardle No 1202 built 1890. New to Logan & Hemingway, Beighton, as their No 21. Sold to JN Scott after use by Naylor's.

0-6-0ST Manning Wardle No 1204 built 1890. New to Logan & Hemingway, Beighton, as their No 19. Sold to T Wrigley after use by Naylor's, thence to Sir L Parkinson & Son Ltd, before passing to Scremerston Main Colliery Ltd, Northumberland.

Ashbourne 0-6-0ST Hudswell Clarke No 439 built 1896. New to Naylor's and later used by them on LNWR Sudbury-Harrow widening. To E Nuttall by 1911.

Heathcote 0-4-0ST Hudswell Clarke No 455 built 1896. New to Naylor's at a cost of £670. To Dowlow Lime & Stone Co (*qv*) after use by Naylor's. Scrapped by TW Ward in July 1952.

Alsop 0-6-0ST Hudswell Clarke No 458 built 1896. New to Naylor's at a cost of £900. To New Haden Colliery, Cheadle, after use by Naylor's. Believed scrapped 1946.

Hartington 0-6-0ST Hunslet Engine Co No 646 built 1896. New to Naylor's and later used by them on MR Armley & Kirkstall widening. To E Nuttall c.1911.

Tissington 0-4-0ST Manning Wardle No 1280 built 1896. New to Naylor's. To Henry Leetham & Sons Ltd, York, after use by Naylor's.